T0258780

Advance Praise

Planning and Designing Healthcare Facilities: A Lean, Innovative, and Evidence Based Approach

"'The rapid developments in health technologies are putting an extra burden on the care infrastructure and its environment. The changing ways to practice medicine dictate the need for contemporary innovations in the planning and design of the physical infrastructure, but perhaps point even more importantly to the quest for dynamic and rapidly adjustable virtual groundwork to support efficient care.

Therefore, the current book edited by distinguished pundits in healthcare innovation Professor V.K. Singh and Professor Paul Lillrank proves to be timely and needed. Without doubt, this book will serve as a useful tool in the rapidly evolving healthcare systems in South and South East Asia, in particular."

Dr. Jaanus Pikani
Chairman
ScanBalt, Denmark

"It is an established fact that well-designed hospitals in terms of architecture, operational processes, and protocols have a significant impact on patient health outcomes. One example is modeling processes based on patient flow analysis (PaFA). Recent advances in big data solutions and machine learning have enabled evidence and data-driven decision making that will guide innovations in the planning and design of healthcare facilities. There are significant opportunities for further enhancement of efficiency in healthcare operations. This book is timely in addressing those opportunities and provides guidance to practitioners in the various approaches they might want to explore and pursue toward this noble goal of a better patient experience and outcome."

Sandipan Gangopadhyay
President and COO
Galaxy Systems, USA

"This is a comprehensive book that covers the planning, design, and control of healthcare facilities, which is a major aspect in the cost of healthcare delivery. It has drawn various lessons on how management science and innovations can help in delivering quality care at low cost."

S. Venkataramanaiah, PhD
Associate Professor in Operations Management
Indian Institute of Management, Lucknow, India

"This book is very much needed to catalyze the innovations and growth in the health sector in developing nations. The spectrum of the content and the background of the contributors are very impressive. It will give readers new and global insights to improve existing healthcare conditions locally. The mix of basic ideas in a futuristic framework covers the whole continuum of putting together best practices in planning and designing healthcare facilities across the world. The suggestions in the book can be looked upon by various stakeholders of healthcare systems in developing nations and could help them overcome the current challenges and be on par with (or better than) developed nations in healthcare facilities."

Saurabh Gupta, PhD
Assistant Professor, Department of Biomedical Engineering
National Institute of Technology, Raipur, India

"This book could not have been launched at a better time. India is reeling under the pressure of providing more hospitals while also matching quality standards internationally. I urge all players in the healthcare industry to study this book so that Indian hospitals can increase the service levels that have not been achieved so far."

Brig (Hony) Dr. Arvind Lal, Padma Shri
Chairman and Managing Director
Dr. Lal PathLabs Ltd, India

Planning and Designing
Healthcare Facilities

Planning and Designing Healthcare Facilities

A Lean, Innovative, and Evidence-Based Approach

Edited by
V.K. Singh and Paul Lillrank

CRC Press
Taylor & Francis Group
Boca Raton London New York

CRC Press is an imprint of the
Taylor & Francis Group, an **informa** business

A PRODUCTIVITY PRESS BOOK

CRC Press
Taylor & Francis Group
6000 Broken Sound Parkway NW, Suite 300
Boca Raton, FL 33487-2742

© 2018 by V.K. Singh and Paul Lillrank
CRC Press is an imprint of Taylor & Francis Group, an Informa business

No claim to original U.S. Government works

Printed on acid-free paper

International Standard Book Number-13: 978-1-138-03226-2 (Hardback)
International Standard Book Number-13: 978-1-315-39350-6 (eBook)

Visit the Taylor & Francis Web site at
http://www.taylorandfrancis.com

and the CRC Press Web site at
http://www.crcpress.com

Contents

Foreword

The health of the general public has improved dramatically since the last quarter of the nineteenth century. The emerging modern medicine played a part, but the steady decrease in infectious diseases and infant mortality has been largely attributed to better nutrition and sanitation. Some historians claim that the cast-iron sewage pipe was the most effective public health innovation ever. It was only after the Second World War that modern medicine could offer therapies that saved lives, altering the course of events in cases where the natural outcome would have been death.

Hospitals and their role in society have changed dramatically. Before modern medicine, hospitals at worst were places where the poor went to die; at best they were sanctuaries and healing environments where patients could rest and be treated by doctors while waiting for nature to run its course. By the 1990s, hospital "emergency rooms" were increasingly being designated "emergency departments" to reflect their association with the new academic discipline of emergency medicine. As science developed theories from which therapies could be derived, the hospital turned into a production site.

The modern hospital has a dual characteristic, which corresponds with the notion widely accepted within health economics that patients seek health services for two concurrent reasons. Health is the ultimate goal; health services are intermediate products. Health as such is both an investment and a consumption good. Health is a form of human capital that provides healthy days for work and other valuable purposes. Health also makes people feel good, like any consumer product or service. From this follows the two value offerings of the modern hospital. It should deliver solutions to medical problems as outcomes, as well as positive experiences of being cared for in a humane and respectful manner. As in all services, it is not only the "what was accomplished" that matters, but the "how it was done" is important as well.

The modern hospital is simultaneously a production site and a healing environment. The "what" is the clinical outcome of a care episode. The "how" is grounded in the skills and service attitudes of staff. But even the most dedicated caregivers find it hard to do their jobs if the physical environment is not supportive. A central issue forming the patient experience is waiting. Time is highly dependent on how the flow of the patient case is designed and managed. All too often the flow runs, literally, into walls. This is where hospitals have something to learn from the most efficient production site ever, the Lean production houses and factories.

Factories offer two major lessons to hospital designers and managers. Quality in its core industrial meaning is conformance to requirements. Quality management is to beat back and contain the inevitable variability that comes with the human condition. If there is a best known way to do things, it must be described and turned into a protocol that is followed without fail. Patient safety is quality assurance and improvement.

The second aspect is flow. Modern factories and hospitals are based on the division of labor and specialization. This means that the patient has to interact with several specialized caregivers and move to specially equipped locations, such as operating rooms and imaging centers. There is both the flow of patients and supplies as they move within the hospital and the flow of service encounters and care episodes; physical and virtual flows. From overlapping phenomena follows complexity. Complexity implies that intuition and common sense are not necessarily sufficient. Therefore, increasing effort should be placed on developing methods for evidence-based hospital design.

This book is a timely effort to discuss various concepts and tools to reduce delivery costs and maintain high quality by means of planning a hospital with an eye on operations. It details experiences from around the globe. The authors strive to integrate several strains of thought: Lean, innovation, patient centricity, and evidence-based designs. This is what the healthcare industry needs.

Dr. B.R. Shetty
Founder and Chairman
NMC Healthcare
Abu Dhabi, United Arab Emirates

Setting Tone of Planning and Designing Healthcare Facilities: Planning to Optimize Operation Cost

Michael Chamberlain

BACKGROUND

Proper hospital design has several potential benefits, but clearly cost is one of the major factors. Given the competitive landscape, it is essential the building and operating cost are not a long term drain on the total cost to deliver healthcare. Fortunately, most organizations have identified ways to reduce the overall build and operating costs while not sacrificing on functionality, efficiency or patient experience.

There are many factors that may contribute to reducing the anticipated cost including:

- Energy consumption
- Square footage
- Capital equipment
- Staffing
- Electronic health record
- Motion and transportation
- Communication

Each of these is extremely important to minimizing cost both individually and in aggregate. The secret is to recognize that each of these is not mutually exclusive. Rather, they collectively can be improved from the existing process while still reducing design and operating cost.

ENERGY CONSUMPTION

The consumption of energy to keep your hospital running properly can have a major impact on the overall operating cost. Whether it is proper lighting for each of the inpatient rooms, running large diagnostic equipment, maintaining the proper temperature, or powering the information data base to store patient records, hospitals not only consume a lot of energy, they put out a tremendous amount of heat.

One of the first rules of applying lean thinking, is to focus the energy on supporting the value add. This means identifying what is needed for the physicians and clinicians to effectively do their job. The second piece is recognizing that not every patient wants or desires the same temperature at all times of the day. It has been shown that a warm blanket may be more effective for comfort than changing the entire room temperature.

Additionally, we need to consider other energy consumption sources. Are lights needed in the entire room or just the area to provide proper diagnosis, treatment or monitoring? Can we add automatic lights that adjust when there is no movement? Finally, can we pick the lights that are most suitable for delivering the proper patient care rather than some standard that is "traditional" to hospital design?

Simple things such as adjusting the temperature between night and day can have a significant impact on the total energy cost. While this is typically standard in many households, it is not always common in hospitals. Adjusting the temperature just a few degrees may not materially change comfort (as the person is sleeping), but when multiplied throughout the hospital, there will be a drastic reduction in energy consumption.

As energy costs will significantly affect the future operating cost, we must quantify what they will be and seek to reduce them. Most organizations take for granted a certain amount of energy consumption based on size, volumes and climate. This is a paradigm that should be discarded as lean design has been shown to reduce energy consumption by 15%–20%. Being prudent with our energy design will also us to capture those savings.

SQUARE FOOTAGE

Our own personal experience tells us that regardless of how much space we have, we are inclined to fill it up with something. It is no different with hospital design, and as a result we need to be as prudent as possible when determining the overall square footage.

The total square footage will be a major contributor to the design, build and operating cost of the hospital. Expand the square footage and you expand everything. Conversely, if you can shrink the overall footprint you will shrink the total cost.

Square footage is first determined by the value added that we must provide to the patients and their families. This means we design the facility around what is needed to deliver patient care in a timely and high-quality manner. This does not mean we design the facility around wasteful processes such as waiting rooms or storage areas. While waiting rooms and storage areas may be necessary, they are not the focal point of the design.

We must also address the flexibility that will have to occur short and long term as it relates to volumes. Short term we need to ensure the staff can be flexed in slow, medium and busy periods. Rooms should be in a manner that allows easy traffic for clinicians and physicians to move easily, safely and quickly. Long term we must recognize that if we do need to expand, which services are most likely to be impacted. Will the facility be able to accommodate expansion in those areas? What if there is a shift in patient mix, are the rooms agile enough to be converted from one treatment area to another?

When designing through a lean lens, we typically target 15%–25% reduction in total square footage. The reason we can save so much space is because we operate in such an efficient manner. Just think about how much cost is wasted because of the single element of waiting. Longer patient wait times affect everything. First, long wait times mean longer lengths of stay. This means people are in the hospital longer and therefore more rooms are required to hold the same number of patients. Second, more waiting means larger waiting rooms. Finally, more waiting means all central areas are larger including the cafeteria, parking and hallways.

The secret is to ensure you design the hospital around value added services versus wasteful processes. Doing this will drastically reduce the footprint and the cost.

CAPITAL EQUIPMENT

One of the key principles around lean design is "right sized equipment." This means we identify all the value add necessary for proper diagnosis and treatment and deliver it in the least wasteful way. In order to do that we need small, agile equipment at the point of use. We must try to avoid large pieces of capital equipment typically referred to as "monuments."

A monument is a large piece of capital equipment that will be used by multiple areas of the hospital. Each monument (such as large diagnostic imaging equipment) must be carefully identified to not impede patient flow. Ideally, we would like right-sized equipment that is placed at the point of use. However, if we do need centralized pieces of large, expensive capital, then it cannot dominate the overall design or we run the risk of sub-optimizing any future design expansion.

Every design has some budget for capital equipment, but how flexible have we been. What if there is a breakthrough technology? Can we leverage the improvements or have our monuments created a permanent impediment to flow and improved quality? What about if our patient mix shifts? Are we agile enough to change staffing and standard work without capital constraints?

The simplest rule is "creativity before capital." This means we look for creative ways to solutions before we automatically resort to large, complex pieces of equipment.

STAFFING

The single largest driver of operating cost in a hospital is labor. While ensuring your people are productive to deliver the proper patient care is extremely important, most people don't realize how that can be facilitated through proper design.

Many organizations have migrated from the historical "individual based care" to a "team based care model." This is important because, quite often rooms or collaborative discussion areas are not designed for a team of people. It is important we consider the following factors when designing a team based care model:

- Have you considered what the "standard work" or proper roles and responsibilities will be for each care team member?
- Have you determined how the standard work may change/flex in slower, medium and busy times?
- Have you identified the proper team based model that allows each care member to operate at the top of his or her license?

- Have you designed the collaborative work areas to be centrally located to the patient rooms?
- Have you determined the total number of people, by discipline, that will be required during slow, medium and busy times?
- Have you right sized the operation to include staff and physicians along with the number of patient rooms and support services?
- Have you quantified what effect proper diagnosis and treatment the first time will have on readmission and volumes in future months?

Answering these questions are extremely important as they all will ultimately affect the staff productivity as well as the overall design and operating cost. A good design means you know exactly who will be doing what in all areas of the hospital during the slow, medium and busy times. As a result, you can create scenarios that right size the staffing for 90% of the time while building in contingency plans for the extreme periods. You are left with a very robust plan that ensures operational success after the building is complete.

ELECTRONIC HEATH RECORD

An effective electronic heath record IT system is obviously very important for ensuring an accurate medical history of each patient. The implementation and operating cost is typically extreme, yet most people do not understand how those costs can be reduced through effective hospital design.

Electronic Health Record (EHR) systems are like any IT system—provide it with accurate and timely information and you can get a good output; provide it with anything less than that and the system will suffer. EHR systems are intended to follow a particular patient process so if you have a great process, you will likely have a simple EHR implementation. This will also result in very little re-work once the system is up and running. However, if you have a very ineffective process, then you be placing an EHR over something wasteful—that is you are actually automating waste.

It is important to first design all of the flows that will make your EHR effective:

- Patient
- Clinician/physician

- Specimen/test
- Medical device
- Pharmaceutical
- Quality/safety/compliance reporting
- Information (medical record)

Once these flows have been properly designed, then you can overlay your electronic medical record. This will allow for the following benefits:

- Reduced lead time to implementation
- Reduced implementation cost
- Reduced rework from anticipated edits/improvements
- Reduced operating costs

MOTION AND TRANSPORTATION

Quite often when we identify the layout of a hospital, we forget about the motion and transportation that are necessary to safely navigate the patients to/from the appropriate venue. Also important, we must ensure the staff can move swiftly from room to room without excess waiting or distance. Organizations quite often make the mistake of designing something to reduce cost only to have decades of wasteful operating costs when they are running the hospital.

A very simple tool—the spaghetti diagram—can be used to determine the total travel distance for any given process for each person. The spaghetti diagram traces the path of the provider or patient to see where and how far they have to be from the beginning of the journey to the end.

As we calculate the total distance traveled we begin to identify wasteful steps. Are people making the same paths multiple times because they are looking for something? Are people crossing paths because materials are not located at the point of use? If the ancillary services that perform diagnostics and testing can't be located at the point of use, are they within some respectable travel distance?

One of the most important aspects of motion and transportation is the proper use of visual management. Visual management means that anyone (i.e., providers, patients, families, vendors, etc.) can successfully navigate where they are going without asking for directions. An efficient layout will keep those individuals from having to distract physicians and clinicians for directions so they may be able to focus on providing patient care. It may seem small, but hundreds of inquiries each day can have a major impact on employee productivity.

COMMUNICATION

Proper communication can have a major impact on cost. As mentioned before, simple visual management techniques can help everyone understand what is happening in their area as well as those around them. Many organizations do the opposite and try to use very centralized, complex systems to communicate internally. While the intent is good, they typically don't improve anyone's knowledge of what's happening or what needs to be done.

The simplest way to test this theory is to map out all the communication flows. Start with the patient and determine what is needed to communicate between the providers, the patient and the families. Raise the altitude and determine what is needed to communicate between departments. Finally, determine what is needed to be communicated between facilities or networks. While technology may be necessary between departments, facilities and networks, it is quite often overcomplicated within a department or service line.

One of the key benefits of a team based care model is the increased communication. Because everyone is involved with the diagnosis and treatment plan, there is no gap in communication. The patient, family and care givers are all up to speed on what has happened and no complex communication system was required to bring things together.

SUMMARY

Cost is typically one of the major components of the final design, but that doesn't mean it can't be reduced while still improving safety, quality and productivity. However, it must be addressed in multiple dimensions and not accepting the status quo of standard room size, capital investments or staffing assumptions.

Most hospital designs are simply copies from previous hospitals. This is problematic because it is highly probable that no waste was designed out of the original design. The key to an effective hospital design is to use a robust methodology where all elements (and workflows) are incorporated. On the surface, this can seem like it may take time, but in fact it will shorten the design and construction lead time and ensure an efficient process when the hospital is in operation.

Summary of Book

V.K. Singh and Paul Lillrank

Chapter 1: Introduction
V.K. Singh and Paul Lillrank

Modern medicine is founded on the scientific pursuit for knowledge about the human body and its pathologies. Science builds theories and tests them against evidence. The scientific method should now be applied to the design of hospitals and health service systems. This is the rationale for evidence-based design.

Chapter 2: Innovative, Lean, and Evidence-Based Design
V.K. Singh

Lean and innovation complement each other. Lean means creating more value for customers with fewer resources. Innovation is a process of translating an idea into goods or services that create value for which the customer is willing to pay.

Evidence-based design (EBD) emphasizes credible evidence to influence design. It works on well-defined problems, applies a multidisciplinary perspective, involves users and customers, establishes quantitative performance measures for critical variables, and uses tests and simulations throughout the design process.

Chapter 3: Concept of a Hospital
Paul Lillrank, Riikka-Leena Leskelä, and Olli Tolkki

The hospital has traditionally been seen as a production site like a factory where flows of material, people, energy, and information combine with fixed assets. In modern manufacturing, the factory has evolved into supply networks. In a similar vein, the modern hospital is seen as a node in a regional service system. A hospital design initiative should therefore begin with a master plan that defines the hospital's place and role in a broader health service system.

Chapter 4: Patient First, Functions Next, and Design Later
V.K. Singh and S.K. Biswas

The evolution of hospital design principles has gone through several stages. The first was "functions follow design," as services had to be adapted to whatever structures were available. Next came "design follows functions." Various professional groups set out their requirements in terms of floor space and layout. More recently, the concept "design follows first patients, then functions" has been adopted. The emphasis now is on integrating the needs of patients, hospital functions, and functionaries in hospital design.

Chapter 5: Green Hospitals and Sustainable Solution to Healthcare Facility
Rajeev Boudhankar

As important parts of the modern urban landscape, hospitals must adopt environmentally friendly and sustainable designs and technologies. Green hospitals use energy, water, materials, and land more efficiently than conventional buildings. With more natural light and better air quality, green buildings contribute to improved health, comfort, and productivity. The LEED 2009 for Healthcare Green Building Rating System is a set of performance standards for certifying healthcare facilities.

Chapter 6: Designing a Patient-Centric Healthcare Facility Using Lean Methodology
John Gallagher, Kim Chaney, and Ron Kwon

2P (Process Preparation) is a Lean design tool that helps to organize the flow of activity in a way that results in the least amount of waste. This chapter details how it worked when Concord Hillside Medical Associates, a multispecialty group practice and part of Harvard Vanguard Medical Associates near Boston, applied it in a major facility design project.

Chapter 7: Creating Safer Healthcare Environments Using an Evidence-Based Design Process
Anjali Joseph, Ellen Taylor, and Xiaobo Quan

A growing body of research shows that the healthcare built environment impacts safety outcomes such as infections, medication errors, falls, and staff injuries. Latent conditions that adversely impact patient safety are built into the physical environment during the planning, design, and construction phases. Design decisions should be proactively evaluated by engaging users from different disciplines such as infection control, nursing, risk managers, and environmental services. Emerging tools such as the safety risk assessment (SRA) toolkit provide a structured way to apply evidence-based design to improve patient safety.

Chapter 8: Evidence-Based Design in Hospitals: Theory to Implementation
S.K. Biswas and V.K Singh

The principles of Lean healthcare support evidence-based design. Lean calls for the identification of all major stakeholders and specifying what they consider valuable. Stakeholder value can be grouped into the basic categories of tangibility, reliability, responsiveness, assurance, and empathy. When these requirements are not met, processes create waste. EBD analyzes the constraints that need to be addressed. The design process covers several stages: initial hypothetical design, process design, service design, and empirical design. These principles are detailed in a case in a hospital in Kolkata.

Chapter 9: Virtual Hospitals of the Future
Sachin Gaur

Information and communication technologies (ICT), particularly smart and wearable devices, have the potential to break the constraints of time and location. Physical installations may turn virtual, and centralized services may be decentralized. Assessing the potential of new technologies, the CIMO methodology of evaluation science can be employed. It asks what is the Context in which technology is applied through what kinds of Interventions, and which Mechanisms are activated to produce which Outcomes.

Chapter 10: Redefining Healthcare of Tomorrow in Smart City
V.K. Singh and Nimisha Singh

The three pillars of a smart city are people, process, technology, and the information flows that bind them together as an optimized whole. The Smart Cities Mission of India under the leadership of Prime Minister Narendra Modi is an initiative toward urbanization. Smart cities require smart healthcare. With the Internet of Things (IoT), layers of smartness are being added to hospitals, such as remote monitoring, chronic disease management, medication management, patient self-management, and workflow management.

Chapter 11: Delivering Inclusive Intelligent Healthcare by Innovative and Comprehensive e-Health System
Kuo Shou-Jen and Lai Chien-Wen

This chapter is based on a case study of Changhua Christian Healthcare System (CCH), Taiwan. CCH has been a pioneer in implementing sophisticated new technologies. The case emphasizes the importance of the combination of high tech with a human touch.

Chapter 12: Planning Safe Hospitals
Sushma Guleria

The Hyogo Framework for Action 2005–2015 (HFA) spells out the challenge to substantially reduce the impact of disasters and to make risk reduction an essential component of development policies and programs. Risk reduction planning should be integrated into the health sector to make hospitals safe from disasters and strengthen their capacity to remain functional in disaster situations. Hospitals need to have disaster management plans and to evaluate their performance by implementing the Hospital Safety Index used widely to gather information for sound decision making.

Chapter 13: Designing Innovative Facilities: Contamination and Security Hazards at Hospitals
Raman Chawla and V.K. Singh

The danger of chemical, biological, radiological, nuclear, and explosive (CBRNE)-related terrorism poses a contamination threat to healthcare institutions. Designing innovative resilience can provide long-term and effective solutions by establishing a rigorous framework that can accelerate adaptation and the ability to recover from any known and unknown contamination security and safety hazards.

Chapter 14: Adapt or Obsolesce: The Evolution of the Singapore Health System
Matthew Saunders

Singapore is a small advanced country with a single-party-dominated political system. This has made it agile and able to respond quickly to changing circumstance in ways that differ from larger and more complex polities. Singapore faces the same challenges as other developing countries, including an aging society, non-communicable diseases, and healthcare cost inflation, while it is well positioned to implement advanced technologies, such as electronic patient records and smart solutions. Singapore highlights the systemic nature of healthcare, where service production, facility design, finance, and regulation require innovative approaches to integration.

Acknowledgments

We could not have completed this book without the support of the people mentioned here. It is my second book with Professor Paul Lillrank, a great academician and researcher, who was a great support to complete this book. This book is a collection of the ideas and practices of both thinkers and doers at the front line of healthcare innovation. We would like to thank each contributor of the book for sharing their experience and knowledge for the benefit of readers. We had a team of people assisting us along the way. We would like to acknowledge the contributions of Michael Sinocchi, publisher at Productivity Press, who was very quick to take the responsibility of publishing through CRC Press. Alexandria Gryder, editorial assistant, who was dedicated to coordinating our project with the publishing house and was always available with quick advice when it was needed.

Iris Fahrer, project editor at CRC Press initiated the editing of my book and her advice was very useful. The contribution of Jennifer Brady, project manager at Deanta is laudable for editing and formatting. She has gone through every word in such detail to make each chapter flawless.

I cannot forget to credit my family and all well-wishers who motivate and assist me whenever it's required that I complete my work in time. This book, along with my first book *Innovations in Healthcare Management: Cost-Effective and sustainable Solutions* published 2015 by CRC Press, has given me much insight and learning in the art of book writing.

Editors

Vijai Kumar Singh, MBBS, retired as surgeon rear admiral after 37 years in national and international assignments. He earned an MBBS, Master in Hospital Administration, Diplomate National Board in Hospital and Healthcare Management, and an MPhil. He was awarded the Distinguished Services Medal for services in Zambia by the president of India and a commendation by Zambia. Dr. Singh was deputy chief medical officer of the United Nations and visited 36 countries; adjunct professor of the Massachusetts Institute of Technology (MIT), Zaragoza, Spain; and consultant to the National Disaster Management Authority. He was president of the Academy of Hospital Administration, founder director of the International Institute of Health Management Research, chairman of the Health Care Division of Quality Council of India, and member of the International Group on Biosafety. He developed a European Foundation for Quality Management (EFQM) model for healthcare in India released by the Union Health Minister. He was adjunct research professor at the International Health Innovation Center, Ivey School of Business, Canada, and director of Healthcare Asia for Lean Healthcare Excellence-Simpler. Dr. Singh was a member of the National Public Health Committee of Confederation of Indian Industry (CII), chairman of the Board of Indian Society of Health Professionals, formerly president and is a fellow of the Academy of Hospital Administration, and a founder director of the International Institute of Health Management Research, New Delhi. Dr. Singh conceived and executed the telemedicine project connecting inaccessible areas with Delhi. He is a consultant in the JCI accreditation system and a consultant and trainer in the application of Lean principles in healthcare. He has planned and executed health/hospital projects by cutting down costs during planning, operations, and transformation of organizations in India and abroad by applying Lean, innovations, and evidence-based principles.

Currently, he is managing director of InnovatioCuris (IC), adjunct professor at the World Health Innovation Network, Odette School of Business, University of Windsor, Canada. Dr. Singh is visiting professor at the Indian Institute of Management, the Indian Institute of Technology, and others. He is Honorary Professor–Australian Institute of Health Innovation, Macquarie University, Australia. He authored the book *Innovations in Healthcare Management: Cost-Effective and Sustainable Solutions* with national and international authors (CRC Press 2015), and launched a global magazine in healthcare innovation titled *InnoHEALTH* in 2015.

 **Paul Lillrank, PhD,** has been professor of quality and service management at Aalto University since 1994. He has served as head of the Department of Industrial Engineering and Management for 8 years and has been academic dean of the school's MBA program. Aalto University was formed in 2010 through the merger of Helsinki University of Technology, Helsinki School of Economics, and Helsinki School of Art and Design.

He earned a PhD in social and political sciences at Helsinki University in 1988 after spending 6 years as a post-graduate student in Japan where he researched quality management in Japanese industry. After graduating, he joined The Boston Consulting Group in Tokyo and later in Stockholm, returning to academia in 1992 as an affiliated professor at the European Institute of Japanese Studies at the Stockholm School of Economics. He has been a visiting professor at the University of Tokyo, served as program director at College des Ingenieurs in Paris, and teaches regularly at the Indian Institute of Technology, Kharagpur, India.

Dr. Lillrank has conducted research in several service industries, such as software, telecom, airlines, and retailing. Recently, his focus has been on healthcare. He has been a pioneer in introducing industrial management methods to the study of healthcare service production. He has co-founded The Institute of Healthcare Engineering, Management and Architecture (HEMA) and The Nordic Healthcare Group (NHG), a consultancy. He has been a frequent speaker and advisor to several healthcare producers and government agencies. His research interests are in healthcare operations management, particularly operating modes, process coordination, knowledge integration through mobile solutions, and regional supply systems. A current topic is innovations in healthcare management, particularly frugal innovations in the Indian context.

Contributors

Swapan Kumar Biswas, MPhil, after a successful practice career spanning 11 years as a clinician, has been involved in healthcare planning, design, and management for the last 24 years. His experience in clinics and management has led to the Lean approach to functional processes. He is presently involved in a number of performance improvement initiatives at the Iris Hospital. He earned an MPhil in hospital and health system management.

Rajeev Boudhankar, MD, has 29 years of experience in the healthcare industry. He earned an MD (internal medicine) from Grant Medical College, Bombay University, and a PhD in hospital and health systems management from BITS, Pilani. Dr. Boudhankar is involved in many hospital projects from the planning stage (drawing board) to operationalization.

Michael Chamberlain is president of Simpler North America. He leads more than 140 proven experts who deliver game-changing Lean enterprise transformations to manufacturing, military, banking, construction, government, finance, and insurance clients every day. His personal expertise in healthcare includes strategy, innovation, convergence, and population health.

Kim Chaney has over 20 years' experience in delivering successful Lean transformations across a range of industries and in multiple countries. He has focused on healthcare improvements in patient visit and between patient visit flows, as well as preoperative, emergency departments, and patient flows in private practice environments.

Raman Chawla, PhD, earned a PhD in toxicology and medical elementology, and is a scientist at the Institute of Nuclear Medicine & Allied Sciences, Defence Research & Development Organisation, India. In the last decade, he has edited 9 books, coauthored 7 national guidelines including medical/CBRN preparedness, conducted 10 industrial mock exercises, and has published 90 papers in journals of international repute.

Lai Chien-Wen, PhD, administrative vice-superintendent of Changhua Christian Hospital (CCH), graduated from Dayeh University with a PhD in electrical engineering and is the assistant professor in the Department of Electrical Engineering, Chung Yuan Christian University. He was also honored to be the advisor to the Logistics Professional Committee, Taiwan Non-Governmental Hospitals and Clinics Association. He is the key person in the Administrative Chief of Preparatory Office to construct the green and intelligent hospital Yuanlin Christian Hospital.

John Gallagher has more than 20 years of diverse Lean experience in multiple industries. John has worked as a senior consultant in the healthcare industry, coaching and developing C-suite level executives on their Lean journey. He is responsible for the innovation practice at Simpler.

Sachin Gaur is a researcher of mobile applications and their applications in the health sector. He was picked as one of the top 10 innovators in India by the Federation of Indian Chambers of Commerce and Industry (FICCI). Part of his field research is covered by broadcast and print media. He earned a double MSc (tech) from Aalto University, Finland and the University of Tartu, Estonia. He has multiple patents issued and has contributed book chapters on topics of innovation.

Sushma Guleria, PhD, earned a PhD in disaster management and is working as a research associate with the National Institute of Disaster Management, Government of India. Earlier, she worked on a World Bank project in the School Environmental Education in India for the Ministry of Environment and Forests. She is a recipient of the World Bank's Young Researcher's Grant Award for Disaster Risk Reduction for the year 2005–2006 from India. She is a trainer in disaster management.

Anjali Joseph, PhD, is Spartanburg Regional Healthcare System Endowed Chair in Architecture and Health Design at Clemson University. She is focused on using simulation and prototyping methods to research and test the effectiveness of promising design solutions that may impact patient safety in high-stress healthcare environments. She earned a PhD in architecture from Georgia Institute of Technology and an M Arch from Kansas State University.

Ron Kwon, MD, FACP, has been site medical director and internist at Atrius Health Concord. His leadership was instrumental in the development of a Lean practice site through innovative Lean design approaches resulting in improved quality, reduced costs, and improved patient and staff satisfaction.

Riikka-Leena Leskelä, PhD, is senior manager at Nordic Healthcare Group Co. Ltd. She earned her PhD in operations research from Aalto University in 2009. Her areas of expertise are analysis of large data sets, healthcare process analysis and improvement, health economic modeling, healthcare system planning, and hospital design.

Xiaobo Quan, PhD, is professor of practice at Washington University at St. Louis, Missouri. He has been actively engaged in healthcare environment research for more than 10 years and has published widely. He earned a PhD in architecture from Texas A&M University and has two professional degrees in architecture from Southeast University in China.

Matthew Saunders is an architect registered in the United Kingdom and senior consultant at MJ Medical London office. He has specialized in health facility design for the last 18 years. He is LEED AP certified combining sustainable design principles with his broad experience of healthcare typologies from working in Europe and Southeast Asia, offering an international perspective on differing economics, cultures, and policies driving healthcare.

Bavaguthu Raghuram Shetty After arriving in the UAE in the early 1970s as a pharmacist from India, saw an opportunity to provide a quality healthcare ecosystem. Accordingly, he founded New Medical Centre in 1975 and today NMC is the largest private health provider in GCC. As founder and chairman, Dr. Shetty has expanded NMC into areas beyond healthcare, such as pharmaceuticals, retail, IT, F&B, and money remittance. He is a member of the Medical Council of the UAE representing private sector healthcare and is setting up Medi-cities at Sanchi, Amaravati, Varanasi, and Mumbai, in India and at Abu Dhabi in the UAE.

Kuo Shou-Jen, Ministry of Education–certified associate professor; superintendent of Changhua Christian Healthcare System, Taiwan. He is commissioner of the SNQ National Quality and National Biotechnology and Medical Care Quality Award Review Committee. He is director of the Taiwan Non-Government Hospitals & Clinics Association. He has led Changhua Christian Hospital, achieved three consecutive accreditations from the Joint Commission International since 2008, and has piloted CCH, receiving a total of 17 certifications from CCPC.

Nimisha Singh earned an MBA in hospital and health management. Her interest is in healthcare quality management, IT, and innovation. She is editor of *InnoHEALTH* magazine and has authored a chapter on Innovation in *Innovations in Healthcare Management: Cost-Effective and Sustainable Solutions* (CRC Press 2015). She is an assessor of the Healthcare Excellence Award based on the European Foundation Quality Model and is certified Bronze in Lean healthcare, by Cardiff University.

Ellen Taylor, PhD, is vice president for research at The Center for Health Design, has more than 25 years of experience, and is an AIA member with an architecture degree from Cornell University and MBA degrees from Columbia University and London Business School. She earned a PhD in human factors and patient safety from Loughborough University in England.

Olli Tolkki is director of sales at Nordic Healthcare Group Co. Ltd. He earned a master's degree from Aalto University School of Business in 2005. His core expertise is healthcare process improvement, healthcare system planning, elderly care improvement, and hospital design.

1

Introduction

V.K. Singh and Paul Lillrank

During the past few centuries, healthcare has slowly emerged as a science-driven profession. Still, only about one-third of what doctors do is based on scientifically justified evidence. Nevertheless, there is a consensus that therapies should ideally be based on theories. No respected professional would apply the reasoning of prescientific medicine, where doctors claimed that if their patient was cured, it was proof of the efficacy of techniques, while if their patient died, it simply showed that the disease was incurable.

In his book, *Bad Medicine*, Professor David Wootton[1] makes the case that Western medicine from Hippocrates to the late nineteenth century did more harm than good. The turning point came in 1865, when Joseph Lister performed the first surgical intervention involving antiseptics. Soon, the idea of aseptic surgery followed, meaning that instead of the surgeon cleaning the scalpel on his coat between patients, instruments were sterilized through boiling. In effect, modern medicine could seriously claim its capacity to save lives only after 1942 when antibiotics were introduced.

As elsewhere, medicine science progressed through adapting the basic principles of methodology. For Hippocrates, every patient and their problem were unique. With such a mind-set, no meaningful categorizations of states, cures, and effects could be collected. Only after symptoms, conditions, diseases, interventions, and outcomes were classified—following the principles of Linnaeus' ordering of the biosphere and the periodic tables in chemistry—could meaningful data be collected. With data on hand, it became possible to compare and set up experiments to collect evidence. Classify, count, and compare.

In many areas of health and welfare, the progress of the scientific method is still painstakingly slow. This applies also to the topic of this book, the facilities and the production sites where health services are performed. Before theory-based therapy and evidential effectiveness, hospitals were warehouses for the sick, sanctuaries where the placebo effect could do its job, or the last place to rest for those who could not afford a bed of their own.

It is obvious that the location and circumstances where a therapy is provided play a role in determining the outcome. A person in a weakened state needs shelter, anybody with an open wound benefits from a germ-free environment. Indeed, the idea of the healing environment, though ancient is still valid. As the medical profession's skills improve and specialization occurs, and when more devices, supplies, and pharmaceuticals are needed, the hospital obeys the same logic of location, concentration, and organization as any production facility. As patient volumes and capital intensity grow, economies of scale and scope come into play. The logic of production and economic forces, form and function, location and access, cost and space, closure and control, efficiency and comfort, advanced toward a dominant design: the general hospital as a multifunctional health factory.

However, advances in technologies, such as information, computing, logistics, clinical methods, diagnostics, and devices, challenge the standard concept and allow for new ideas. Increasing wealth and housing standards erode the hospital's monopoly on healing environments. With cheap and portable devices together with smartphones and wearable sensors as hubs of information gathering, aggregation, and analysis, the imperative of the centralization and concentration of facility-based services gives way to ambulatory field–based services. The hospital can be disaggregated to the "hot floor" where invasive therapies are carried out; the "hotel" where patients recover under observation; the out patient department to which patients commute for therapies; the emergency department with rapid reaction stand by assets; as well as assisted housing and social care. All can in various ways be nested within an urban landscape. A plethora of different arrangements can be imagined to follow the discontinuation of the hospital as the primary production site. Some caution, however, is required.

While progress in some technologies, particularly electronics and communication, has been breathtaking, it is good to keep in mind that not all technologies follow Moore's law in doubling performance every three years. Batteries are a crucial element of the mobile Internet, yet the progress of battery technology has, as measured by the weight–power ratio, proceeded at a turtle's pace of 4% per year. It will take 35 years for performance to double. When technology meets human behavior, anything can happen.

While it is exciting to play with visions of what might come, it is prudent to focus on what is possible. The history of medicine shows that something becoming possible does not yet guarantee it being implemented. It took two centuries from Leuwenhoek's discovery of bacteria to the formulation of the germ theory of diseases. To the modern mind, the 50 years between the invention of anesthesia and its application in surgery seems incomprehensible. Powerful incumbents have resisted every disruptive innovation. Professionals tend to identify with their current competencies and resist radical change. While Wootton demonstrates the harm of Hippocratic prescientific medicine, he strongly emphasizes that this is not a case of malice, evil, or ignorance. Most of the doctors were sincere and dedicated, but while doing their best they did not know what they were doing. They just lacked evidence-based methods.

The evidence-based approach to hospital design seeks to break with a number of traditional lines of thinking and practice. Some of these are the assumptions that a hospital is first and foremost a building where patients come to stay in bed and patiently receive scheduled therapies and undergo monitoring. Buildings can be described with floor space and room requirements. Planning can be a top-down process based on intuition and authority that pays little attention to how patient processes, staff movements, and logistic flows actually happen. Patients and staff representatives may be asked for their opinion, based on the superficial assumption that anybody can, in his or her head, translate 2-D drawings into a dynamic view of what will actually happen. There is the benevolence trap, the assumption that everything that is done with good intentions automatically creates value and nothing can be wasteful.

The general hospital is still a valid concept and is not going to disappear anytime soon, particularly in parts of the world where public health is poor, resources are scarce, and a majority of people are underserved. While visions are always welcome, the task at hand, and the theme of this book, is to improve on the dominant design, the standard general hospital.

The notions that facilities are important and that the scientific method is supreme lead straightforwardly to the call for evidence-based hospital planning. A number of design and planning principles have emerged and several of them are described in the following chapters.

REFERENCE

1. Wootton, David: *Bad Medicine: Doctors Doing Harm since Hippocrates*. Oxford University Press, Oxford, 2007.

2

Innovative, Lean, and Evidence-Based Design

V.K. Singh

CONTENTS

INTRODUCTION

Healthcare affordability is a major concern in poor and emerging countries, while rich and developed nations continue to spend and demand more, as in the United States where annual healthcare spending per capita was $8602 (17.2% of gross domestic product [GDP]) in 2011, yet people are still not happy. Cost containment is possible using an evidence-based system and quality tools such as Lean, and judiciously using technology and innovation. The aim is to deliver healthcare at optimum cost keeping quality in mind. The concept of affordability needs to be further considered as what is affordable for one person may not be so for another person. Healthcare delivery comes at a cost that can be optimized, but the cost needs to be considered from the planning and design stage of a hospital as the operational costs of healthcare delivery are dependent on how well a hospital has been planned and designed. The planning team should have expertise in innovation, Lean, and EBD, as knowledge of these new concepts is considered essential. There are various cost centers in healthcare delivery such as pharmaceuticals, devices, diagnostic, and processes, which need to be controlled by these methods. Information technology (IT) has a big role to play and its use in planning, designing, and operations is vital. This chapter discusses these concepts and how they can be integrated to reduce costs.

LEAN AND INNOVATION

Lean and innovation are two sides of the same coin and complement each other. Lean means creating more value for customers with fewer resources. The Lean approach, a concept developed by Toyota, has been adopted by healthcare over the last few years. The goal is to provide value to the customer by continuously improving processes that have zero waste. It is estimated that there is approximately 90% waste in various manufacturing processes; however, it is not possible to remove all waste in healthcare because, unlike cars, patients and healthcare providers are not robots and patients are bound to ask for things that typically would be waste but cannot be eliminated. I define this as *essential waste*. It is estimated that 60%–65% of healthcare waste can be removed. There are eight types of waste: transportation (unnecessary movement of patients and materials); inventory (equipment and medicines stored over long periods), just-in-time inventory; motion (unnecessary movement of people, searching for investigation results, etc.); waiting everywhere in a hospital be it registration, diagnostics, pharmacy, operations, and so on; people not listened to and their talent not exploited; overprocessing (unnecessary ordering of tests that are not required); overproduction (preparing drugs that are not required); and defects such as medication errors, wrong operations, and so on. Efforts should be made to remove waste to add value to the customer experience and transform healthcare. Lean thinking aims to improve quality, reduce the cost of healthcare delivery, and increase profitability and the morale of providers. Listen to the voice of the customer—the patients and their families. The facilities are not for the providers but for the customer, which implies that the customer's requirements should be integrated at the planning stage. Learn from your current circumstances and bring in a fresh pair of eyes. Go to the place where the work is being done, and list any changes suggested by staff. The staff then become owners of such changes in processes. Some minor changes can make a big impact on day-to-day work schedules. Do a comprehensive review of the organization's workflow and downstream effects and create mock-ups and prototypes. Plan development and operations concurrently with design and construction. Listen to the views of staff and plan equipment from the drawing board stage to the design stage. The guiding principle of Lean is standardization. Synchronize the approach of the technology and construction implementation schedule.

Lean has linkages with the Donabedian model, a conceptual model that provides a framework for examining health services and evaluating the quality of healthcare.[1] According to the model, information about quality of care can be drawn from three categories: "structure," "process," and "outcomes."[2] Structure describes the context in which care is delivered, including hospital buildings, staff, financing, and equipment. Process denotes the transactions between patients and providers throughout the delivery of healthcare. Finally, outcomes refer to the effects of healthcare on the health status of patients and populations.[2] Avedis Donabedian, a physician and health services researcher at the University of Michigan, developed the original model in 1966. Process improvements remove waste to reduce cost and simultaneously improve outcomes. It implies that Lean can be applied to the structure and processes with the outcome of reduced healthcare delivery costs.

Innovation is a process of translating an idea into goods or services that create value for which the customer is willing to pay. Innovation involves the application of information, imagination, and initiative in deriving greater or different values from available resources. It includes all processes by which new ideas are generated and converted into useful products. Innovation has become a buzzword that everybody wants to use but without understanding its meaning. There are many types of innovation, such as frugal innovation, reverse innovation, and disruptive innovation. In 2009, the word "indovation" was coined by Navi Radjou of the University of Cambridge, which is an abbreviated version of "Indian innovation." Hospital innovation has two components, operations and infrastructure, and both are applied in hospital planning and design. Flow and functional diagrams are created before infrastructure design to provide minimum movement of patients, staff, and supplies. Technology allows the collection of reliable real-time data, and analysis and collation can reveal problems and help test solutions.[3]

Lean thinking can make many small improvements to processes and can integrate innovative ideas backed by technology. These could achieve a significant price reduction and could be scaled in various settings.

EVIDENCED-BASED DESIGN (EBD)

EBD is a field of study emphasizing credible evidence to influence design. This approach has become popular in healthcare to improve patient and staff well-being, patient healing, stress reduction, and safety.

EBD suggests that well-designed physical settings play an important role in making hospitals safer, improving the recovery of patients, and reducing the frequency of hospital-acquired infections. The findings support the importance of improving effective ventilation systems, a good environment, appropriate lighting, better ergonomic design, and improved floor layouts and work settings. It also improves the staffs' work environment.

Zimring et al. have identified the following 10 strategies for EBD[4]:

1. Start with known problems, such as hospital-acquired infections, patient satisfaction, and staff performance, and envision new solutions.
2. Use a multidisciplinary approach, but ensure that senior leaders demonstrate the support necessary to achieve change.
3. Include patients and families.
4. Seek cost efficiencies.
5. Use decision-making tools to keep process on track.
6. Establish quantitative criteria linked to incentives.
7. Use strategic partnerships to accelerate innovation.
8. Support and demand simulation and testing throughout the process.
9. Use a 30- to 50-year cycle perspective to determine the return on investment.
10. Communicate frequently with all stakeholders about the desired outcomes and potential benefits.

LEAN AND EBD

Lean and EBD have close links and complement each other in reducing healthcare delivery costs while maintaining quality. The EBD principles are closely related to Lean management.[5]

- Identify the outcome value and the activities that produce or con- tribute to it.
- Identify the wasteful activities that do not create value.
- Identify the stream of value-creating activities and organize them into processes.
- Apply tools and automation to achieve just-in-time flows.
- Codify best practices into standards and foolproof practices.

INNOVATION, LEAN, AND EBD

The application of innovation, Lean, and EBD in planning and design- ing and their benefits have been explained. In subsequent chapters, these concepts will be discussed using various case studies where they have been applied and have accrued the desired results. The development of newer concepts such as virtual, intelligent, smart hospitals, and hospital with- out walls is based on these principles and integrating IT into healthcare systems. Lean, innovation, and EBD have been deliberated in the book *Innovations in Healthcare Management: Cost-Effective and Sustainable Solutions*, which is suggested for further reading.

SUMMARY

The concept of Lean, innovation, and EBD need to be adopted to reduce healthcare delivery costs and maintain quality. The focus on patient needs is based on real-time data collated by IT systems and they should be included right from the planning and design stage of healthcare facilities to reduce operation costs. The future development of healthcare delivery is advancing and soon it will include artificial intelligence (AI), which I call "assisted intelligence," in the planning, design, and operation of hospitals; however, technology should not take over, we should be masters of technology.

REFERENCES

1. McDonald KM, Sundaram V, Bravata DM, et al. (2007). *Closing the Quality Gap: A Critical Analysis of Quality Improvement Strategies* (Vol. 7: Care Coordination). Rockville, MD: Agency for Healthcare Research and Quality (US).
2. Donabedian, A. (1988). The quality of care: How can it be assessed? *JAMA*. 260 (12): 1743–48.
3. Biswas SK, Singh VK. (2015). Hospital planning and design innovation for Lean operation. In V K Singh and P Lillrank (eds) *Innovations in Healthcare Management: In Cost Effective and Sustainable Solutions* (pp. 107–30). Boca Raton, FL: CRC Press.
4. Zimring CM, Augenbroe GL, Malone EB and Sadler BL. (2008). Implementing healthcare excellence: The vital role of the CEO in evidence based design. White Paper Series 3/5, Evidence-Based Design Resources for Healthcare Executives, Center for Health Design.
5. Spoerl B. (2012). How to get hospitals to think "lean": 5 Key Principles. Retrieved from: http://www.beckershospitalreview.com/strategic-planning/how-to-get-hospitals-to-think-lean-5-key-principles.html

3

Concept of a Hospital

Paul Lillrank, Riikka-Leena Leskelä, and Olli Tolkki

CONTENTS

INTRODUCTION

A hospital is part of a service network and needs to define its position and business model within such a network before detailed planning starts. This chapter focuses on the very first steps in hospital planning when important strategic issues must be addressed.

Decisions made at the planning stage of a hospital have an impact on its life cycle. The hospital, in turn, influences the regional service system that manages patient flows and complementary health and well-being services. In the first world, to construct, furnish, and equip a hospital costs about the same as running it for two years. If the building does not support efficient and flexible processes, it will become a sinkhole for unnecessary costs. A big hospital can drain resources from other activities and inhibit alternative solutions. Therefore, there is a need for increased and strategic planning at the initial stage of a hospital project.

Florence Nightingale was to hospitals what Frederick Taylor was to factories; the first to apply systematic, analytical, and evidence-based thinking to production. Since Taylor, the factory has metamorphosed from a stand-alone smoke-belching building into hubs of global supply networks. The hospital is changing from a shining building on a hill to a node in a health service ecosystem. This has been driven by changes in demand. In Nightingale's time, demand was most typically a wounded soldier, who received some treatment from which he either died or was discharged as an invalid; that is, a health problem subject to intensive care for a finite period. Nowadays, most demand is the mirror image: chronic diseases with long gestation requiring low-intensity monitoring and occasional therapies that continue till the end of life. Consequently, the concept of a hospital must change.

In this chapter, we discuss the early stages when a master plan needs to be developed for a hospital and its processes, before the technical planning starts and architects are employed. To this end, the fundamental nature of a hospital as a service production unit is explicated by comparing hospitals and factories.

HEALTH FACTORY

People with medical problems need help. So do their families and local community leaders. Governments need to show that they care about public health, investors need objects with long-term prospects, and professionals need places to work.

But why hospitals, if that means big buildings with many co-located activities under a central management? Why can't healthcare be organized like a bazaar with a number of different professionals plying their trade as independent operators while sharing some necessary infrastructure? Why are hierarchical organizations needed to integrate and coordinate activities in large units? This is, indeed, a core issue of organizations. The various answers developed by, among others, Nobel laureates Ronald Coase[1] and Oliver Williamson,[2] form a line of thought called the *theory of the firm.* The key concepts are integration, coordination, hierarchies, markets, and transaction costs.

A hospital is a productive organization with a purpose. The organization exists to integrate and coordinate the activities of various clinical specialties and provide an infrastructure of sites, buildings, equipment, maintenance, and supply chains.

Integration is the task of assembling, joining, and merging components consisting of various technologies, resources, and skills with the aim to create an integrated offering that is valuable to users. For example, a mobile phone is an agglomeration of technologies, such as processors, memories, radio signaling, software, materials, mechanics, and design. People with corresponding skillsets represent each of these technologies. None of these people alone can run the show and design a device that maximizes the influence of the technology they represent. For a device to be of value, the parts must submit to the whole. Technology companies typically have hierarchies where the upper echelons force an integrated solution out of rival technology factions. In healthcare, the equivalent is to take various informational inputs about a patient and merge them into a diagnosis and a care plan.

Once an integrated design has been achieved, it needs to be produced in sufficient volumes. A number of resources, components, and activities need to be organized into processes with task flows, schedules, deadlines, and controls. This is coordination, the administrative effort to ensure that the right things are done at the right time in the right way in the right place. Thus, integration means fusing together a number of inputs into a whole, while coordination is to arrange discrete activities into a process. In healthcare, this means the execution of a care plan following various coordinated tasks, routines, and patient processes.

In healthcare, the principles of integration and coordination have not attracted the same level of attention as in manufacturing. A large part of service production is immaterial, such as information gathering, analysis, and decisions. Service production systems do not have the same obvious physical manifestation as, say, an assembly line or the pipelines of a petrochemical plant. In a traditional hierarchical hospital, integration is performed through the authority of the chief clinicians, who may or may not consider the inputs of other parties. There are hospitals with formalized care pathways for common ailments, while other hospitals' patient processes are executed ad hoc.

The current management model in many hospitals is not favorable for the coordination of patient processes. Some hospitals could be described as a set of independent professionals in an organization that feeds them resources. In the early stages of planning a new hospital, there is a need to discuss and define a new management model.

If a health service consists of one patient with a clear-cut problem, such as a broken bone, which is served by a production unit consisting of one doctor and one nurse, the problems of integration and coordination are not overwhelming. However, if a patient case is complex, including multi-morbidities requiring complex diagnostics using various data sources, several procedures, medication, ward care, and rehabilitation, then integration and coordination become pressing concerns. The thing to be integrated and coordinated, the unit of analysis, is a patient case. Integration is akin to product design. It takes diagnostics, clinical decision making, and the establishment of a care plan, which may have to be amended based on how the patient reacts to various treatments and what can be afforded. If several subspecialties and stakeholders are involved, hierarchy and administrative boundaries may turn into obstacles. As the care plan is executed, the more tasks there are, the more coordination is needed. Compared to manufacturing, managerial problems are amplified by the fact that integration and coordination need to be done separately for each patient. While most patients fall under a known diagnostic category that calls for a routine care process, each patient is still an individual.

Up to the twentieth century, hospitals were facilities where people were brought to die, or asylums where sick people were isolated from the world. As clinical medicine has advanced, hospitals have become institutions to produce health. As more was accomplished, more was asked for. Hospitals faced increasing volumes of patients and had to go into mass production and employ economies of scale.

Economies of scale is a central mechanism in industrial production. As production units grow in size, they produce higher volumes, from which follows that the unit cost drops. This is the cornucopia of industrial capitalism: the more you produce the cheaper it gets. Large production units offer several benefits. Division of labor and specialization—the primary drivers of productivity—can be used to the full. A large organization can allocate capacity more efficiently. It can afford expensive capital equipment, such as radiological diagnostics and specialized operating theaters. It can exploit scale in support functions, such as maintenance, laundry, and food services. As a result, hospitals have been growing by adding functions and layers of hierarchy.

While the benefits of scale and hierarchy are obvious, each organizational innovation carries the seeds of its own destruction. As hierarchies grow taller, coordination becomes more complex. As scale increases, the marginal benefits diminish and at some point turn into diseconomies of scale. A hospital may become too big to fail, and too big to manage. Hospital designers must get back to basics.

The original dilemma explicated by the pioneers of the theory of the firm was the traditional solutions to integration and coordination: hierarchies or markets. Hierarchy means that an organization is formed like a pyramid. There is a vertical line of authority and reporting relations. If two players at the same level in the hierarchy can't agree, say software and hardware, surgeons and radiologists, a manager who has authority over both solves the issue higher up. The tool used is administrative fiat, the legitimate power to reward and punish, and to hire and fire. Obviously, the real world is seldom as neat and orderly as the organization chart. Hierarchical organizations tend to be rife with conflicts, factions, and intrigues.

The other solution is to have a market. The suppliers of various components and skillsets are each an independent legal entity trading in a market. The end user, filling his or her shopping cart with what is deemed to be necessary and worthwhile, does the integration. If the end user lacks the skills and knowledge, professional integrators can be employed. For example, in the automobile industry, the big brand original equipment manufacturers do the assembly and marketing of vehicles of which about 90% are made out of purchased parts. Travel agents offer integrated all-inclusive packages to some customers, while other travelers may integrate their own schedule up to the last bus ride. In some countries, the family doctor serves as an integrator to his or her patients by procuring specialized services from hospitals and other caregivers.

Market-based solutions offer many benefits. Each market actor is forced to deal with customers and thereby needs to flexibly respond to customer needs. The end users or integrators can choose what they need, select from alternatives, and apply competitive pressure. While market solutions work nicely in some walks of life, they are unsuitable for others. The end user may not have the information and knowledge to integrate complex issues. Some relations may be akin to a spot market, where no continuity or trust between players can be assumed, and opportunistic behavior is a real risk. There are transaction costs. A shopper in a market needs to search, select, evaluate, pay, and monitor a trade. This can be risky, technically impossible, and economically costly. Thus, the hierarchies versus markets dilemma is explained by the theory of transaction costs. The most efficient solution is that which optimizes transaction costs. If transaction costs are high, it may be more efficient to rely on hierarchies and administrative fiat and absorb the costs of bureaucracy. If transaction costs are low and risks manageable, market solutions are preferable. Both markets and hierarchies can be used. In some health systems, market solutions are employed in support services, such as cleaning and laundry, and increasingly in specialties with clear-cut tasks and outputs, such as radiology and routine laboratory diagnostics, while the core clinical processes are kept within the hierarchy.

Transaction costs can be reduced by various means, such as trust and long-term relations between players, improved information systems for selection and monitoring, and more sophisticated contracting and contract governance. A third way between hierarchies and markets first emerged in the post-war Japanese automobile industry. Suppliers are independent, but tied to integrators through long-term relations. This is known as relational contracting, supply chain management, and demand–supply networks.

The consequences for hospital design are formidable. A hospital does not have to be a vertically integrated production system that within one organization supplies everything a patient may need. Healthcare is increasingly perceived as a network of goods and service suppliers that can find various ways to integrate and coordinate the patient's journeys. A more recent idea is to view health services as an ecosystem. While a network consists of actors connected through trading relations and contracts, an ecosystem, in addition to these, includes relevant actors that do not have formal relations, but nevertheless influence each other. For example, a bike helmet manufacturer may not trade or even talk with emergency departments. Still, the design and usage of helmets significantly affect the volume and type of head injuries that come in for treatment. Indeed, the most significant public health innovation ever was the cast-iron sewage pipe.

If factors driving transaction costs and economies of scale change, the concept of a hospital may as well change, likewise as the concept of a factory has changed with the advent of electric power, demand–supply chains, bar codes, and recently additive manufacturing and 3-D printing.

The overall consequence is that a hospital is not necessarily a standalone, all-purpose health factory. As one player in a health service network, a hospital can position itself in various ways. There are many strategy options to consider before a design effort is initiated. A hospital may consider itself a specialized supplier to a preselected segment of patients offering a narrow range of highly specialized services. For example, the Shouldice Hospital in Canada, which only performs hernia operations; Coxa Hospital in Finland, which is a focused production system for knee and hip joint replacement surgery; and Arvind Eye Hospital in India, which has a standardized production line for cataracts. A geriatric facility, such as Jorvi Hospital in Finland, can define its strategic position as a support function for home care. Narayana Hrudayalaya in Bangalore strives to be a global center of excellence for pediatric cardiac surgery. There is, obviously, a lot of room for all-purpose general hospitals that offer a wide range of services to a region. But these also need to think carefully about their position within a network of general practitioners (GPs) that refer patients, as well as units that provide community care, rehabilitation, and preventive health. Thus, before thinking of buildings, hospital designers need to think about networks.

SERVICE NETWORKS AND THE DEVIL'S TRIANGLE

A service network is made from service provision points (SPP) and their connections. In health services, a majority of service encounters are time and location constrained, that is, a patient and a caregiver need to meet at a certain place at a certain time. Telemedicine can be used to amend this constraint, but only in contacts where information can be digitalized.

Each SPP has three generic characteristics. First, since the SPP has a physical location, there will be a distance between it and the point of need. An SPP may be in service around the clock or office hours only. If demand exceeds supply, there will be waiting times. Thus, location–time access is a basic feature of an SPP.

Second, an SPP has a range of different services that are not substitutes for each other. An SPP may treat trauma, but not provide dental care. Thus, a main feature is the variety of non-substitutable offerings at one SPP.

Third, the services can be provided at variable specialization levels that are substitutes for treatment of the same problem. A paramedic, a GP, a trauma specialist, or a highly specialized orthopedist can treat a broken bone. The levels of specialization carry different costs. To cover these, the expensive specialist capacity needs to be fully utilized.

The three basic attributes of an SPP—location–time access, variety, and specialization—constitute a trilemma, a three-factor optimization problem with no obvious solution, called the devil's triangle.[3] The solutions are constrained by the catchment areas that provide the service volume, which in turn determines the capacity utilization rate, which in turn is the basis for investment decisions (Figure 3.1).

The higher the level of specialization, the larger the catchment area and the worse the location access. In dense urban areas, this is not necessarily a problem, but in rural and remote areas it becomes a pressing issue. If an SPP wants to offer an easy access next-door service, it may not afford a large variety of services and high specialization levels. If a hospital wants to offer the highest level of specialization, it may have to limit variety. A hospital that wants to accept all comers with a broad variety will have to compromise access and specialization.

An illustration of the devil's trilemma is found in retailing. The traditional solution has been local merchants and mom-and-pop corner shops that rely on convenience, that is, an access maximization strategy. They offer a limited variety of goods at prices that must support low-volume operations. If the catchment area offers sufficient demand volume, small players can band together and form a bazaar to overcome the constraints of variety. Increasing wealth has led to specialization maximizers, who focus on single brands and professional quality goods and offer expert advice at a price. Modern logistics and the automobile created the variety maximizers, typically hypermarkets with over 50,000 items on sale, with moderate specialization and poor location access to those without cars. When a Wal-Mart locates in a region, it brings devastation to the small fry.

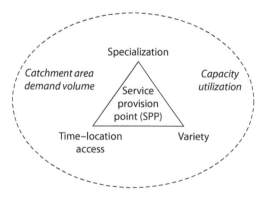

FIGURE 3.1
The devil's triangle.

Similar strategies can be observed in health services. Traditional healers and family doctors offer convenient access. Super-specialty hospitals grab the high end and locate on the main street. Multispecialty hospitals offer everything that is needed on one campus.

The constellation in retailing has been challenged by innovators. Convenience stores combine local access with large efficient supply chains, driving out traditional vendors. Specialty shops congregate at upscale malls. Variety maximizers offer free bus services and home deliveries of bulky items. E-commerce and network shopping is a game changer in retailing. They are bound to disrupt hospitals, too.

BUSINESS MODEL OF A HOSPITAL

As any organization with a mission, a hospital needs a business model that defines its strategy and operations. A useful conceptual tool for this purpose is Osterwalder's business model canvas (BMC)[4]. A business model should include definitions of the following issues, as illustrated in Figure 3.2:

- Customer segments: Whom do you serve? A whole population in a region or one or several segments?
- Customer relations: How are relations with patients and other stake-holders formed and managed?

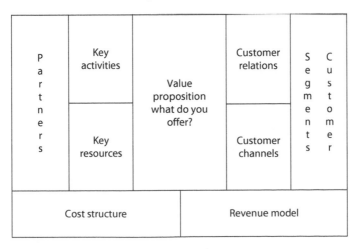

FIGURE 3.2
The business model canvas.

- Channels: How do patients communicate with, and reach the hospital? What kinds of gatekeepers are there?
- Value proposition: What is the hospital supposed to deliver and which are the value drivers?
- Key resources: Buildings, personnel, equipment, accommodation service, outpatient facilities
- Key activities: Core and support processes
- Key partners: Suppliers, financiers, regulators, universities, vocational schools
- Cost structure
- Revenue model

The BMC is used to clarify how different issues impact each other. Different customer segments ask for different value propositions, which require different key activities, which require different resources and partners. A Coxa-type hospital focusing on patients in need of an artificial knee or hip joint needs to build relations with GPs and the orthopedic community, invest in single-purpose resources, and develop processes with industrial efficiency.

CUSTOMER'S SEGMENT: WHO ARE SERVED?

Customer segmentation can be approached in two overlapping ways. First, segments can be defined based on the served populations within a catchment area, that is, the region from which a hospital draws most of its patients. Regional hospitals in publicly financed health systems typically have a catchment area to serve without much competition. In market-based systems, a typical segmentation is based on purchasing power or insurance coverage. There are high-end and low-end hospitals. A hospital can focus on demographic categories, such as the elderly, women, children, or veterans.

A second segmentation principle is based on demand upon arrival. The basic classifying variables are urgency and severity. Typical arrival categories and corresponding key resources and key activities are given in Table 3.1.

Customer Relations

By definition, a customer is an individual or a legal entity who has the capabilities to choose, pay, and use a product or a service. A patient is

TABLE 3.1

Examples of Demand Categories and Corresponding Value Propositions, Key
Resources, and Key Activities

Arrival Category	Value Proposition	Key Resources	Key Activities
Random emergency	Save and stabilize	24/7 emergency team	Triage
Predictable urgency (birthing)	Timely access	Birthing unit	Midwifery
Severe non-urgent (cancer)	Cure	Specialists	Multistep processes
Electives with ward care	Procedure	Operating rooms, wards	Capacity allocation, scheduling
Unclear problems	Diagnosis and care plans	Laboratories, imaging	Clinical decision making
Recovering patients	Rehabilitation	Healing environment	Monitoring, therapies
Chronic conditions	Disease management	Long-term wards, hospices	Care routines

first and foremost a user or benefactor of a service. However, the value
of the service affects others, such as family, community, employers, and
ultimately society. Patients who pay out of pocket and have the capability
to shop around are customers in the full meaning of the word. There are,
however, instances where the role of the customer is split among several
actors. In an insurance-based health system, the insurance company is
the primary payer that may also have a say in the choice of caregiver and
care types. In publicly funded systems, these roles fall to the appropriate
authorities. In occupational health systems, employers pay their part and
tend to make demands, such as fast recovery.

In health networks, patients often first approach a GP or family doctor,
who gets the role of a chooser, or at least has a significant impact on the
choice.

Customer Channels

Customer channels refer to the ways by which patients or other relevant
actors approach and access a hospital. The basic categories are walk-in
patients and those with an appointment, that is, on-demand and on-
schedule patients. A further categorization is walk-in versus wheel-in, that
is, those who come by their own devices and those who need help.

The types of entry impact resources and activities. In many hospitals, there are specific entry points for wheel-in emergencies and walk-in on-schedule cases.

A more difficult and unpredictable issue concerning the customer channels are digitalized services; will there be a need for a patient to physically visit a hospital in the future? Most likely the answer in some cases will be "no" and therefore the need for facilities may be smaller in the future.

Value Proposition: What Is Delivered?

The core of a business model is the relation between segments and value: what is offered to whom?

At one extreme, a hospital may offer everything to everybody. This is often the case in publicly financed systems, where the government demands that a hospital serves a regional population and nobody in need can be turned away. The limiting factor becomes the availability of specialized resources. Following the logic of the devil's triangle, the region may not have the volumes to support sufficient capacity utilization of expensive specialists. In such cases, a partnership with central and university hospitals is required. Thus, a key issue is to decide what to do and what not to do.

In situations where a hospital faces a competitive market, it may find it wise to focus on something and limit access to everything else. A typical focus strategy is to pick a demographic segment. There are children's and women's hospitals, geriatric hospitals for the elderly, and military hospitals for the services. Focus may be put on arrival characteristics, which produces specialized emergency and trauma hospitals. Supply-based focus strategies may concentrate on body systems, disease types, or principal methods. There are eye hospitals, cancer clinics, surgical hospitals, and psychiatry units. Focus can be anchored in certain processes, such as surgical factories doing only cataracts or joint replacements. Finally, there are hospitals where the focus is on care outcomes, such as terminal care, detoxification, or rehabilitation units.

Key Activities

Key activities, that is, what is done at a hospital, obviously follows from who is served for what purpose. Activities are typically described as processes. They can be defined as a planned and purposeful series of linked steps each contributing to the expected outcome. At the core of a process is a value chain. It is determined by the clinical technologies used and can be described as the necessary things that need to happen to a patient's medical condition in order to achieve the expected goal. A value chain is enacted by various tasks and routines performed by both caregivers and patients. Thus, a process is a description of activities, what is done to and by a patient, while a value chain is a description of the changes in the medical state that need to happen to a patient.

The best practices and available resources of clinical medicine determine the value chain. Value chains change as technologies and care methods improve. Processes, on the other hand, can be designed in many ways but still achieve the same results. Some processes may do it slowly at great expense, while others generate a swift even flow at low cost. There are various methodologies for designing, managing, and improving processes, such as Lean, the theory of constraints, and Agile management.

Processes can be categorized and grouped in various ways. The level of standardization gives standard processes with identical repetition of given tasks. These are mostly found in diagnostics and support services, and can be made subject to automation. Routine processes deal with cases that are similar but not identical, requiring case-by-case choices between alternatives and individual judgments. Most processes in healthcare are routine and need to be managed as such by involving standardized components (e.g., laboratory tests), decision heuristics, and support. Finally, there are non-routine processes that typically appear in very rare cases and require unique problem-solving skills.

Another aspect to processes is the division between continuous flows and discrete processes. A process involving two or more discrete steps, that is, steps that are performed at different times, different locations, or by different personnel, needs to be connected by handovers. Each step needs to consider what has been done before and what is planned to come next. Handovers are managed by verbal communication and/or documentation. A typical problem is that handovers are done poorly leading to situations where the left hand does not know what the right hand is doing. There are basically two ways to deal with this. Using multiskilled teams so as not to unnecessarily split therapies into discrete steps can reduce the number of handovers per patient. Where handovers are unavoidable, they can be managed by real-time patient information systems and accompanying protocols.

Processes are grouped into bundles or care pathways. A fundamental design choice is should processes be organized around patient journeys or around functional clinical specialties. Both solutions have their merits and demerits, which depend on the chosen segments and value propositions. High-volume routines can be organized into production lines that offer something like prepackaged journeys to patients. For other types, resource centers and specialized units are better solutions.

Key Resources

The key resource in healthcare is personnel. In wealthy societies, personnel costs are up to 80% of the total cost, if the personnel component of purchased goods and services is counted. Thus, recruiting, training, and other human resource issues are crucial. Particularly in remote areas, the availability of staff can become the most crucial factor in deciding on a hospital's location.

Key Partners

A hospital is a node in a health service network. If it has an emergency department, it will get patients directly from the point of need. For other cases, typically there is a supplier of patient flows, such as family doctors, GPs, care homes, and other hospitals. A hospital that has a limited variety of offerings and/or is not able to offer services at the highest level of specialization has to found partnerships with other hospitals with complementary competencies. At the output side of a hospital there is a need for partners, such as rehabilitation centers, community care, and family doctors, to monitor the progress of discharged patients.

When the elements of the BMC are sufficiently clear, call in the architects and engineers.

CASE: KAINUU HOSPITAL

Our cases are from Finland, where the healthcare system is a decentralized version of the British Beveridge model. Two-thirds of healthcare finance comes from taxes, a nominal fee is paid at the point of care. Most of the service production is operated by municipalities, which may outsource some or all service production to private providers. Municipalities band together to form districts to run hospitals. While patient choice of caregiver has been expanded recently, and some specialized single-procedure hospitals (Coxa) have been established, in practice each hospital serves a catchment area and needs to cater to all types of demand. Patients can't be turned away for non-clinical reasons, for example, the inability to pay. This makes for a quite different situation compared to countries where hospitals serve overlapping catchment areas and compete for patients.

Finland, as with all Beveridge model health systems, is struggling with a set of global problems: cost inflation, increase in demand due to aging and medicalization, long waiting times, and a variety of private service providers eroding the tax-financed public provision principles.

The public service system is organized on traditional lines based on urgency (walk-in vs. appointment) and severity (primary vs. secondary). This produces four types of organizations:

- Primary emergency: Walk-in patients with urgent but not severe issues.
- Primary scheduled: Patients with non-urgent, non-severe ailments request appointments.
- Secondary emergency: Urgent and severe cases, including ambulance patients.
- Secondary scheduled: Patients with referrals.

A recent health policy debate has focused on network issues. First, while specialist hospital care is generally perceived as efficient, especially in urgent cases, there is growing dissatisfaction with primary care, particularly long waiting times for non-urgent appointments. The relation between primary and specialist care is perceived as problematic. Patient journeys that include several providers tend to be long and confusing even with all providers being public operators under a common finance and governance system. The coordination of complex flows is an issue. Thus, there are initiatives calling for closer organizational integration between primary and specialist care. This has largely been achieved in emergency care by combining generalists and specialists in common emergency care units.

Second, as the burden of disease has shifted from curable emergencies toward long-term and lifestyle-related problems, the cooperation between social and medical care becomes an issue.

Third, Finland has a low population density, particularly in the north. The tax bases of the local hospital catchment areas are insufficient to support specialized expensive services. This is accentuated by the question of birthing. A birthing unit with 24/7 emergency capabilities to minimize the risk of perinatal deaths and injuries, requires a minimum of a thousand births per year. About 25% of the current regional hospitals do not have such volumes. The solution is to keep the units but accept the higher unit costs and possibly drain resources from other sectors. Alternatively, patients will have to travel to central hospitals, which increases the risk of on-the-road deliveries. Decision makers face a nasty trade-off. The problem is accentuated by the fact that a 24/7 birthing unit and a general emergency unit can share some resources. If the birthing unit goes, the emergency unit will soon follow. Under economic constraints, regional hospitals are forced to consider a number of network-related options.

Case Kainuu

Kainuu is a nine-municipality region in northeastern Finland close to the Russian border. It has a population of 80,000 inhabitants, of which half are concentrated in Kajaani, the regional capital. Outside the city, the population density is low leading to long-distance travel.

The central hospital of Kainuu has reached the end of its technical life span; thus, there is a need for massive renovation or the construction of new buildings (Figure 3.3).

The leaders of the hospital wanted to renew the concept of the hospital and change the way the service production was organized jointly with the building of a new facility. The objective was to create a modern hospital with both modern facilities and a modern way of producing services.

An exceptional feature of Kainuu is that the hospital is part of the larger Kainuu social and healthcare organization, which is responsible for all the social and healthcare services in the region. Usually, secondary care is produced by a separate organization, while individual municipalities produce primary care and social services.

Key issues to be solved in the planning process were, first, should there be a 24/7 emergency care unit? Would babies be delivered in the hospital in the future? The small size of the hospital district catchment area means that the unit cost of 24/7 emergency care is high. On an average year, there are about 700 births in the region, significantly below the stipulated volume. As the central government finances municipalities, there is a risk

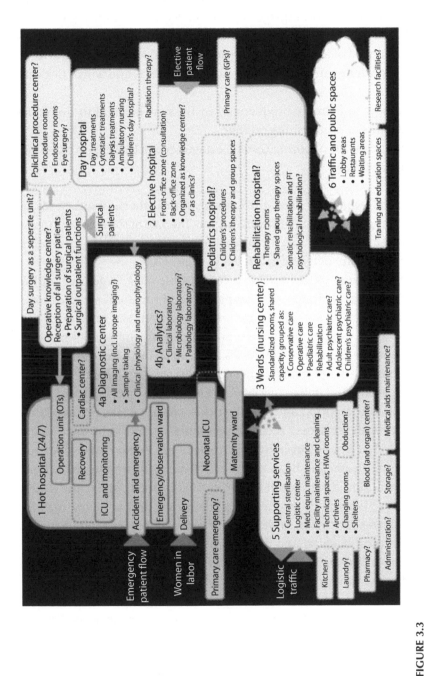

FIGURE 3.3
The basic structure of the Kainuu Hospital.

of government-level intervention and closure of fully equipped birthing units.

Second, how to secure sufficient and good-quality doctors and nurses in the future when the working-age population decreases in the region.

Third, how to manage the aging population and the increasing numbers of people in need of a variety of medical and social services. How to allocate resources for primary, secondary, and social care, and where to locate the facilities.

Finally, how to increase productivity in the new hospital to overcome the constraints of diminishing revenue.

The main concept planning results, categorized according to the BMC model, are as follows.

> *Customer segments*: Given the circumstances, the hospital needs to serve the whole population of Kainuu. The size of the elderly population requires some specific arrangements. The role of the hospital in the healthcare network is defined in Figure 3.3.
>
> *Value proposition*: The hospital is responsible for a larger part of the care episode. Primary care outpatient and inpatient services from Kajaani healthcare center are collocated with the hospital facilities. They used to be in a separate building some 2.5 km away. A separate ward and processes are established for those elderly patients with other challenges besides acute medical problems (e.g., dementia), where geriatric consultations, physical and occupational therapists, and social worker consultations are available. Social care services, including psychiatry and substance abuse rehabilitation, however, are not co-located, as easy time–location access is deemed to be important in these services. Organizational integration across several locations, that is, the hospital and health centers, is done by pediatrics, gynecology, and primary care for children sharing the same chief physician. Doctors rotate between the central hospital and the local health centers.
>
> *Customer relation:* The hospital is positioned as a full service hospital with emergency care services and neonatal delivery 24/7.
>
> *Channels*: The hospital accepts walk-in for emergency care, ambulance, and referral patients. The hospital will also provide specialist and consultation services for the health centers in order to reduce the need for a hospital visit.

Key resources: Resources used to be organized according to clinical specialties. A functional organization is based on an emergency department, bed wards, ambulatory care, and so on. As specialists are a scarce and most valuable resource, technology is used to provide e-services so that specialists can be physically somewhere else.

Key activities: The hospital is organized around four activity blocks. The first is the hot hospital. Operating theaters, intensive care and cardiac care units, and diagnostics are situated next to the emergency care department. The second block is the elective hospital including a polyclinic procedure center and rehabilitation. The third block is the wards that serve all patients who need to stay overnight. The fourth block consists of analytics, laboratories, and imaging. The fifth is supporting services, and the sixth is traffic and public spaces.

Due to the small size of the hospital and comparatively low volumes, a patient process–based design could not be applied, as dedicated pathways would not receive a sufficient amount of patients. Almost all doctors need to work for both the acute and elective care processes. The nursing staff, which used to be organized by medical specialty, is organized according to the blocks to ensure the flexible use of personnel to match the varying demand.

Key partners: Primary care, although partly integrated into the hospital, is the main partner that feeds patients into the hospital. For patients with chronic diseases, the hospital and primary care health centers form designated teams including specialists from the hospital, thereby eliminating the need for referrals to specialist consultations. As the size of the catchment area restricts the levels of specialization, a partnership is formed with the nearest university hospital in the city of Oulu.

As illustrated in Figure 3.4, the hospital defines itself as an acute and general hospital, where a set of diagnoses and treatments offer a defined set of variety. The nearby primary care focuses on people; patients stay the same while their diagnoses change over time.

The Kainuu Hospital is still under construction but according to *pro forma* calculations the productivity of the hospital will be about 10% higher than before. The mission, services, and profile of the hospital are more clearly defined then before, which facilitates the adaptation of changes in the future.

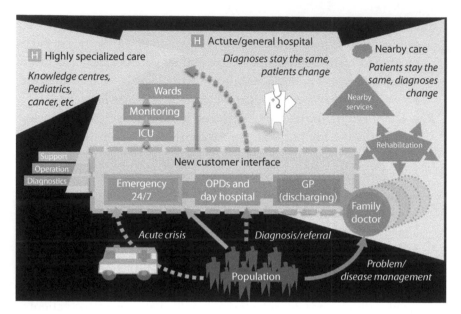

FIGURE 3.4
The Kainuu Hospital as a node in a network.

SUMMARY

Advances in medicine, information, and communication technologies and shifts in cost structures and population bases affect hospital design. The devil's triangle illuminates some basic trade-offs that need to be made. The BMC helps in defining the specific choices that need to be made. The Kainuu Hospital case illustrates that local conditions are powerful constraints to what can be feasibly done. Different circumstances will produce different designs that will expand the space of possible alternatives.

REFERENCES

1. Coase R., 1937. The nature of the firm. *Economica*, 4 (16), 386–405.
2. Williamson O., 1981. The economics of organization: The transaction cost approach. *The American Journal of Sociology*, 87 (3), 548–577.
3. Lillrank P., Torkki P., Venesmaa J., and Malmström T., 2011. Regional Healthcare Service Systems: A Conceptualization of the Meso-Level of Healthcare. SRII Global Conference, San Jose, CA.
4. Osterwalder A., Pigneur Y., Smith A., 2010. *Business Model Generation*, Wiley, New York.

4

Patient First, Functions Next, and Design Later

V.K. Singh and S.K. Biswas

CONTENTS

INTRODUCTION

Hospital design and planning concepts have evolved rapidly over the last few decades. The starting point was "functions follow design." Hospital facilities were created in any existing building such as an old barracks or a jail. Care functions had to be squeezed within the existing walls. This was followed by "design follows functions." New facilities were designed as per the needs of hospital functions and functionaries. Fixed assets, such as operating rooms, imaging equipment, and laboratories, were arranged to maximize capacity utilization. Patients had to adapt to the requirements of functions. More recently, the concept "design follows first patients, then functions" has been adopted. The emphasis now is on integrating the needs of patients, hospital functions, and functionaries in hospital design. Integration by definition means optimization. No party can get everything they want. The parts have to submit to the whole, which is a basic integrative principle. Here, it is the needs of the patient. This should be kept in mind when new tools and technologies, such as information and communication technology (ICT), evidence-based planning (EBP), Lean process thinking, and innovation and life-cycle cost analysis are being used.[1] This chapter lays out the basic concepts of patient-centric hospital planning and design.

PATIENT FIRST

In a world with innovations, yesterday's luxury is today's routine; tomorrow it will be a basic necessity. It used to be that patients had to travel to their hospital to be told their laboratory results. Now, they can be sent via e-mail. Such capabilities should be included when designing a hospital information system.

A hospital is an alien environment to most people. Patients dread going there. When care can't be administered at home, hospital visits and stays are necessary. A hospital should be planned to be patient friendly and homely. Many studies have investigated patients' perceptions, attitudes, and requirements toward a hospital. In general, they are a homely atmosphere, a supportive environment, good physical design including acoustics and visuals, access to external areas, and provision of facilities for recreation and leisure. Patients come to hospitals from diverse cultural and religious background and such diverse requirements should be considered. Being sick and hospitalized is a social event; therefore, hospitals should cater to the needs of relatives, friends, and visitors. There are patients and visitors who are disabled and their needs should be integrated during planning.

Patients are looking for compassion, courtesy, and competence and we should emulate many good aspects of the hospitality industry when designing a healthcare facility, and train staff as they are trained by hotels. We should make comparisons of hospitals with hotels, while in hospitals the sick are admitted, in hotels healthy people are checked in. Hospitals have functional areas like operation suites, laboratories, specialized areas, and medical equipment as well as the functionalities that exist in hotels such as dietary services, housekeeping, and security services etc. Another example is to create a Disney experience in hospital to energize patients. All of these inputs should be integrated at the planning stage. Lean teaching is to listen to the "voice of the customer," which is the patient in the hospital context. The facility should be so designed that the patient markets the hospital by word of mouth, as this is a far stronger tool than advertising.

The patient faces uncertainty and is apprehensive hence he needs to be constantly communicated with and informed about his treatment and health. Communication is another area of concern to be included as a planning parameter.

In 1948, the World Health Organization (WHO) defined health as "A state of complete physical, mental, and social wellbeing not merely the absence of disease or infirmity." This definition is too comprehensive for practical use. It is not useful in chronic cases for which there is no cure. An alternative definition is focused on peoples' ability to adapt to various conditions. While the upside "complete wellbeing" is difficult to define and measure, the downside is easier. The first obligation of health-care is to "do no harm." The WHO partners with the Joint Commission International (JCI) accrediting health-care organizations to improve health-care systems to protect patients. Patient safety as defined by the WHO and the JCI includes many important planning considerations. One central consideration is infection control. It demands air conditioning with air changes, temperature control, high efficiency percolate air (HEPA) filtering, positive/negative pressure for barrier or reverse barrier nursing, sterilization, and waste management. Despite their best efforts, hospitals are dangerous places. Patients should not be kept hospitalized for longer than necessary. Therefore, home care, day care, and hospitals without walls are important safety considerations.

FUNCTIONS NEXT

After patient needs, process optimization, and safety have been secured, the functions should be considered. Some functions, such as operating theaters (OT), procedures in operation, emergency services, intensive care units (ICU), laboratories, and blood banks are hot areas with activity round the clock. The location of such functions should be determined by flow analysis. The concept of a control room monitoring critical activities round the clock backed by a customized hospital information system has been created at Iris Hospital in Kolkata, India. IT systems can be used to manage patient flows, particularly bringing together all the information needed for swift discharges. As IT systems can be hacked, cybersecurity is also a patient safety issue.

DESIGN LATER

Hospital design is a truly complex undertaking. Several requirements have to be integrated over a number of systems, not only physical layouts, but also the flow of patients that has to be synchronized with the flow of tasks performed by caregivers; the in- and outbound material flows, and the IT systems that enable real-time management. Iris Hospital is an example of a planning approach that started with patient requirements, and proceeded to work flows and departmental integration applying Lean and innovative, evidence-based design. These concepts are described by case studies in Chapter 8 of this book.

SUMMARY

The newer hospital planning and design concepts have revalorized the healthcare delivery system. If planning is done well it decreases operational costs and improves efficiency and patient satisfaction. Well-planned healthcare facilities will transform healthcare delivery systems.

REFERENCE

1. Biswas S.K. and Singh V.K.: Chapter 7 in *Innovations in Healthcare Management: Cost-Effective and Sustainable Solutions* by V.K. Singh and Paul Lillrank, published in 2015 by CRC Press, Boca Raton, FL.

5

Green Hospitals and Sustainable Solution to Healthcare Facility

Rajeev Boudhankar

CONTENTS

INTRODUCTION

Green hospital concepts will play an important role in the curative process in time to come. Instead of being referred to as a place that houses healthcare amenities, hospitals of tomorrow will now focus on wellness and be transformed into welcoming spaces in which to get well.

Health administrators are increasingly looking to introduce green initiatives and environment-friendly practices into the design, building, and management of healthcare facilities. This shift to sustainable healthcare facilities is primarily centered around reducing the carbon footprint of hospitals and incorporating modern "green building" design elements into the healthcare environment to improve patient care and allow hospital occupants to feel more at ease.

As hospitals typically use significantly more resources and produce more waste than comparably sized commercial buildings, the effective deployment of environmentally driven strategies to improve resource management is of critical importance in the development of sustainable healthcare facilities. The World Health Organization (WHO) too, has urged hospitals to proactively address the environmental footprint of the healthcare sector by reducing power consumption and utilizing alternative energy generation through the recycling and conservation of resources.

A range of energy efficiency measures, which rightly form the starting point for many global green hospital initiatives, are being adopted both in the renovation of existing facilities and in the construction of new hospitals. Core measures include the use of energy-efficient medical equipment and lighting systems in hospitals to reduce their energy expenses, as well as the deployment of technologically advanced energy management systems that leverage on-site renewable energy sources.

These transformational energy solutions, coupled with the implementation of efficient water management and a focus on the reuse of resources, can greatly reduce the overall environmental impact of healthcare facilities, increase efficiency, and reduce the cost of operations.

Besides the goal of reducing their carbon footprint, hospitals are also looking at how to increase the amount of daylighting and natural ventilation into the healing environment. To raise the standards of patient care, a sustainable hospital design should also look at improving indoor air quality.

Ultimately, a well-preserved and ecologically sound environment is critical for good health, and there is a tremendous opportunity for the healthcare sector to optimize resource management and improve site sustainability in future hospital settings.[1]

Let Us First Understand What Is Meant by "Green Building" and Why We Should Go Green

So, What Are Green Buildings?

"Green" or "sustainable" buildings use resources such as energy, water, materials, and land more efficiently than regular standard or conventional buildings. With more natural light and better air quality, green buildings typically contribute to improved employee health, comfort, and productivity.

Financial Benefits of Green Buildings

Green buildings provide financial benefits that conventional buildings do not. These benefits include energy and water savings, reduced waste, improved indoor environmental quality, greater employee comfort/productivity, reduced employee health costs, and lower operations and maintenance costs.

Generally, buildings account for one-sixth of the world's freshwater withdrawal, a quarter of its wood harvest, and two-fifths of its material and energy flows.

Hence, it would be justifiable to say "building green" is an opportunity to use our resources efficiently while creating healthier buildings that improve human health, build a better environment, and provide cost savings.

DEFINITION—GREEN HOSPITALS

A green hospital building can be defined as one that enhances patient well-being and aids the curative process, while utilizing natural resources in an efficient and environment-friendly manner.

Help Reduce Long-Term Energy Consumption While Improving the Health of Patients and the Community!

Patient health, community health, and environmental health are all negatively affected by multiple aspects of hospital construction, design, and maintenance. Increasing numbers of studies have found correlations between the materials used in hospitals and human disease. For instance, volatile organic compounds such as formaldehyde, acetaldehyde, naphthalene, and toluene are released into the air from particle board and carpets. These toxins, breathed in by patients and hospital staff, have been correlated with longer patient recovery times and more staff sick days. The inadequate ventilation found in most hospitals also contributes to poor indoor air quality and pollution. The production of polyvinyl chloride (PVC), which is widely used in the production of intravenous (IV) bags, plastic tubing, and other healthcare supplies, releases the carcinogen dioxin, which has been associated with a number of other health problems, including developmental defects, endometriosis, learning disabilities, and endocrine disorders. Mercury—a component of thermometers, blood pressure cuffs, and other supplies—is widely found in hospital waste released into the air and water. Other chemicals used to clean and maintain hospitals add additional toxins to the environment.[3]

The green hospital movement began a few years ago following the U.S. Green Building Council's (USGBC) release of their Leadership in Energy and Environmental Design (LEED) standards for building construction. Although initial construction costs are higher, green hospitals have been shown to reduce long-term energy costs. In addition, there is a growing consensus among the healthcare profession that pollutants generated by medical facilities must be reduced. Moreover, green hospital design has been linked to better patient outcomes and staff retention. In the past few years, a number of newly constructed and renovated hospital buildings have strived for and received LEED certification.

The LEED certification building requirements include specific commitments to minimizing the use of resources, maximizing energy efficiency, and releasing minimal waste into the surrounding environment. The specifications to be met include criteria that fall under the following categories:

- Sustainability of the site
- Water efficiency
- Energy and atmosphere
- Materials and resources
- Indoor environmental quality
- Innovation in design

Designing a green hospital according to these requirements would not only fulfill our obligation to the local area as an environmentally friendly neighbor, but would also offer many economic advantages that would serve the hospital well into the future. With reduced expenditure on energy, water, and waste production, the hospital would have greater potential to reduce its operating costs. Can a building help cure you?

Research shows that a well-designed hospital building can actually accelerate the curing process. Increasingly, therefore, designers are focusing on green strategies to enhance the positive impacts on patients and staff in hospitals. Design professionals need to know how their buildings will enhance a cure—through spatial and physical ambience.

Benefits of Green Hospitals[2]

- Can reduce patient recovery time
- Eliminates sick building syndrome (SBS) for both patients and staff
- Reduces stress levels in hospital workers, thus improving quality of care
- Lower energy and water consumption

Focus Areas for Green Hospital Design

1. Lighting
2. Indoor air quality: Passive and active measures
3. Green housekeeping
4. Clean and green interior building materials
5. Gardens and landscape

In the architectural planning and design of green hospitals, an overarching consideration is to ensure that the floor plate facilitates efficiency. An efficient floor plate design will reduce the construction footprint of a hospital—thus benefiting both the owner (lowered construction cost) and the patient (fast, smooth, and efficient transit through the hospital).

Lighting

A good hospital design should maximize daylight and optimize the artificial lighting requirement. Daylighting is the controlled admission of natural light from the sky (direct and diffused) into a building, to reduce the use of electrical energy for lighting.

Benefits of Daylighting and Views in Hospitals (Figure 5.1)

- Proven to have positive effects on patients in hospitals.
- Enhances the health and well-being of the patients and reduces the stress levels of hospital employees, thus improving quality of care.

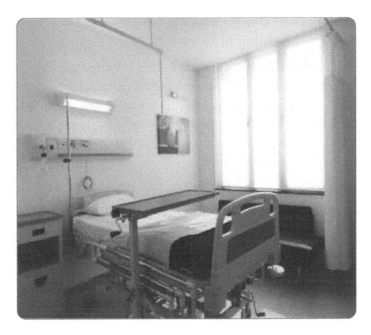

FIGURE 5.1
Natural light in a patient's room.

- Combats seasonal affective disorder, or winter depression, through connectivity to natural vistas.
- Improves facility's overall operational efficiency.

It is a well-known fact that

- Humans naturally synthesize 90% of their body's requirement of vitamin D through the skin's exposure to sunlight.
- Buildings can save up to 20% of their cooling energy load by optimally substituting artificial lighting with daylighting.

Artificial lighting is required in sensitive areas of a hospital, including operating theaters (OTs), medical dispensaries, and interior corridors and passages. However, with rising energy costs and high initial investment, it is imperative to reduce the operational cost of lighting in hospitals by combining natural lighting and efficient artificial lighting.

Some of the Passive Design Aspects to Enhance Natural Lighting in Hospitals

- Design glazing facades to provide both a view and daylight
- Install translucent skylights that have soothing colors
- Provide transparent and operable openings to green courtyards
- Consider ledge seating at windows, thereby engaging nature in the curative process

Some of the Design Aspects to Enhance the Efficiency of Artificial Lighting in Hospitals

- Use occupancy sensors in passageways, storage rooms, laboratories, and so on
- Install low-energy light-emitting diode (LED) lighting to save on indoor lighting energy costs (up to 40%)
- Use task lights to provide illumination in task areas such as consulting rooms, laboratories, and wards

Indoor Air Quality by Passive and Active Design

As restoring and safeguarding health is the main purpose of healthcare facilities, indoor environmental quality is considered critical to green hospitals.

Must Do's for Good Indoor Environment

- Install permanent entryway systems such as slotted systems, grates, or grilles at all primary entrances, to capture dust particles.
- Use certain species of indoor plants that not only produce oxygen but also reduce indoor pollutants such as volatile organic compounds (VOCs) from air.
- Improve fresh air by providing courtyard spaces with native and adaptive plant species, which are free from any allergic effects.
- Use zero-VOC interior materials.

Green Housekeeping

The accumulation of dust, soil, and microbial contaminants on surfaces is a potential source of nosocomial (hospital-borne) infections. Effective and efficient cleaning methods and schedules are therefore necessary to maintain a clean and healthy environment in healthcare buildings.

Today, housekeeping policies and procedures increasingly focus on making a positive environmental impact. Typical measures include:

- Insist on cleaning products that meet environmental standards
- Provide personnel training for safe handling and disposal of hospital waste
- Consider waste recycling wherever feasible

Clean and Green Interior Building Materials (Figure 5.2)

Hospitals may inadvertently contribute to illness by exposing patients and staff to a host of pathogenic germs and toxins that enter the hospital premises through the medium of a large number of infected patients.

- Ensure that hospital surfaces have the capability to repel or resist the growth of pathogenic germs and bacteria. Patented interior surfaces are now available that resist bacterial and fungal growth (Figure 5.2). These include countertops, tiles, vinyl flooring, and so on.
- Consider using copper-based interior materials. Recent research has shown that copper is a good material for common "touch" surfaces

FIGURE 5.2
Germ-resistant surface.

in hospitals (door handles, light switches, faucets, countertops, etc.) due to its microbial-resistant properties.
- Use indoor flooring that does not emit, absorb, or re-release indoor pollutants such as VOCs and dust.

Gardens and Landscape (Figure 5.3)

Gardens and landscape are an aesthetic delight and promote the wellness of patients in hospitals. Persons exposed to plants have higher levels of positive feelings (pleasantness, calm) as opposed to negative feelings (anger, fear).

Various research studies show that recuperation from stress is faster and complete when patients are exposed to natural settings than any other form of built environment.

Benefits Achieved by the Rated Green Hospitals[2]

- Better indoor air quality
- 20%–40% energy savings
- 35%–40% water savings
- Good daylighting
- No sick building syndrome
- Faster patient recovery

FIGURE 5.3
Landscaping around a hospital.

LEED 2009 FOR HEALTHCARE: OVERVIEW AND PROCESS[4]

The LEED 2009 for Healthcare Green Building Rating System is a set of performance standards for certifying healthcare facilities. The intent is to promote healthful, durable, affordable, and environmentally sound practices in building design and construction.

Prerequisites and Credits in the LEED 2009 for Healthcare Address 7 Topics

- Sustainable sites (SS)
- Water efficiency (WE)
- Energy and atmosphere (EA)
- Materials and resources (MR)
- Indoor environmental quality (IEQ)
- Innovation in design (ID)
- Regional priority (RP)

LEED 2009 for Healthcare Certifications Is Awarded According to the Following Scale

Certified 40–49 points
Silver 50–59 points
Gold 60–79 points
Platinum 80 points and above
"Green Building Council of India" recognizes buildings that achieve one of these rating levels with a formal letter of certification.

When to Use LEED 2009 for Healthcare

LEED for Healthcare was written primarily for inpatient and outpatient care facilities and licensed long-term care facilities. The rating system may also be used for medical offices, assisted-living facilities, and medical education and research centers. LEED for Healthcare addresses the design and construction activities for both new buildings and major renovations of existing buildings. A major renovation involves major heating, ventilation, and air-conditioning (HVAC) renovation, significant envelope modifications, and major interior rehabilitation. For major renovation of an existing building, LEED for Healthcare is the appropriate rating system. If the project scope does not involve significant design and construction activities and focuses more on operations and maintenance activities, LEED for Existing Buildings: Operations and Maintenance is more appropriate because it addresses the operational and maintenance issues of working buildings.

LEED 2009 FOR HEALTHCARE PROJECT CHECKLIST[4]

Sustainable Sites: 18 Possible Points

Prerequisite 1: Construction Activity Pollution Prevention—Required
Prerequisite 2: Environmental Site Assessment—Required

- Credit 1 Site Selection: 1 point
- Credit 2 Development Density and Community Connectivity: 1 point
- Credit 3 Brownfield Redevelopment: 1 point
- Credit 4.1 Alternative Transportation—Public Transportation Access: 3 points
- Credit 4.2 Alternative Transportation—Bicycle Storage and Changing Rooms: 1 point
- Credit 4.3 Alternative Transportation—Low-Emitting and Fuel-Efficient Vehicles: 1 point
- Credit 4.4 Alternative Transportation—Parking Capacity: 1 point
- Credit 5.1 Site Development—Protect or Restore Habitat: 1 point
- Credit 5.2 Site Development—Maximize Open Space: 1 point
- Credit 6.1 Stormwater Design—Quantity Control: 1 point
- Credit 6.2 Stormwater Design—Quality Control: 1 point
- Credit 7.1 Heat Island Effect—Non-roof: 1 point
- Credit 7.2 Heat Island Effect—Roof: 1 point
- Credit 8 Light Pollution Reduction: 1 point
- Credit 9.1 Connection to the Natural World—Places of Respite: 1 point
- Credit 9.2 Connection to the Natural World—Direct Exterior Access for Patients: 1 point

Water Efficiency: Nine Possible Points

Prerequisite 1: Water Use Reduction—Required
Prerequisite 2: Minimize Potable Water Use for Medical Equipment Cooling—Required

- Credit 1 Water Efficient Landscaping—No Potable Water Use or No Irrigation: 1 point
- Credit 2 Water Use Reduction—Measurement and Verification: 1–2 points
- Credit 3 Water Use Reduction: 1–3 points
- Credit 4.1 Water Use Reduction—Building Equipment: 1 point
- Credit 4.2 Water Use Reduction—Cooling Towers: 1 point
- Credit 4.3 Water Use Reduction—Food Waste Systems: 1 point

Energy and Atmosphere: 39 Possible Points

Prerequisite 1: Fundamental Commissioning of Building Energy Systems—Required
Prerequisite 2: Minimum Energy Performance—Required
Prerequisite 3: Fundamental Refrigerant Management—Required

- Credit 1 Optimize Energy Performance: 1–24 points
- Credit 2 On-Site Renewable Energy: 1–8 points
- Credit 3 Enhanced Commissioning: 1–2 points
- Credit 4 Enhanced Refrigerant Management: 1 point
- Credit 5 Measurement and Verification: 2 points
- Credit 6 Green Power: 1 point
- Credit 7 Community Contaminant Prevention—Airborne Releases: 1 point

Materials and Resources: 16 Possible Points

Prerequisite 1: Storage and Collection of Recyclables—Required
Prerequisite 2: PBT Source Reduction—Mercury—Required

- Credit 1.1 Building Reuse—Maintain Existing Walls, Floors, and Roof: 1–3 points
- Credit 1.2 Building Reuse—Maintain Existing Interior Non-structural Elements: 1 point
- Credit 2 Construction Waste Management: 1–2 points

- Credit 3 Sustainably Sourced Materials and Products: 1–4 points
- Credit 4.1 PBT Source Reduction—Mercury in Lamps: 1 point
- Credit 4.2 PBT Source Reduction—Lead, Cadmium, and Copper: 2 points
- Credit 5 Furniture and Medical Furnishings: 1–2 points
- Credit 6 Resource Use—Design for Flexibility: 1 point

Indoor Environmental Quality: 18 Possible Points

Prerequisite 1: Minimum Indoor Air Quality Performance—Required
Prerequisite 2: Environmental Tobacco Smoke (ETS) Control—Required
Prerequisite 3: Hazardous Material Removal or Encapsulation (Renovations Only)—Required

- Credit 1 Outdoor Air Delivery Monitoring: 1 point
- Credit 2 Acoustic Environment: 1–2 points
- Credit 3.1 Construction Indoor Air Quality Management Plan—During Construction: 1 point
- Credit 3.2 Construction Indoor Air Quality Management Plan—Before Occupancy: 1 point
- Credit 4 Low-Emitting Materials: 1–4 points
- Credit 5 Indoor Chemical and Pollutant Source Control: 1 point
- Credit 6.1 Controllability of Systems—Lighting: 1 point
- Credit 6.2 Controllability of Systems—Thermal Comfort: 1 point
- Credit 7 Thermal Comfort—Design and Verification: 1 point
- Credit 8.1 Daylight and Views—Daylight: 2 points
- Credit 8.2 Daylight and Views—Views: 1–3 points

Innovation in Design: Six Possible Points

Prerequisite 1: Integrated Project Planning and Design—Required

- Credit 1 Innovation in Design: 1–4 points
- Credit 2 LEED Accredited Professional: 1 point
- Credit 3 Integrated Project Planning and Design: 1 point

Regional Priority: Four Possible Points

- Credit 1 Regional Priority: 1–4 points

LEED 2009 FOR HEALTHCARE

100 base points; 6 possible Innovation in Design and 4 Regional Priority points

Certified 40–49 points
Silver 50–59 points
Gold 60–79 points
Platinum 80 points and above

Let me share some of the measures initiated for a LEED Platinum–rated hospital project in Mumbai, India, to make the LEED jargon a little more understandable for "the non-technical layperson" under various LEED prerequisites.[5]

SUSTAINABLE SITES (FIGURES 5.4 THROUGH 5.6)

Sustainable sites　　　　**Possible points 13**　　　**Achieved 10**

Credit 6.1 stormwater management quantity control
Credit 6.2 stormwater management quality control

Ring wells

Mesh filters

Grass pavers

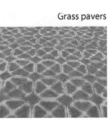
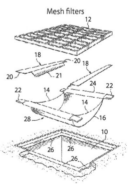

3 ring wells
Stormwater drain holding tank capacity 87KLD
Reducton post development imperviousness is more
80% removal of total suspended solids

FIGURE 5.4
Sustainable sites.

Sustainable sites   **Possible points 13**   **Achieved 10**

Credit 7.1 heat island effect, non-roof
Credit 7.2 heat island effect, roof

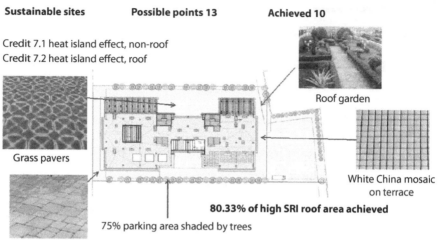

Roof garden

Grass pavers

White China mosaic
on terrace

80.33% of high SRI roof area achieved

75% parking area shaded by trees

Concrete pavers of SRI 35 for site development

FIGURE 5.5
Sustainable sites.

Actual pictures   Grass pavers   High SRI pavers

Native plantation on roofs

FIGURE 5.6
Sustainable sites.

WATER EFFICIENCY (FIGURES 5.7 AND 5.8)

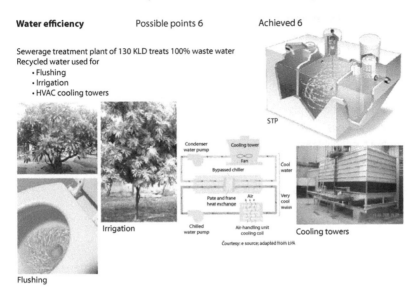

| Water efficiency | Possible points 6 | Achieved 6 |

Sewerage treatment plant of 130 KLD treats 100% waste water
Recycled water used for
  • Flushing
  • Irrigation
  • HVAC cooling towers

STP

Irrigation

Cooling towers

Courtesy: e source; adapted from EPA

Flushing

FIGURE 5.7
Water efficiency.

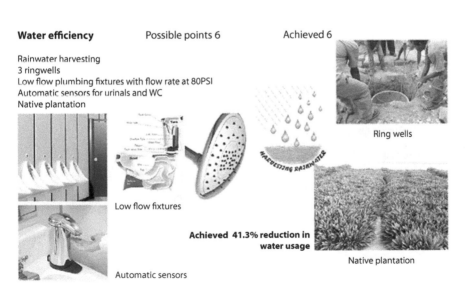

| Water efficiency | Possible points 6 | Achieved 6 |

Rainwater harvesting
3 ringwells
Low flow plumbing fixtures with flow rate at 80PSI
Automatic sensors for urinals and WC
Native plantation

Ring wells

Low flow fixtures

Achieved 41.3% reduction in water usage

Native plantation

Automatic sensors

FIGURE 5.8
Water efficiency.

ENERGY AND ATMOSPHERE (FIGURES 5.9 THROUGH 5.19)

Energy analysis and simulation

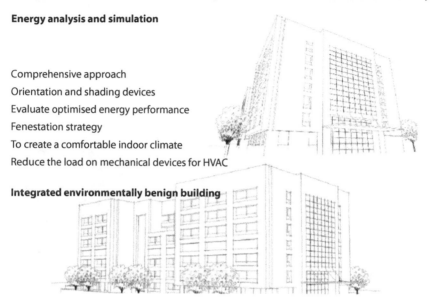

Comprehensive approach

Orientation and shading devices

Evaluate optimised energy performance

Fenestation strategy

To create a comfortable indoor climate

Reduce the load on mechanical devices for HVAC

Integrated environmentally benign building

FIGURE 5.9
Energy and atmosphere.

Fenestation

Double glazed unit

Capacity to retain and reflect heat

Double glazed units with high performance reflective glass of 1.2 U value

SC (all)   : 0.62

VLT   : 75%

Shading device : installer

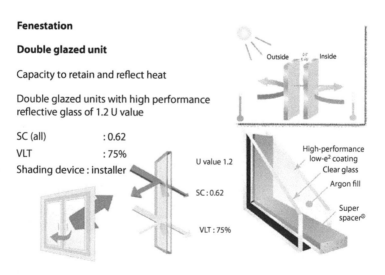

FIGURE 5.10
Energy and atmosphere.

Envelope

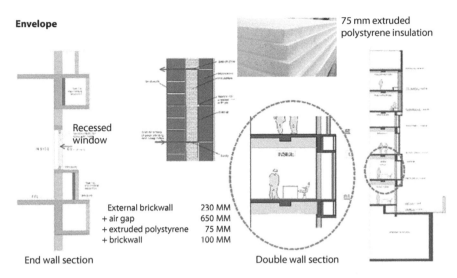

75 mm extruded
polystyrene insulation

Recessed
window

External brickwall	230 MM
+ air gap	650 MM
+ extruded polystyrene	75 MM
+ brickwall	100 MM

End wall section

Double wall section

FIGURE 5.11
Energy and atmosphere.

Actual pictures

Recessed windows

FIGURE 5.12
Energy and atmosphere.

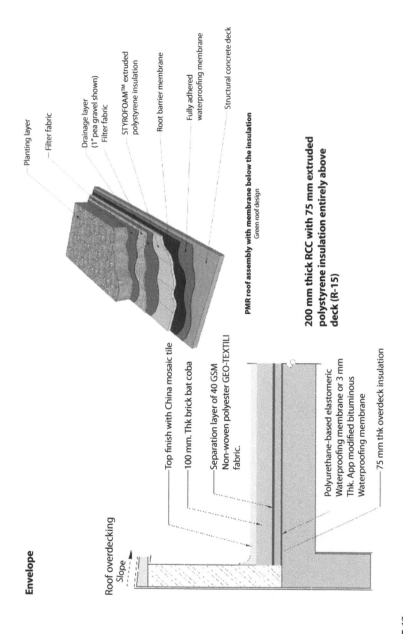

Envelope

Planting layer

Filter fabric

Drainage layer
(1" pea gravel shown)

Filter fabric

STYROFOAM™ extruded
polystyrene insulation

Root barrier membrane

Fully adhered
waterproofing membrane

Structural concrete deck

PMR roof assembly with membrane below the insulation
Green roof design

**200 mm thick RCC with 75 mm extruded
polystyrene insulation entirely above
deck (R-15)**

Roof overdecking

Slope

Top finish with China mosaic tile

100 mm. Thk brick bat coba

Separation layer of 40 GSM
Non-woven polyester GEO-TEXTILI
fabric.

Polyurethane-based elastomeric
Waterproofing membrane or 3 mm
Thk. App modified bituminous
Waterproofing membrane

75 mm thk overdeck insulation

FIGURE 5.13
Energy and atmosphere.

Energy optimization

- Use of R-134 A refrigerant is free of HCFC and HALONS
- State of art HVAC
- Metering equipments for collection of data, analysis, and rectification
- 84% hot water generated by solar thermal collectors
- Windmills generate green power off-site equivalent to 90% of total requirement

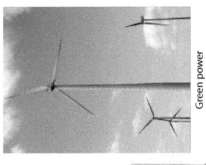

State of art HVAC

R-134A Refrigerant

Solar thermal collectors

Metering equipments

Green power

FIGURE 5.14
Energy and atmosphere.

Lighting

- Efficient and intelligent lighting system with LED/CFL combination
- LED for cove lighting
- Activity-wise distribution to achieve optimum LUX level
- Occupancy sensors in public toilets
- Carefull circuiting for efficient lighting stratergy

Achieved overall LPD of 0.54 w/sqft

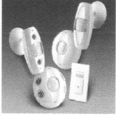

FIGURE 5.15
Energy and atmosphere.

Actual pictures

Cove lighting

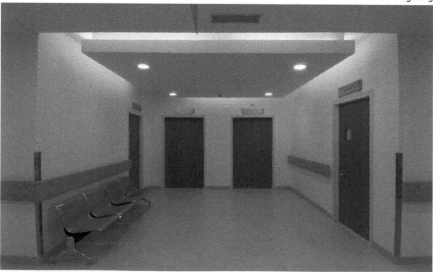

FIGURE 5.16
Energy and atmosphere.

Actual pictures

Task light

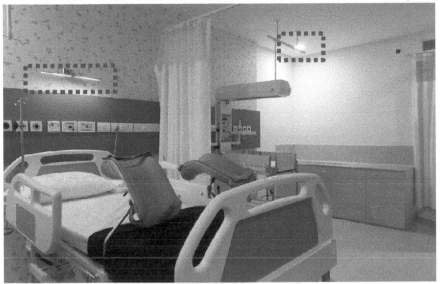

FIGURE 5.17
Energy and atmosphere.

S.no	Equipment	Numbers and capacity
1	Chillers	2 Nos. of 200 TR water cooled screw
2	Transformers	2 Nos. of 750 kVA
3	DG sets	2 Nos. of 500 kVA
4	UPS	2 Nos of 60 kVA + 4 nos. of 10 kVA
5	Solar hot water system	12,000 L/day
6	Sewage treatment plant	130 KLD

Green features

- Water-cooled screw chillers (ARI COP of achieved overall HVAC load 1TR/500 sqft)
- Low water loss cooling towers
- Efficient variable volume pumping system
- AHUs with airfoil fans and variable frequency drive
- Demand controlled ventilation with CO_2 sensors in air path
- Heat recovery system for areas with large fresh air requirements
- Pressured independent VAV systems

FIGURE 5.18
Energy and atmosphere.

Savings

End use	Energy consumption (×1000 kwh)		Energy savings %
	Baseline building	Proposed building	
Space cooling	1,226.6	729.10	40.56
Heat rejection	33.6	16.90	49.63
Space heat	0	0	0.00
Hot water	554.1	—	100
Ventilation fans	805.5	197.10	75.33
Pumps and auxiliaries	209.7	166.10	20.80
Miscellaneous equipment	1,515.3	1515.30	0.00
Interior lighting	1,189.6	777.40	34.65
Total building consumption	5534.325	3,401.90	38.53
			40.07

FIGURE 5.19
Energy and atmosphere.

MATERIALS AND RESOURCES (FIGURES 5.20 AND 5.21)

Material and resources parameters

96.3% waste generated diverted from landfills
Factory made furniture and sized glass panels — hence no wasteage
80% use of recycled steel manufactured through induction furnace

Factory made furnitur

Recycled steel

Sized glass panels

FIGURE 5.20
Material and resources.

Material and resources parameters

Use of 72% regional material
36.40% material harvested locally
FSC certified wood

Regional and locally harvested

FSC certified wood

FIGURE 5.21
Material and resources.

INDOOR ENVIRONMENTAL QUALITY (FIGURES 5.22 THROUGH 5.26)

Indoor environment quality parameters

No smoking premises
MERV 13 filters
CO_2 sensors
30% increase in fresh air delivery
Temperature for spaces designed at 23°C ± 1°C
Temperature sensors in return and supply air duct
Humidity sensors in return air duct
Relative humidity not to exceed 60%

NO SMOKING

MERV 13 FILETERS

CO_2 sensors

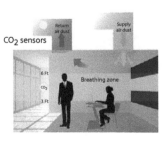

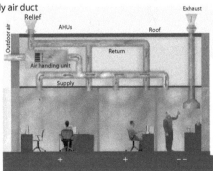

FIGURE 5.22
Indoor environment quality.

Low VOC material

Low emitting adhesives and sealants
Low emitting paints
Low emitting carpets
Composite wood and agrifiber products
Chemical and pollutant source control

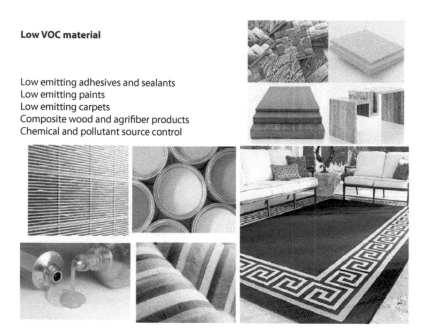

FIGURE 5.23
Indoor environment quality.

Controllability

Controllability of systems, lighting
Controllability of systems, thermal comfort

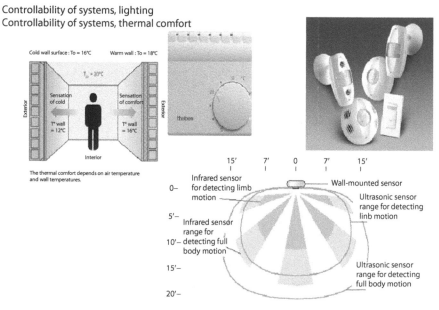

FIGURE 5.24
Indoor environment quality.

Daylight stategy

Provision of skylight

Large fenestation strategy

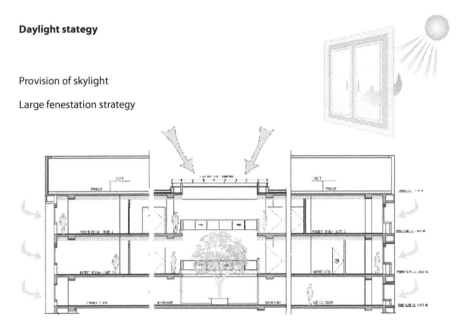

FIGURE 5.25
Indoor environment quality.

Actual pictures

FIGURE 5.26
Indoor environment quality.

INNOVATION IN DESIGN (FIGURE 5.27)

Innovation and design process   Possible points 5   Achieved 5

Attempted	Not attempted			
1		Credit 1.1	Innovation in design—exemplary performance in water use reduction WE credit 4	**41.3% reduction in use of water**
1		Credit 1.2	Innovation in design—exemplary performance in construction waste management MR credit 2	**96.79% construction waste management**
1		Credit 1.3	Innovation in design—exemplary performance in regional materials MR credit 5	**72.05% regional material**
1		Credit 1.4	Innovation in design—exemplary performance in recycled material MR credit 4.2	**29.75% recycled material**
1		Credit 2	LEED accredited professionals	
5	0			

FIGURE 5.27
Innovation and design process.

SUSTAINABLE OVERVIEW[5] (FIGURE 5.28)

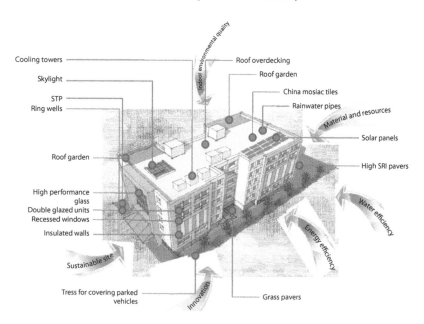

Cooling towers
Skylight
STP
Ring wells
Roof garden
High performance glass
Double glazed units
Recessed windows
Insulated walls
Sustainable site
Tress for covering parked vehicles

Indoor environmental quality
Roof overdecking
Roof garden
China mosiac tiles
Rainwater pipes
Material and resources
Solar panels
High SRI pavers
Water efficiency
Energy efficiency
Innovation
Grass pavers

FIGURE 5.28
Sustainable overview.

GREEN FEATURES OF ENERGY SAVING IN BIOMEDICAL EQUIPMENT

The following are some of the various electrical energy saving techniques utilized in a green hospital:

LED Lights in Operating Theater

The shadowless surgical lights in OTs are now losing the race to a new-generation of LED lights. These LED lights consume at least 20% less electrical energy than conventional lights. Moreover, LED lights have a much longer life compared with conventional lights, hence, the energy consumption of LED lights remains far less than conventional lights even over a period of time.

Green hospitals have installed systems of LED lights in OTs used specifically for cardiac, neuro, and orthopedic surgeries.

Care Dose on Computed Tomography Scan

The computed tomography (CT) scan installed in green hospitals has a special feature called a care dose in x-ray dose monitoring and delivery. The care dose feature understands the patient's category and adjusts the x-ray dosage that is to be delivered to the patient accordingly and keeps it to a minimum. The less the x-ray dose delivered, the less the amount of electrical energy consumed, thereby contributing to energy saving.

Water Pressure–Driven Washer Disinfector

A washer disinfector is an inevitable machine in a super-specialty hospital. Many green hospitals have a washer disinfector system. The specialty of a washer disinfector system installed in a green hospital is that it is predominantly more water driven than electricity driven. The revolving washing pistons are rotated because of water pressure and not because of electricity. The amount of energy needed to drive the pistons is much less than if it was electrically driven, thus contributing to energy saving.

X-Ray View Box

The x-ray film viewing panels installed in green hospitals also utilize LED strips instead of conventional tubes. These are installed around the hospital in various departments. Thus, the energy saving per unit is multiplied and, hence, the total amount of energy saved is even greater.

Pneumatically Driven Respiratory Support Systems

Respiratory support systems such as ventilators and bilevel positive airway pressure (BiPAP) machines are a must in a set up where there are high numbers of intensive care beds in the intensive care unit (ICU), the neonatal intensive care unit (NICU), and the pediatric intensive care unit (PICU). These machines are powered by a central gas supply along with electricity, thereby consuming less energy than systems driven by a compressor unit.

A few other techniques that contribute toward electrical energy saving are as follows:

- Most equipment has the facility of automatic cut-off from the mains supply once the batteries in the system are fully charged. Hence, these machines consume less electrical energy compared with other machines.
- Many machines with display units have a brightness adjustment feature as display units are one of the major factors that require very high amounts of electricity. Thus, by optimizing the brightness of the display units of various machines in the hospital, excessive consumption of electricity is prevented.
- A few machines have a standby mode feature where the processing unit and the display unit shut off the intake of power and still remain on. This again reduces the unnecessary consumption of energy.

These are a few of the techniques implemented in the biomedical equipment used in green hospitals, which have helped to save energy because, after all, ENERGY SAVED IS ENERGY GAINED.

SUMMARY

Hospital Industry Issues We Addressed

Issue 1

Hospitals are enormous consumers of energy due to the 24/7 operation of high-end biomedical, engineering, and other equipment, thereby inflating energy costs.

Energy efficiency measures planned from project stage. Examples are solar panels, use of natural lighting, motion sensors, variable frequency drives (VFDs) for air handling units (AHUs) and cooling towers, high coefficient of performance (COP) energy-efficient chillers, and LED lights.

Issue 2

- Increased carbon footprint of hospital industry.
- Recycled material used for construction.
- Recycling—sewage and water treatment plant.
- Use of R-134A refrigerant that is free from hydrochlorofluorocarbons (HCFC) and halons.
- Low VOC material.

Issue 3

Increased cost of healthcare.

Initiatives would bring operational efficiency in terms of electricity savings, reduced water bills, and reduced length of stay (LOS), which are passed on to patients in terms of affordable tariffs/healthcare costs compared with similar hospitals with similar expertise and infrastructure.

REFERENCES

1. Smart Healthcare, July 6, 2014. Designing Green Hospitals of the Future: Tommy Tan. Available a Hospital and Healthcare Management website www.hhmglobal.com/knowledge-bank/articles/designing-green-hospitals-of-the-future.
2. Technical Bulletin, 2014. Green Hospitals, From Indian Green Building Council, CII Sorabji Godrej Green Business Centre, Hyderabad, India. Available at www.igbc.in/igbc/html-pdfc/technical/Green%20hospitals.pdf.

3. PSR-Medical Alliance to stop Global Warming-ANISA-Project Green Hospitals. Petition Postcard, Vision 2010: A Healthier Future, Fred C. Rothstein CEO, University Hospitals Case Medical Center, Cleveland, OH 44106.
4. LEED 2009 for Healthcare. www.usgbc.org.
5. Architect Sandeep Shikre. Green Building Presentation, IGBC, 2007. (USGBC®, U.S. Green Building Council® and LEED® are registered trademarks of the U.S. Green Building Council.)

6

Designing a Patient-Centric Healthcare Facility Using Lean Methodology

John Gallagher, Kim Chaney, and Ron Kwon

CONTENTS

INTRODUCTION

The healthcare landscape continues to change rapidly, presenting unprecedented challenges in the quest for improving patient access and quality, while at the same time reducing costs. In working toward these goals, it is often done at the "expense" of physician and staff burnout. External competitive forces at play as well as practices are losing market share to "minute clinics" and concierge medicine practices that have easier access. The ability to streamline care across the entire continuum, reduce space and overhead costs, and provide easy access and patient flow are all of ever-increasing importance.

In 2009, Harvard Vanguard Medical Associates (HVMA) in Boston worked with Simpler Consulting to adopt Lean methodology as their management and operating system for consistently delivering care to their patients. HVMA is a not-for-profit, multispecialty group medical practice operating in eastern Massachusetts. It was founded in the late 1960s as part of Harvard Community Health Plan and has 17 locations in the Boston metro area.

In 2010, Concord Hillside Medical Associates, a multispecialty group practice that is part of HVMA located about 30 miles west of Boston. The Concord practice has 30+ internists and pediatricians, gynecologists, and behavioral health specialists, along with 160 staff and it cares for 34,000 covered lives.

We faced the realities of the need to improve head on with the expiration of the lease on our current practice facility. We had outgrown our existing site and were unable to add services (e.g., pharmacy and imaging) necessary. Senior leadership made it clear that if the organization was going to make a multimillion dollar financial investment in a new clinic, it would have to be innovative.

In a traditional facility planning endeavor for new facilities, many paradigms exist. The usual things you hear are

- "We need bigger offices and please make sure they all have windows."
- "We need MORE rooms so that we can bring in more patients."
- "We need bigger rooms."
- "We need to have the newest, best, and highest-tech (*generally the most expensive and more of a barrier to flow!*) equipment."

While these things would be nice to have, they rarely add value from the patients' perspective. In the original planning stages, the new practice needed to be 43,000 square feet to support the current population trends. The total investment was just one of the concerns. Patient flow times through the practice were long and most the time that the patient was in the building was spent waiting. Each room had different setups based on the perceived needs of the physician, making it difficult for staff to work in different areas. As a result, physicians often had to leave the room during patients' visits to find necessary supplies and equipment. Supplies were stored in multiple locations with no semblance of flow. The design of the new space needed to be more patient-centric. It would take a different methodology to improve the space for physicians, staff, *and* patients.

Rather than approach the issue in a traditional way, the leadership of the Concord practice chose to use a Lean approach to design the new facility. We chose to use the Lean tool of 2P (Process Preparation) as the primary tool to design our new building.

Imagine, as a patient, you can see your clinicians when you are scheduled to see them—and that during your visit, you have access to most of the services you need all in one building, and that you can find them easily and without delays. And imagine that all your calls and questions in between your scheduled visit are answered with prompt, friendly advice—that's outstanding service. It was these types of patient needs and wants that leadership wanted to address.

But, we also had a series of internal challenges to address. There was variation in work and communication, leading to frustration for patients and care providers. The layout of the old building made it difficult for patients to find their way around. Very few of us were well versed in Lean and so we needed to intensively expose the clinicians and staff to an unfamiliar system that, to them, in some ways seemed counterintuitive. Physicians, by nature, tend to be skeptical and slower to embrace change. One way that we could show them the possibilities was with a Lean event to standardize rooms so that they saw an improvement to their workflow with the Lean tools. Early in the journey, Dr. Kwon said, "Our challenge was to create a patient-friendly and inviting clinical space while being mindful of costs and building regulations. We needed to pay attention to 'the voice of the patient' and balance that with the needs of the clinic staff and physicians. The physical space had to enable the newly designed workflows to not only exist but to improve efficiency through the elimination of waste."

Leaders made the decision to use the Lean tool of 2P to design the new facility and the flows inside the facility.

USING 2P IN FACILITY DESIGN

2P is a Lean design tool that helps to organize the flow of activity in a way that results in the least amount of waste. A waste in a process can be identified in eight "forms":

1. Transportation: All patient, staff, and material movement
2. Inventory: All stock and corresponding control systems
3. Motion: Reaching, bending, searching
4. People potential: Not using the problem-solving skills of your people
5. Waiting: Queuing, idle time (e.g., waiting rooms)
6. Overprocessing: Unnecessary activities, overcomplicated

7. Overproducing: Too much and too early
8. Defects: Result in inspection and rework

2P at its most basic form is a planning process that is used for complex change where flow is not obvious. It is used when "how" flow applies is difficult to see and helps to get the buy-in of key stakeholders. We use 2P for large-scale flows, or in the case of Concord's practice, when there is change involving relocation.

There are seven steps in the process of completing the 2P tool:

1. Business case: How does this work/event link to the overall goals of the organization?
2. Backbone and fishbone: What is the main "thing" that needs to flow? In the case of a car factory, it is the car. For a hospital or clinic, it is patients. Where does the process start and finish? And, what are the main value-added steps?
3. Seven flows: Map the seven supporting flows of
   a. Supplies: Where are your supplies needed and where do they come from? What stops them from flowing?
   b. Components: Do you get "kits"? How do we get these closest to where they will be used?
   c. Staff in the flow: Who are the required staff? What skills? How many?
   d. Data: What data is required to let the value-adding steps flow? Schedules, quality, test results
   e. Information: Instructions and essential knowledge required such as process instructions, standard work, and key point sheets
   f. Equipment: What equipment is required and is it "right sized" for flow? Is the equipment reliable?
   g. Finished items: What do we do at the end of the flow?
4. Matrix the seven flows: Start with the primary flow and map in a picture how the seven flows feed in.
5. Seven ways: Experiment with the physical configuration required to get the flow. Generate seven different versions. The least waste way (and fun!) is to use cardboard cutouts to design the seven ways.
6. Beauty contest: Use Lean principles to assess each concept and take the best three (the "prettiest") forward in the process.
7. Simulation: Take the best three solutions and simulate how they would work. Highlight the best aspects of each.

8. Create a first pass of the new standard work to assist in calculating staffing requirements and equipment/material needs.
9. Implementation plan: What are the projects, events, and just-do-its required to implement the changes. Develop a to-do list and assign owners and completion dates.

USE OF 2P AT CONCORD HILLSIDE MEDICAL ASSOCIATES

We kept foremost in our mind the focus of adding value to patients. We included representatives from the core services: internal medicine, pediatrics, laboratories, radiology, and pharmacy in the planning and implementation. We also included facilities personnel, as well as secretaries, patients, and the architects throughout the process. All team members should be included and can add value to the process.

The first mechanical step in our journey was to create a master project plan. We identified the necessary completion date (which in this case was the successful opening of the new practice) and identified key decision makers, decision points, and freeze points. A freeze point was a point in the plan that could not be passed unless a certain set of criteria that the decision makers had identified were satisfied. We also needed to identify the activities in the design that required the use of the 2P tool. We chose five main activities:

1. Check-in (physical check-in and call center)
2. Examination rooms
3. Physician-medical assistant "pod"
4. Ancillary support flows of laboratory and radiology
5. Pharmacy (due to time constraints, we also completed and placed the overall layout of the building, placing all five of the main activities into the building layout. Normally, this would be done as a separate activity.)

The pace of the events was critical as well. There was the pending expiration of the lease, regulatory approvals, architectural design time, construction time, and minimization of patient schedule interruptions. We held five week-long 2P events over the course of 8 weeks starting in late 2011, focused on the main activities. We prepped each activity with voice of the customer (VOC) data. We translated "feelings" into objective information. Personal space and sense of privacy translated into distance and esthetics. Patient friendly translated into easy way-finding through the flow of the building and less wait time. We prepped for each activity with customer and supplies volume data (through actual current demand rates as well as marketing supplied growth projections). We considered and selected the right team members for each of the 2P activities. We researched key requirements such as the Department of Public Health, Occupational Safety and Health Administration (OSHA), and the Health Insurance Portability and Accountability Act (HIPAA) regulations. These were critical to the success, time line, and budget of the project.

We also had to prioritize the 2P activities starting with the core layout for care delivery to the patient, which included the physician, medical assistant, and examination room needs, to create a "pod." Next came the service lines of how many pods would be needed and which day of the week based on demand. This helped us to determine the most efficient layout pattern for the pods.

Other factors that had to be considered included:

Ensure every step in the process adds value for the patient: If not, we worked to eliminate as many non-value-added steps as feasible. For example, registration had financial responsibility for the collection of any co-pay and for providing the physician team with notification of the arrival of a patient all at one stop for the patient rather than separate waiting points.

Placement of facility on new property: We had to consider things such as road access, the topography of the property, and the overall position of the building so that the mobile magnetic resonance imaging (MRI) truck could easily attach itself to the building for days of services.

Visual management of flow: Visual management is critical to any Lean implementation. Visual management is accomplished via managing for daily improvement (MDI) through daily huddles of leadership and staff so that they can see at a glance the status of the day's work. So, in the design we had to consider where this visual management would be located so that there was ample room for the teams to gather/huddle.

2P EVENTS: CREATING THE DESIGN BASED ON OBJECTIVE CRITERIA

Overall, for each 2P event, we were guided to consider the ideal condition in objective terms. The teams worked to consensus on work processes and design based on criteria evaluations. By using specific criteria, we made decisions based on data, not just "feelings." Also, doing the work in this way *and* with a multidisciplinary team allowed us to understand the interdependency between the work of various departments and services. We were able to see that making the total process work in the least waste way for all was much more important than our individual preferences.

For each 2P event, we went through a similar set of exercises:

1. Identifying key functions for value
   a. We identified the key functions for a successful flow. We used VOC and other data to consider what makes each step of the function critical as a descriptor to quality/value.
   b. For example, the steps of the check-in process are: patient presents, patient pays co-pay, patient is directed to the next step, physician team is notified that patient is ready to be seen. For each of these steps, we identified the features that add value, such as for Step 2, the patient values privacy, security, and ease and accuracy of transaction.
2. List and rank criteria

   We listed the criteria that we would use to measure our success and weighted the criteria. Based on a "standard" list, we generated lists for each of the 2P events. The standard criteria were
   - Least walking for patients and staff
   - Supports the staffing model
   - Way-finding
   - Security and safety
   - Privacy
   - Line of sight
   - Healthy, therapeutic environment
   - Least square footage required
   - Agility to manage volume fluctuations
   - Best people flow

- Access
- On-stage/off-stage
- Simple
- Scalable

We then ranked each criterion in order of importance making sure to consider the patient first through the VOC data, then we considered the importance to the staff. We also made sure to include the importance of the design that would generate the most revenue per square foot.

3. Identifying the seven concepts

For each function (e.g., check-in) we went through each step (e.g., patient pays co-pay) and identified the factors critical to adding value. We brainstormed seven different ways to do the function in small groups (coming up with seven ways is challenging, but be firm on this), then we debriefed as a group to allow everyone to have input into the concepts. The team came to a consensus on the top three ways for each step based on added value and gave each step a catchy phrase (this helps with playful, creative energy), for example, "Citgo" indicated a large visual indicator that allows patients to immediately know where to go for check-in, like the large Citgo sign in Boston indicates the location of Fenway Park from a distance! We merged these top ways into seven concepts and displayed them visually in a cloud (Figure 6.1).

4. Optimizing the selected concept

During this step, we compared the favorite concept to all other concepts and identified any other specific features we might want to include, being sure to consider the original seven flows while doing this exercise. Figure 6.2 shows an example of a visual way to compare concepts.

This activity allowed us to see the impact (positive, negative, or neutral) of each of the seven concepts for each key function. In Figure 6.2, the DATUM column represents the team's favorite concept. Often in this process, the team created a hybrid concept by using the favorite (DATUM) and then adding components of other ideas that function well within the favorite design.

5. Create mock-ups

Creating mock-ups of possible layouts was the next step. With mock-ups, ideally you are using cardboard cutouts of the actual size of the design. If a work surface is 2' wide by 4' long, then the

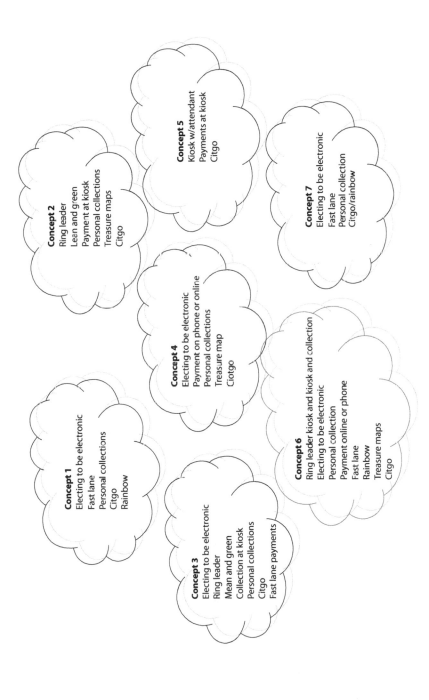

FIGURE 6.1
Example of check-in event.

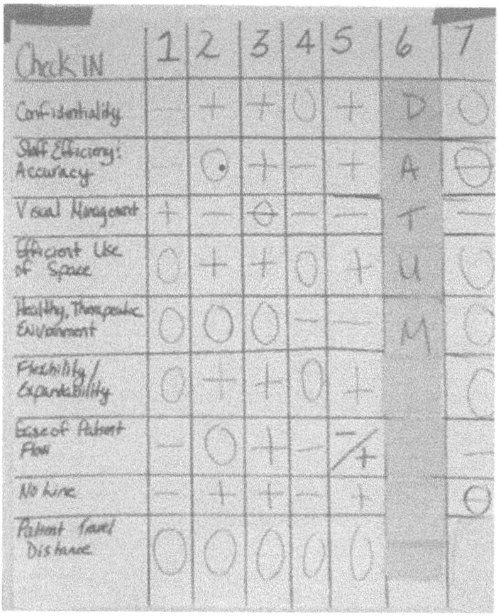

FIGURE 6.2
Concept comparison: Seven flows.

mock-up cardboard piece is that size. By doing the mock-ups, we were able to simulate the actual proposed design. Simulations and the resulting discussions led us to change aspects of the design that we had been wedded to previously; for example, we dropped the idea of using kiosks for registration, which *had* been a given, because we realized it did not add value for the patient. The simulations also increased engagement in the process.

6. Process at a glance worksheets

We created process at a glance worksheets (Figure 6.3 shows the process at a glance worksheet for check-in and the people, equipment, supplies, etc., needed *for each activity*) to identify items we would need for chosen concepts and these worksheets fed the completion plan.

7. Creating the completion plan

After the design simulations were complete and verified against the design, a completion plan with responsibilities and accountabilities was created. Each project manager/"owner" of the 2P event was responsible for making sure that actions were completed on time and as planned. We developed a management system for reporting on the progress of the completion plans including:

FIGURE 6.3
Process at a glance example.

- A steering committee for the internal medicine and pediatrics groups that held each other accountable to the due dates.
- Lean rapid improvement events (aka Kaizen events) that worked with teams to modify the current flow and prove out concepts. These events created flow in the old building similar to what we would experience in the new building.
- Mission control: Mission control rooms were created to visually manage all of these activities, allowing the steering committees to communicate the status with physicians, staff, and leadership at the local and division levels.

REFLECTIONS ON 2P PROCESS

After completing the 2P activities and subsequent improvement events, it was clear that the transformation was not only improved flow, but also a cultural shift in the organization. We saw that major shifts in thinking, analysis, and problem solving had occurred. Our staff became conversant with Lean problem solving and the applications were extended into all facets of the practice. Visual management systems helped us to teach the process, follow the application, and adhere to the process. It was also critical in our ability to sustain the changes we had created. With our goal of the new building as a reward, it made changes to the way we work easier to accept. Ongoing communications via weekly meetings with staff and clinicians and frequent updates were essential to maintaining our momentum and preventing loss of focus and burnout. There was also constant effort to maintain real-time feedback, asking our staff and clinicians what worked well and what did not work well for them. Through all of us and persistent encouragement from the sensei involved, we stayed on path and were educated back on path if we veered. We learned to be continuously present in the gemba (the place where the work occurs), so that the staff and clinicians would always know that we were committed, engaged, and approachable.

RESULTS OF 2P WORK

a. **On time and on budget:** Our new building opened in June 2013 on time and on budget. We closed the old building on a Friday afternoon and opened the new building serving our patients on the following Monday morning. Clearly, this is one of the most critical outputs of the effective use of the 2P process. It provides a time-based schedule and the ability to problem solve and adjust. In general, 2P has been shown to reduce the number of change orders during the building process, which can sometimes add up to 20% or more additional cost in traditional project management.

b. **Standardization of rooms:** The standardization of rooms resulted in less patient waiting and less wasted provider care time. By knowing how many of each item should be in the examination room every day, we centralized inventory, restocking and ordering the medical supplies through our facilities department.

c. **Reduce space requirements:** The original clinic design was for 43,000 square feet, but the resultant space identified and needed, determined through the 2P process, was only 38,000 square feet, a nearly $2 million reduction in the required capital investment from the original plan. This also allowed for the addition of imaging and visual services, which were revenue enhancements for the practice at *no* additional square footage.

d. **Improved patient flow:** The average cycle time for a patient visit was reduced by greater than 20%, freeing up time for other deferrable tasks needed such as prescription refills and calls to patients about results. Other improvements noted by patients were ease of navigation, less waiting time, and improved communication. Patient satisfaction scores improved at a double-digit rate measured by the likelihood to recommend our practice.

Two years after occupancy of our building, it seems so obvious to everyone that this was the right thing to do and no one wants to return to the previous situation where physicians and staff wasted time hunting for supplies *and* each other to satisfy our patients. Our patients continue to tell us that the building makes them feel comfortable and assured that they are receiving high-quality care. Indeed, the patients feel more respected, and this is the result of a process that promotes respect for people (patients and staff). One can only achieve great value with great effort. But, one also needs the necessary tools to accomplish great effort and Lean methodology, including 2P, provides those tools. Skilled and experienced facilitators are absolutely necessary as the process is demanding and can be difficult to manage, given the variation in the individuals involved.

Another by-product of this work has been the cultural change that has occurred. Both personally and professionally, the opportunity to participate in this 2P journey has been rewarding. Future leaders were identified and allowed to succeed. We have all gained enlightenment as leaders, clinicians, consultants, and team members because of it.

CHALLENGES TO IMPLEMENTING 2P WORK

The implementation of 2P work is not easy. It is intense and time-consuming. There are several potential barriers that anyone implementing 2P needs to be aware of and ready to address.

Lack of Lean experience: We overcame this barrier with intense classroom training and participation on rapid improvement events teams. Immersion through participation in both is critical to success.

Need for physician engagement: As stated before, physicians, by their nature, are slow to embrace significant change so we needed to get the physicians on board early. What worked was providing the tangible benefits early. For example, the thought of standardized examination rooms makes eminent sense, yet it was only after we had created the rooms and the clinicians were using them that we increased engagement. We had to provide the actual experience for our clinicians to provide ample time to adjust and reach a state of endorsement. Also, when we looked at space requirements, we decided that the physicians needed smaller offices and they would be co-located with their medical assistant. When we were able to do the 3-D mock-up and had physicians and staff experiment with the space, we achieved consensus on this design.

Cultural change is difficult: Physicians have always been trained to be the "captain of the ship"—always in charge and directing/ordering what they feel is necessary. However, with changing workflows and certainly in the design of the new building, physicians had to become more a part of the team, relinquishing control to staff and non-staff team members, that is, the "wishes and best interests of the group." It is extremely important that in the midst of this type of change (or any large change), administrative leadership remains steadfast and continues to communicate the common goals that we must reach.

Rapid pace of events: Our pace was intense and there was always the pressure of time, as we had to meet deadlines to enable the architects, engineers, and builders enough time to meet construction deadlines. We had to balance these demands with keeping the clinic running smoothly and this was not always easy. One of the ways that we addressed this was "holding harmless" our physicians by compensating them for their lost clinic time when they participated on planning and rapid improvement events. We also did adjust staffing to fill in for personnel on events. This made it essential to demonstrate that the resources were well spent and the use of physicians/clinicians on events did not compromise patient care in any way.

Missing process considerations: "Different" ways to manage the care of patients such as value-based care (pay for outcomes such as quality) versus fee for service (pay for each encounter that occurs, regardless of outcomes).

Existing job roles: Jobs may diversify in the 2P designs. For example, the roles of the medical assistant may need to be expanded to include inbox management, resulting, and/or callbacks. These are tasks that might normally be handled by another individual in the system. Regardless, the design goal is not to eliminate positions, but rather to ensure that the person has time available to complete the tasks in the most efficient manner.

We addressed these challenges through the use of both Simpler consultants/coaches and dedicated, employed Lean resources in the practice. During these events, there were "opportunities" for drama and increased emotions. Professional facilitation was a must. Also, leaders able to address poor behavior *and* recognize/reward positive behavior were critical to success.

SUMMARY

In conclusion, while the 2P process in and of itself is not a guarantee of the results we achieved, it can be a most effective tool when coupled with a Lean transformation operating system, a management system such as MDI, and a strong leadership group to carry out the changes. The 2P process has the ability to facilitate culture change in an organization through the structure process, a multidisciplinary approach, and successful results. By improving our layout and space through the 2P process, we improved our everyday processes for care providers and the experience and outputs our patients have when they visit. We will continue to strive to get to the preferred target state of:

Imagine, as a patient, you can see your clinicians when you are scheduled to see them—and that during your visit, you have access to most of the services you need all in one building, and that you can find them easily and without delays. And imagine that all your calls and questions in between your scheduled visit are answered with prompt, friendly advice—that's outstanding service.

7

Creating Safer Healthcare Environments Using an Evidence-Based Design Process

Anjali Joseph, Ellen Taylor, and Xiaobo Quan

CONTENTS

INTRODUCTION

A majority of patient safety–related adverse events are avoidable and the piecemeal approaches to quality improvement over the past years have contributed to marginal improvements. The healthcare system is complex and includes many different components, including the people, processes, technology, organizational culture, and the built environment. A growing body of research shows that the healthcare built environment is an important latent component of the healthcare system that impacts patient and staff safety outcomes such as healthcare-associated infections (HAI), medication errors, falls, and staff injuries. Often, the physical environment features that negatively impact patient safety are incorporated into the building during the facility design process due to lack of awareness about how these features interact with other system components to impact patient safety. There is a huge opportunity to use the context of a facility design project to initiate comprehensive systemic improvements that help to improve patient and staff safety.

IMPORTANCE OF CREATING SAFE, HIGH-QUALITY HEALTHCARE-BUILT ENVIRONMENTS

Since the release of the Institution of Medicine's report *To Err Is Human*,[1] patient safety improvements have remained elusive, despite a host of interventions.[2] The study by Landrigan and colleagues[3] of 10 North Carolina hospitals over 10 years found 25.1 harms per 100 admissions. Levinson's[4] Department of Health and Human Services' Office of the Inspector General's report found that 13.5% of hospitalized Medicare patients experienced adverse events and a further 13.5% experienced temporary harms. All of these harms significantly impact the nation's healthcare bill, with 1.5 million errors estimated to contribute an additional $19.5 billion annually as found in a medical claims study by the Society of Actuaries.[5] Perhaps one reason for the troubling gaps is that all of the variables that contribute to safe and quality care have not been examined together. One of those less-considered variables is the physical environment, which shapes every patient experience and all healthcare delivery, including those episodes of care when patient harm occurs.

It has become increasingly clear that the problem of patient safety does not lie solely in the hands of clinicians or frontline healthcare staff. The healthcare system has many inherent latent conditions (holes and weaknesses) that interact in complex ways resulting in adverse events.[6] A growing body of research shows that features in the built environment such as light, noise, air quality, room layout, and others contribute to adverse patient safety outcomes such as HAI, medication errors, and falls in healthcare settings.[7,8]

The conceptual model in Figure 7.1, based on the work of Vincent, Taylor-Adams, and Stanhope[9] and Reason,[10] shows the role of the physical environment elements as the latent conditions that contribute to patient safety. Often, these latent conditions that adversely impact patient safety are built into the physical environment during the planning, design, and construction of healthcare facilities. For example, the location of emergency departments and intensive care units might necessitate the transport of critically ill patients over long distances, potentially causing patient complications. Handwashing sinks located in inconvenient or inaccessible locations might result in poor handwashing compliance among physicians and nurses.

Given the ongoing investments in healthcare facility renovation and design around the world, there is an urgent need to systematically identify and eliminate built environment latent conditions that impact patient safety during the planning, design, and construction of healthcare facilities. Design teams themselves are often unfamiliar with the possible built environment impact on patient safety and even less familiar with ways to incorporate these concerns into the design process. While fields such as aviation and other high-risk industries have been able to harness human factors, engineering, and cognitive science that result in the preferred human response and, consequently, improved safety, no similar method currently exists for the design of new healthcare facilities or major renovation projects.

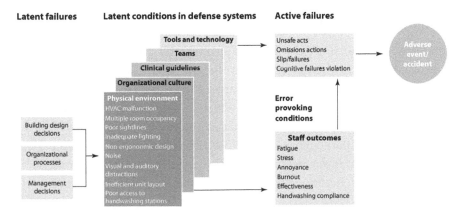

FIGURE 7.1
Conceptual model showing the role of the physical environment as a latent condition or barrier to adverse events in healthcare settings.

USING AN EVIDENCE-BASED DESIGN PROCESS TO DESIGN FOR SAFETY

Evidence-based design is the process of basing decisions about the built environment on credible research to achieve the best possible outcome.[11] The Center for Health Design (CHD), a non-profit organization, is committed to assisting healthcare organizations achieve this goal through their Pebble Project program (http://www.healthdesign.org/pebble), a research initiative that engages healthcare organizations during their facility design and construction projects. Team members use research findings to inform their decision making and then conduct additional research to evaluate the effectiveness of the implemented design strategies. A growing body of research exists linking the design of the built environment with healthcare outcomes. Evidence-based design practitioners use this research, often supported by additional input from best practices and stakeholders, to make key healthcare facility design investment decisions that may impact safety. The design of the healthcare-built environment has been linked to improvements in four key areas—HAI, medication errors, patient falls, and staff injuries.

EVIDENCE LINKING FACILITY DESIGN WITH PATIENT AND STAFF SAFETY

Healthcare-Associated Infections

Since HAI are transmitted through air and water and contact with contaminated surfaces, the physical environment plays a key role in preventing the spread of infections in healthcare settings. The evidence shows that single-bed patient rooms with high-efficiency particulate air filters and with negative or positive pressure ventilation are most effective in preventing airborne pathogens.[12,13] Single-bed patient rooms are also easier to clean and have fewer surfaces that act as reservoirs for pathogens.[7,14] Additionally, the higher sink-to-bed ratios in single-patient rooms is associated with better handwashing compliance—a key factor associated with the spread of HAI.[7] Bronson Methodist Hospital in Kalamazoo, Michigan, found that HAI rates among all patient-care units declined by 11% (0.89–0.80 infections per 1000 patient days) when they moved from an older hospital with mostly semiprivate rooms and shared bathrooms to a new hospital with all private rooms with bathrooms.[15,16] Moreover, among the six patient-care units that changed from semiprivate to private room design, the infection rate declined by 45%.[15] In addition, easy access to alcohol-based rub dispensers (high sink-to-bed ratio and easy physical access) in patient rooms has been linked to improved handwashing compliance.[17-19]

Medication Safety

A growing body of research suggests that medication safety is markedly influenced by the physical environmental conditions in areas where medication-related activities occur. These conditions include light levels, sound and noise, work space design to mitigate interruptions and distractions, and work space organization.[20,21] Performance on visual tasks such as dispensing medications improved in an outpatient pharmacy at higher illumination levels.[22] Poor acoustic environments with hard sound-reflecting surfaces may contribute to low speech intelligibility, which may also contribute to errors.[20] Acuity-adaptable rooms that enable patients to stay in the same room as their acuity level changes reduce the need for transfers and associated breakdowns in communication that potentially result in error. Hendrich and colleagues found that after a move to an innovative acuity-adaptable cardiac comprehensive critical care unit at Clarian Methodist Hospital, patient transfers decreased by 90% and medication errors by 70%.[23,24]

Patient Falls

It is widely accepted that the physical environment—including environmental features, such as the placement of doorways, handrails, and toilets, the flooring type, and the design and location of hazards such as furniture—can contribute to patient falls and associated injuries. Because most of the studies in this area have involved multifaceted interventions to reduce falls, the independent impact of any single design strategy remains to be evaluated.[25] Hendrich and colleagues[26] found that most falls occurred when patients attempted to get out of bed unassisted or unobserved. In their study, when patients moved from a centralized unit with semiprivate rooms to decentralized units with single-patient rooms that included a family zone, the number of falls was reduced by two-thirds. Creating space that can accommodate family members (who can help or call for aid) in the patient's room, along with better visibility from the nurses' station, represent promising design interventions.

Staff Injuries

Healthcare employees are at serious risk of contracting infectious diseases from patients due to airborne and surface contamination.[27-29] Factors such as poor ventilation and fungal contamination of the ventilation system that have been linked to the spread of HAI among patients may also impact staff. For example, one study that examined the relationship between indoor environmental factors and nasal inflammation among nursing personnel found the contamination of air ducts with *Aspergillus fumigatus* to be the source of infection.[29] A study conducted in the wake of the severe acute respiratory syndrome (SARS) epidemic in China found that isolating SARS cases in wards with good ventilation could reduce the viral load of the ward and might be the key to preventing outbreaks of SARS among healthcare workers, along with strict personal protection measures in isolation units.[30]

Lower back pain is a pervasive problem among nursing staff and is a result of poor fitness, long periods of standing, and efforts far exceeding workers' strengths.[31,32] Patient lifting in particular is a major cause of injury to healthcare workers. According to Fragala and Bailey,[33] 44% of injuries to nursing staff in hospitals that result in lost workdays are strains and sprains (mostly of the back), and 10.5% of back injuries in the United States are associated with moving and assisting patients. Reducing injuries that result from patient-lifting tasks not only results in significant economic benefit (reduced cost of claims, staff lost workdays), but also reduces pain and suffering among workers. Ergonomic programs, staff education, a no manual lift policy, and use of mechanical lifts have been successful in reducing back injuries that result from patient-handling tasks.[32,34-36]

WHAT DOES IT TAKE TO MAKE SAFETY A PRIORITY DURING THE FACILITY DESIGN PROCESS?

While improving safety for their patients and staff is a key priority for most healthcare organizations, they do not often understand the role of the built environment in promoting safety. To ensure that teams consistently focus on safety throughout the design process requires a commitment to safety by all team members starting with the healthcare organization's leadership. The healthcare organization should take several key steps at different phases of its healthcare facility design project to ensure a consistent and committed focus on safety.

Some steps to be considered during strategic planning, facility master planning, and process and operational planning include:

- Focus on safety as both a strategic and an operational goal, as reflected in your mission, vision, and values statements.
- Examine root cause analysis and other performance improvement projects to identify safety improvement opportunities.
- Identify specific safety goals for the project (e.g., reduce patient HAI, falls, medication errors, staff musculoskeletal injuries, injuries associated with patient and staff violence).
- Identify fiscal improvement targets for safety outcomes that the project will help to achieve.
- Begin a return on investment analysis for equipment purchases (e.g., ceiling-mounted lifts, ultraviolet gamma irradiation) needed to support identified safety goals.
- Consider the role that safety has on the brand recognition of your organization.
- Include safety as a key priority in the guiding principles for the project.
- Hire an architecture-engineering firm and project team with proven expertise in designing for safety.
- Orient the design team to your safety culture and priorities.
- Identify safety as a high priority during the visioning session used to launch the project.
- Communicate the project vision and goals to key stakeholder groups (board, medical staff, staff, patients, community).
- Provide the key stakeholders with an overview of evidence-based design features that research reveals contribute to improved safety outcomes.
- Align processes of care using safety as a focus.
- Assign multidisciplinary staff members to support the facility project.

Some steps to be considered during the programming and design phases include:

- Develop a functional program that accommodates safety features to support goals.

- With the design team, develop statements that highlight how the proposed safety features will improve the organization's safety metrics.
- Identify the baseline, preoccupancy safety metrics that will be used for comparison purposes during post-occupancy measurements.
- Review the evidence and complete a safety risk assessment (SRA) to identify specific safe design features that will be included in the project.
- Identify environmental safety features missing in your present environment for comparison purposes and to facilitate an understanding of care processes that may require reengineering.
- Use different tools such as virtual tools and mock-up rooms to understand how design features may support safety culture and processes.
- Ensure that the design supports the desired safety concepts of operation from all perspectives: patients, family and visitors, the community, staff, material movement, equipment and technology use.
- Ensure that critical safety design features are not lost (e.g., during design development, value reengineering) during the programming and design phases.

Some steps to be considered during the construction and commissioning phases include:

- Ensure that critical safety design features are not lost/removed during construction.
- Finalize care processes' reengineering based on the design of the new facility.
- Modify your existing comprehensive safety program to reflect the safety design features and reengineered processes of care.
- Establish training programs, which integrate the new safety design features, equipment, and reengineered care processes.
- To the degree possible, implement the new care processes in your current environment.
- As appropriate, inform key stakeholders about the emerging safety-focused design features.
- Collect the final preoccupancy measures for targeted safety outcomes.

USING A PROACTIVE SAFETY RISK ASSESSMENT APPROACH TO DESIGN SAFER HOSPITALS

Following the steps outlined will help an organization stay focused on safety as they go through the long and complex healthcare facility design project. Additionally, conducting an SRA early in the design process will help the team prioritize the key design features that will support safety outcomes for patients and staff. The 2014 Guidelines for Hospital and Outpatient Facilities from the Facility Guidelines Institute (FGI) (used extensively in the United States for designing and renovating all health-care facilities) now includes a section on conducting an SRA.[37] The SRA is described as "a multidisciplinary, documented assessment process."

It is intended to proactively identify hazards and risks and mitigate the underlying conditions of the environment that contribute to adverse safety events. These include infections, falls, medication errors, immo-bility-related outcomes, security breaches, and musculoskeletal or other injuries. The process includes an evaluation of the population at risk, and the nature and scope of the project. It takes into account the models of care, operational plans, sustainable/green design elements, and perfor-mance improvement initiatives of the healthcare organization. The SRA also proposes built environment solutions.

The SRA is started during the planning phases of a project and contin-ues to evolve with additional levels of detail throughout the project's life cycle. The SRA enables a multidisciplinary group of stakeholders, which may include architects, facility managers, risk managers, infection control professionals, clinical staff, and patients, to collectively discuss key design decisions from the lens of how they might impact patient and staff safety.

Although many organizations regularly assess safety and identify risk management strategies, applying these concepts to the built environ-ment may be new to some. The CHD, through a three-year grant from the Agency for Healthcare Research and Quality (AHRQ) and additional financial support from the FGI, has developed a tool to support the SRA included in the 2014 guidelines.

The SRA toolkit developed by the CHD includes a safe design road map, risk data, and design considerations for six safety areas including hospital-acquired infections, medication safety, falls, psychiatric injuries, security, and patient handling.[38] The tool is based on research evidence in each of these areas linking the design of the physical environment to health outcomes. The purpose of the tool is to allow healthcare design decision makers (architects, owners, risk managers) to proactively evaluate the impact of proposed designs on health outcomes and to help design environments reduce the risk of harm to patients and staff. Design considerations in each of the six areas are supported by rationale statements that include research citations and various tags for sorting and filtering. A user guide provides background and recommendations for toolkit implementation.

SUMMARY

The physical environment is an important tool in the quality and safety improvement toolkit available to healthcare administrators and providers. There is increasing awareness among designers, healthcare administrators, and clinicians about the important role of the physical environment in improving patient and staff safety in healthcare. It is important to proactively evaluate design decisions from the perspective of their potential impacts on patient safety. It is also critical to engage users from different disciplines such as infection control, nursing, risk managers, and environmental services when making facility design decisions that can impact patient and staff safety. Emerging tools such as the SRA toolkit provide a structured way to use an evidence-based design process for improving patient safety in healthcare facilities.

REFERENCES

1. Kohn L, Corrigan J, and Donaldson M, editors. *To Err is Human: Building a Safer Health System*. Washington, DC: National Academy Press; 1999.
2. Wachter RM. Patient safety at ten: Unmistakable progress, troubling gaps. *Health Affairs* (Project Hope). 2010;29(1):165–73.
3. Landrigan CP, Parry GJ, Bones CB, Hackbarth AD, Goldmann DA, and Sharek PJ. Temporal trends in rates of patient harm resulting from medical care. *The New England Journal of Medicine*. 2010;363(22):2124–34.
4. Levinson D. *Adverse Events in Hospitals: National Incidence among Medicare Beneficiaries*. Washington, DC: U.S. Department of Health and Human Services, Office of the Inspector General, 2010 OEI-06-09-00090.
5. Society of Actuaries. Study finds medical errors annually cost at least $19.5 billion nationwide [press release]. Society of Actuaries 2010.

6. Reason J. Human error: Models and management. *British Medical Journal.* 2000;320:768–70.
7. Ulrich R, Zimring C, Zhu X, DuBose J, Hyun-Bo S, Choi Y-S, et al. A review of the research literature on evidence-based healthcare design. *Health Environments Research & Design Journal.* 2008;1(3):61–125.
8. Joseph A, and Rashid M. The architecture of safety: Hospital design. *Current Opinion in Critical Care.* 2007;13:714–19.
9. Vincent C, Taylor-Adams S, and Stanhope N. Framework for analysing risk and safety in clinical medicine. *British Medical Journal.* 1998;316(11 April):1154–57.
10. Reason J. Human error: Models and management. *British Medical Journal.* 2000;320(7237):768–70.
11. The Center for Health Design. Evidence-based Accreditation and Certification (EDAC) 2008 [cited 2015 4/2/15]. Available from: https://www.healthdesign.org/edac/about.
12. Passweg JR, Rowlings PA, Atkinson KA, Barrett AJ, Gale RP, Gratwohl A, et al. Influence of protective isolation on outcome of allogeneic bone marrow transplantation for leukemia. *Bone Marrow Transplant.* 1998;21(12):1231–38.
13. Sherertz RJ, Belani A, Kramer BS, Elfenbein GJ, Weiner RS, Sullivan ML, et al. Impact of air filtration on nosocomial *Aspergillus* infections: Unique risk of bone marrow transplant recipients. *The American Journal of Medicine.* 1987;83(4):709–18.
14. Joseph A. *The Impact of Design on Infections in Healthcare Facilities.* Concord, CA: The Center for Health Design; 2006.
15. Van Enk RA. Modern hospital design for infection control. *Healthcare Design.* 2006;6(5):10–14.
16. Joseph A, and Hamilton K. The Pebble Projects: Coordinated evidence-based case studies. *Building Research and Information.* 2008;36(2):129–45.
17. Vernon MO, Trick WE, Welbel SF, Peterson BJ, and Weinstein RA. Adherence with hand hygiene: Does number of sinks matter? *Infection Control and Hospital Epidemiology.* 2003;24(3):224–25.
18. Kaplan LM, and McGuckin M. Increasing handwashing compliance with more accessible sinks. *Infection Control.* 1986;7(8):408–10.
19. Bischoff WE, Reynolds TM, Sessler CN, Edmond MB, and Wenzel RP. Handwashing compliance by health care workers: The impact of introducing an accessible, alcohol-based hand antiseptic. *Archives of Internal Medicine.* 2000;160(7):1017–21.
20. Flynn EA, Barker KN, Gibson JT, Pearson RE, Smith LA, and Berger BA. Relationships between ambient sounds and the accuracy of pharmacists' prescription-filling performance. *Human Factors.* 1996;38(4):614–22.
21. Lin AC, Jang R, Sedani D, Thomas S, Barker KN, and Flynn EA. Re-engineering a pharmacy work system and layout to facilitate patient counseling. *American Journal of Systems Pharmacy.* 1996;53(13):1558–64.
22. Buchanan TL, Barker KN, Gibson JT, Jiang BC, and Pearson RE. Illumination and errors in dispensing. *American Journal of Hospital Pharmacy.* 1991;48(10):2137–45.
23. Hendrich A, and Lee N. Intra-unit patient transports: Time, motion, and cost impact on hospital efficiency. *Nursing Economics.* 2005;23(4):157–64.
24. Hendrich A, Fay J, and Sorrells A. Effects of acuity-adaptable rooms on flow of patients and delivery of care. *American Journal of Critical Care.* 2004;13(1):35–45.

25. Ulrich RP, Quan X, Zimring CP, Joseph A, and Choudhary R. *The Role of the Physical Environment in the Hospital of the 21st Century: A Once-in-a-Lifetime Opportunity*. Research. Concord, CA: The Center for Health Design, September 2004.

26. Hendrich A, editor. Case study: The impact of acuity adaptable rooms on future designs, bottlenecks and hospital capacity. *Impact Conference on Optimizing the Physical Space for Improved Outcomes, Satisfaction and the Bottom Line*. Atlanta, GA: The Institute for Healthcare Improvement & The Center for Health Design, 2003.

27. Kromhout H, Hoek F, Uitterhoeve R, Huijbers R, Overmars RF, Anzion R, et al. Postulating a dermal pathway for exposure to anti-neoplastic drugs among hospital workers: Applying a conceptual model to the results of three workplace surveys. *The Annals of Occupational Hygiene*. 2000;44(7):551–60.

28. Kumari DN, Haji TC, Keer V, Hawkey PM, Duncanson V, and Flower E. Ventilation grilles as a potential source of methicillin-resistant *Staphylococcus aureus* causing an outbreak in an orthopaedic ward at a district general hospital. *The Journal of Hospital Infection*. 1998;39(2):127–33.

29. Smedbold HT, Ahlen C, Unimed S, Nilsen AM, Norbaeck D, and Hilt B. Relationships between indoor environments and nasal inflammation in nursing personnel. *Archives of Environmental Health*. 2002;57(2):155–61.

30. Jiang S, Huang L, Chen X, Wang J, Wu W, Yin S, et al. Ventilation of wards and nosocomial outbreak of severe acute respiratory syndrome among healthcare workers. *Chinese Medical Journal*. 2003;116(9):1293–97.

31. Brophy MOR, Achimore L, and Moore-Dawson J. Reducing incidence of low-back injuries reduces cost. *American Industrial Hygiene Association Journal*. 2001;62(4):508.

32. Miller A, Engst C, Tate RB, and Yassi A. Evaluation of the effectiveness of portable ceiling lifts in a new long-term care facility. *Applied Ergonomics*. 2006;37(3):377–85.

33. Fragala G, and Bailey L. Addressing occupational strains and sprains: Musculoskeletal injuries in hospitals. *AAOHN Journal*. 2003;51(6):252–59.

34. Garg A, and Owen B. Reducing back stress to nursing personnel: An ergonomic intervention in a nursing home. *Ergonomics*. 1992;35(11):1353–75.

35. Joseph A, and Fritz L. Ceiling lifts reduce patient-handling injuries. *Healthcare Design*. 2006;6:10–13.

36. Engst C, Chhokar R, Miller A, Tate RB, and Yassi A. Effectiveness of overhead lifting devices in reducing the risk of injury to care staff in extended care facilities. *Ergonomics*. 2005;48(2):187–99.

37. Facility Guidelines Institute. *FGI Guidelines for Design and Construction of Hospitals and Outpatient Facilities*. Institute FG, editor. Washington, DC: Facility Guidelines Institute, 2014.

38. Joseph A, Taylor E, and Quan X. *Safety Risk Assessment Toolkit*. Concord, CA: The Center for Health Design; 2015 [cited 2015 9/1/15]. Available from: https://www.healthdesign.org/chd/learning_tools_and_resources/safety_risk_assessment_toolkit.

8

Evidence-Based Design in Hospitals: Theory to Implementation

S.K. Biswas and V.K. Singh

CONTENTS

INTRODUCTION

The UK House of Commons was extensively damaged during the Second World War. The question of its reconstruction was taken up on October 28, 1943, when Sir Winston Churchill stated:

We shape our buildings and afterwards, our building shapes us.....[1]

Now, nearly 74 years later, this statement still holds true, especially from the perspective of the planning and operation of hospitals.

A hospital begins either as a desire to meet the healthcare needs of communities or to achieve the business objectives of owners and entrepreneurs. From the architect's drawing board or computer, the outcome is a set of "good for construction" drawings. The drawings reflect the detailed dimensions, the location of various building structures, and the services and interiors layouts. These are then passed on to the construction company to execute, at which time the building's layout and location are set. As a result, and in order to open on time, the operational management has to compromise with the departments or reorient them. In essence, we shape our buildings and afterward they shape us!

Several innovations and the development of new technologies have compelled us to change. Information and communication technology (ICT) and the application of management tools, such as the Lean approach (LA), are prime examples. There has also been a paradigm shift in health delivery processes and patients' outlook. Leveraging these has become imperative for any modern hospital to stay competitive.

As the Joint Commission International (JCI) stated:

> Building more of the same, will freeze into place persistent problems which hospital must already contend - such as unsafe care, hospital acquired infection and worker fatigue - that otherwise could be mitigated through application of evidence based design.[2]

In the twenty-first century, the challenges for the hospital sector are to run a hospital in a cost-effective way and yet deliver a quality service.

Globally, the rising input costs of delivering healthcare services far exceed expected revenue. In an era of perfect market competition,[3] rival providers offer comparable and homogeneous services.

Users, on the other hand, are resolute in their demands for safe and quality care. They are cost sensitive and yet press the competitors for much more, including

- Improved **tangible** ambience
- **Reliable** and safe clinical outcome of their illness
- **Responsiveness** to their needs (discounted, accountable services)
- **Assurance** for their safety
- **Empathetic** approach from the hospital personnel

Consequently, the hospital management has a dilemma during the operational phase: to meet the demands in an effective and efficient manner, or to keep the operational expenses under control. With a demand-versus-delivery impasse imminent, the hospital management must ensure that from the conception stage of the hospital, the outdated approach is avoided, while capital costs are kept to a minimum.

In order to do this, management tools such as the LA could be adopted. This is applicable at both the hospital design stage and during operation. The bedrock of the LA is evidence-based design (EBD) that relies less on individual opinion and experience and more on the best practices and protocol followed globally.

In the last decade, we have seen exemplary changes in the operation of banking, insurance, hotel, travel, cashless purchase, supply chain, and many other sectors. This has been made possible initially due to the evolution of and then due to the revolution in ICT. This practice is now creeping into the healthcare realm to improve its outcomes.

This chapter attempts to describe the principles of the LA, and its synergy with EBD. It analyzes standards and guidelines based on research findings and the recommendations of peer groups for a quintessential hospital. And finally, we share some real-life experiences of its application in a hospital in Kolkata.

LEAN APPROACH

The LA is not especially new. It is a merger of two aspects of management. In the 1950s, marketing had started to put the emphasis on the customer. Customers' needs and their satisfaction were seen as the main drivers of success in business. To understand customers, they should be segmented into groups with homogeneous needs. Marketing, however, has never paid much attention to production. As long as there is a scarcity of goods, producers do not pay attention to customers. If the product is without errors,

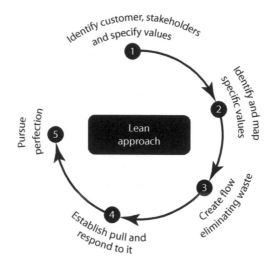

FIGURE 8.1
The Lean approach.

that is good enough. Customers can take it or leave it. As economies and wealth grow and supply becomes abundant, there will be buyers' markets. Both production efficiency and customer needs need to find a common focus. Customer value is the relation between what you give as a price and what you get as a product or service. Production efficiency reduces what you give; customer focus improves what you get. The modern adaption of the LA to hospitals is summed up in Figure 8.1.

IDENTIFY CUSTOMER AND STAKEHOLDERS AND SPECIFY VALUE

It is common knowledge that the end users of a hospital are the patients or customers who use the facilities and pay for them. The caregivers, staff, and owners are also important. They are the stakeholders. The caregivers (doctors, nurses, and technicians) who manage the patient's illness are crucial stakeholders. As are the administrative and support staff who keep the system running, as well as the owners who, quite reasonably, expect a return on their invested capital.

So, what values may these various customers and stakeholders expect from the hospital?

Patients

The patients or customers value the tangibles, such as cleanliness, hygiene, and an ergonomically designed space for their care. At the same time, they expect a reliable clinical outcome. They demand transparency in billing; quick throughputs on admittance and discharge; and responsive, reassuring, and empathetic staff. They expect natural light, reduced noise, privacy, and communicability with relatives, which have far-reaching consequences for their recovery. The patient's relatives, likewise, want frequent informational updates and counseling regarding the condition of their relative.

Doctors, Nurses, and Paramedics

This group appreciates management systems and processes that give top priority to patient care and safety. Where the flow of clinical information is in real time, a reassuring environment may be formed, for which the following of their directives without error is a critical requirement. Well-trained, experienced personnel demand measures to correct error-prone processes and administration's focus on the prevention of nosocomial infections. In summary, professionals appreciate a work environment where they can concentrate on their work and see the results of it; not spending time on administration hassles or correcting errors.

Staff

Staff expectation of a hospital is that its very design minimizes the physical stress and strain of patient handling. Protocol-based processes logically embedded in the hospital information system (HIS), such as in ICT, greatly reduce the effects of their mundane tasks. The HIS has automatic sentinel protocols, able to better disseminate information through short message services (SMS). A pneumatic transportation system (PTS) helps to alleviate their physical stress, and the frequency of unnecessary movements. The staff would find the environment designed on training and skill development motivational.

Owners

They would readily back efficient processes run by teams of professionals, and the systemic work culture tuned to avoid wastage of resources. Their aspiration would be for a fair return on the capital invested in the project.

Analysis of Customer and Stakeholders Value

In order to analyze the purpose of a hospital project, one needs to document the customer's values or desires. Each of the stratified customers and stakeholders, as defined previously, desires the implementation of the values that they cherish. A fishbone diagram provides a sneak peek of the possible needs (Figure 8.2). The values attribute relates to

Tangibility

Defined as any deliverable that the customers' sensory systems pick up, such as ambience, taste of food, cleanliness of beds and toilets, the surrounding greenery, unnecessary excessive noise, smells, ergonomics that prevents falls and injuries, and so on.

Reliability

Delivering what has been promised and accredited, such as quality of care, reliable clinical outcome, proper systems maintenance, avoidance of nosocomial infection or medical error, and so on.

Responsiveness

This translates into a hospital's readiness and willingness to provide services in a prompt and timely manner. It needs good and effective communication throughout the hospital, teams of well-trained, enthusiastic caregivers, and less superfluous movements.

Assurance

To perform the services necessary for patient care requires skills and professionalism. Issues related to patient safety need enablers such as regularly updating employee's knowledge through continuous training, staff satisfaction, reward and recognition, return on investment from the perspective of owners, and so on. All of this together builds assurance.

Empathy

This is manifested in the clean and neat appearance of hospital staff, their polite and respectful behavior, their demonstrated teamwork, and their maintaining a feedback loop while delivering service.

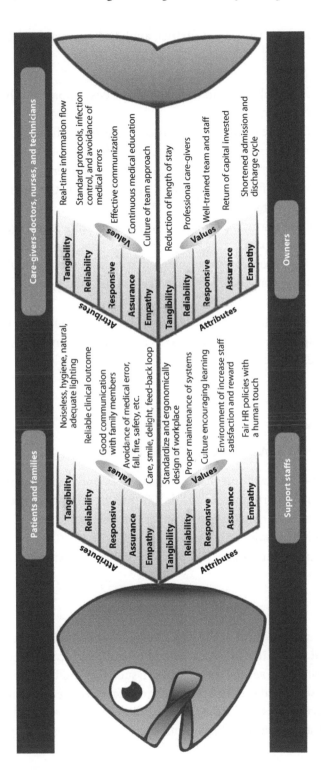

FIGURE 8.2

Fish-bone analysis of customer's and stakeholder's value.

In the next step, the values are further analyzed against the following queries:

- **What** do these values mean in terms of the cost impact on the project and returns on investment?
- **Why** should these be taken up for incorporation in the project? Will there be any differentiation in services as compared to other hospitals? Will there be any value-addition to the customer?
- **Where** do these fit into the design stage and then the operational stage of the hospital?
- **When** will the changes be conceived, tested, executed, and evaluated to gauge their impact?
- **Who** will be responsible for implementation and monitoring?
- **How** will they work to benefit the various customer needs?

These steps help to define, prioritize, and document the intent or purpose of the design/process change, as well as its subsequent implementation. It facilitates the next step of the LA.

IDENTIFY AND MAP SPECIFIC VALUE

LA involves all of the customers and stakeholders previously mentioned, and enables them to participate in the design/process change of the hospital. The effort put in during this time shapes the final outcome and should thus reflect what they value.

In LA, there are certain organizing tools to enable this. Among them are

Six-S

The various values or desires of the customers and stakeholders are identified and **sorted** according to issues related to staff, service quality, time, and cost. Priorities are **set** for these issues. Issues that are unsolvable and not critical are **scrubbed** out. Issues related to **safety** are specially analyzed and settled. An overall **standard** approach/solution is derived, and finally, these solutions are **sustained** throughout the project/process change cycle (Figure 8.3).

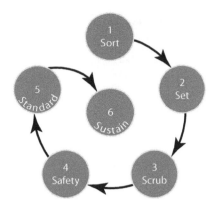

FIGURE 8.3
The Six-S.

Handouts

A handout is a document that quantifies the processes and subprocesses, along with the efficiency of resource usage. It provides key data regarding the efficacy of various processes, and leads to an EBD and operation. Broadly, it provides an input into what to do (**responsibility**), how to do it (**knowledge**), doing the actual work (**action**), and learning from the outcome (**feedback**). The process helps to make decisions based on data, rather than opinions.

Spaghetti

This is a visual reflection of the to-and-fro movement of staff, materials, and other resources. It is a representation of the physical space and its proposed processes (Figure 8.4). The approach allows an analysis of resources to identify probable wasteful uses and to work out possible alternatives (Figure 8.5).

Downtime

Downtime is an acronym for the various aspects of service delivery:

Defective processes, **O**verproduction within the system, supererogatory **W**aiting time, **N**on-utilization of staff, non-essential **T**ransportation involving staff and materials, needless **I**nventory and blocking of working capital, unreasonable **M**otion of staff and materials, and **E**xcessive

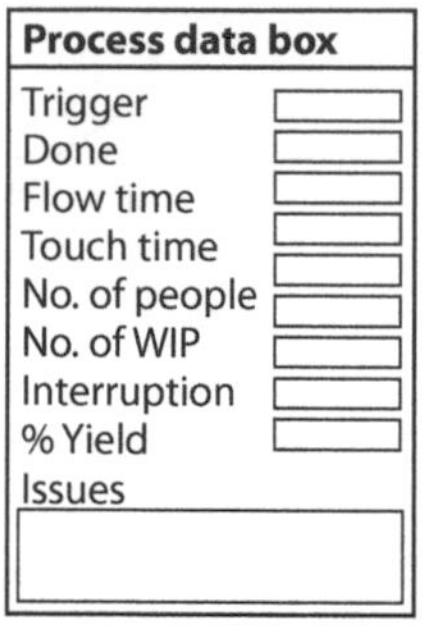

Process data box
Trigger
Done
Flow time
Touch time
No. of people
No. of WIP
Interruption
% Yield
Issues

FIGURE 8.4
The handouts.

Spaghetti map to record matrix from process data box
Activity routes
Receive inventory
Medicine distribution
Inventory supply

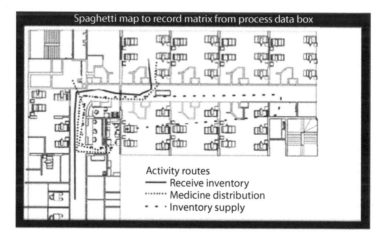

FIGURE 8.5
The Spaghetti mapping.

processing while delivering services. A design approach that looks into each of these attributes and values and works through consensus finds the best alternate solutions, resulting in better outcomes for all the customers and stakeholders defined earlier.

Defects	**T**ransport
Overproduction	**I**nventory
Waiting	**M**ovement
Non-utilization	**E**xcess Processing

A3 Approach

This is a template done on a sheet of A3 paper based on the problem-solving and documentation process. The template summarizes the findings from the previous exercise and helps further analysis. The data are put under nine boxes, as shown in Table 8.1, to ensure the visibility of the outcome of the exercises to the stakeholders. These include:

TABLE 8.1

Steps for Lean A3 Approach

Reason for Action

The values expressed by the customers and stakeholders are prioritized with tools such as Six-S. They are further analyzed for quality, cost, staff issues, and time line.

Initial State

A reflection of the current stage or **Current Stage Value Stream Analysis** (CSVSA). The issues are presented as numeric and/or graphical data. Their input comes from the process data sheet, and the spaghetti and handover map. It sets baseline values for the issues that are to be addressed.

Target State

Through research, field survey, and focus-group discussion, the best practices to follow are visualized, discussed, and finally benchmarked. It reflects the **Future State Value Stream Analysis** (FSVSA), also represented as numeric and/or graphical data for better understanding by the stakeholders.

Gap Analysis

The gap between the CSVSA and the FSVSA is iterated, both qualitatively and quantitatively, using the fishbone analytic approach. Here, evaluation is based on queries, such as What, Why, Where, When, Who, and How. The **cause–effect** on or of any given issue may be scrutinized and correlated through this approach.

Solution Approach

Following the gap analysis, probable solutions are derived and developed. The solutions focus on methods to improve quality, cost, staff issues, and time line.

Rapid Improvement Event (RIE)

The solutions are tested for feasibility and practicality of implementation. Lessons learned are improved on for the next stage.

Completion Plan

Based on the findings from the RIE, time line and the responsibility for execution are set for implementation. A key step would be to educate and train the operational staff during the execution of the altered processes.

Confirmed State

This is based on the difference in matrix between FSVSA and CSVSA. At this stage, issue outcomes are measured to determine how close their achievements have been to the target.

Insight

This is the final stage where we reflect what needs to be done to pursue perfection.

CREATE FLOW AND ELEMINATE WASTE

The outcome of the exercise is a system in which processes are not uneven and overburdened with the wasteful allocation of resources. The objective at this stage of the design/process change is to develop a smooth relationship between issues relating to stakeholders, methods, materials, money, and time. The cliché "Anything that does not add value to the customer is WASTE" holds true.

ESTABLISH PULL AND RESPOND TO IT

The conventional hospital design follows a "**Push**" system. Space or resources for various disciplines are allocated largely in a decentralized, dedicated, and specialized manner. Once the hospital is operational, there is little scope for change, since all the resources are allocated more or less permanently. A design/process change based on the "**Pull**" system, however, is largely centralized, shared, and generalized, thereby avoiding resource wastage. The efforts to eliminate the wasteful use of resources are put into the processes through the participation of all the stakeholders of the hospital. A consensus is arrived at by observing, collecting data, and analyzing the best outcomes. By streamlining the entire attribute mentioned in the acronym **DOWNTIME** explained earlier, the avoidance of uneven flow and overburdened systems in a hospital is ensured. Staff are encouraged to multitask and deliver services promptly when needed. Communications are aided by ICT in the HIS to make them meaningful. For example, inventories are pulled from the central store when the demand arises. Their storage is not based on a hypothetical assumption.

PURSUE PERFECTION

The final outcome of the exercise through LA is to strive for perfection in delivering patient care. When new processes are introduced, one needs to continue monitoring and making changes where and when necessary. A hospital, in which processes are linked with the backbone of ICT, requires constant upgrading of its software with new reports mined from the data to analyze and improve the processes. In time, the new hospital personnel must be adequately trained to follow the processes and enhance them to the extent a given hospital's environment permits.

EVIDENCE-BASED DESIGN

EBD is a field of study where rational evidence is incorporated into a design. The ethos of EBD is gradually being embraced in the health domain to improve patient well-being and healing, stress relief for staff, and overall safety. EBD obtains its ideas and nomenclatures from disciplines such as environmental psychology, architecture, neuroscience, and behavioral economics.

The hospital's surroundings play a big role in reducing the stress experienced by patients and their families as well as caregivers. The healthcare environment is multifaceted. It is a place of cure and care for the patients and their families, a place for staff to earn their livelihood, a business surroundings, and a cultural environment for the organization to pursue its mission. The EBD addresses issues of the customer and stakeholders values or desires (defined earlier) for hospitals. It is based on the ideology that at each stage of the planning and execution, evidence is gathered, measured, correlated, analyzed, improved, and documented. It is also a cross-functional communication tool for the forward–backward exchange of information between all stakeholders in the project/process change. It helps them in the decision-making process. This approach allows the design to be based on evidence from the past as well as the present and into the future, in a logical manner, as shown in Figures 8.6 and 8.7 and Table 8.2.

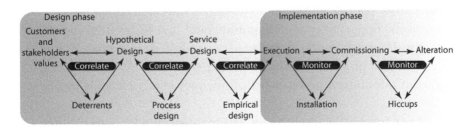

FIGURE 8.6
The flow in the project cycle with the EBD approach.

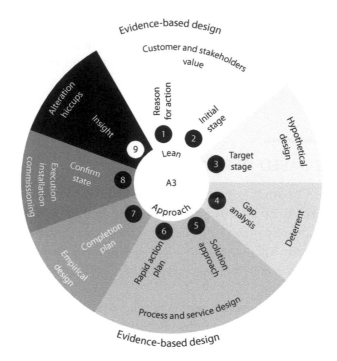

FIGURE 8.7
Synergy between Lean A3 and the EBD approach.

EVIDENCE-BASED DESIGN IN ACTION

IN AN ARTICLE, JOHN G. REILING [4] STATED:

When SynergyHealth, St. Joseph's Hospital of West Bend, Wisconsin, decided to relocate and build an 82-bed acute care facility, it recognized the opportunity to design a hospital that focused on patient safety. Hospital leaders believed if a facility design process was "engineered properly, it would enhance patient safety and create a patient safe culture; however, little information was available to give direction.

The management conducted a national learning laboratory. They drew knowledge and experience about patient safety from the available literature. They invited experts from the healthcare profession and other fields, including transportation, spacecraft design, and systems engineering. They involved the board members, staff, physicians, and facility design team.

The outcome of the effort was a set of top 10 recommendations as guideline for the design team to follow:

1. Design failure mode effort analysis (FMEA) at each design stage.
2. Standardize the location of equipment, supplies, room layout, and care processes.
3. Involve patient/families in the design process.
4. Use an established checklist for current/future design.
5. Bring critical information for decision making close to the patient.
6. Reduce noise.
7. Use adaptive systems that will allow function in the future.
8. Articulate a set of principles by which everything is measured.
9. Begin equipment planning on Day 1.
10. Begin mock-ups on Day 1.

Iris Hospital is a 180-bed multispecialty hospital in Kolkata. This project was a part of the diversification plan for a group of local entrepreneurs, who wanted to enter the vibrant healthcare domain with a greenfield project. The brief given to the design and execution team was to address the various shortcomings apparent in existing public and private hospitals. The ethos of the brief was to bring forth a hospital that differentiated its services by leveraging ICT and organizing teams of well-trained employees who followed standardized protocols and processes, curbing wastage of resources while delivering services to the patients.

The design and the project team of Iris Hospital chose to leverage the foregoing recommendations and the outcome was as follows.

1. **Design FMEA at each design stage**

    The team's efforts focused on simulating the **place** (physical environment) with **processes** that would be followed by operational **personnel** to ensure the safety and quality care of **patients** with a wide range of **products** (services), provided to them at a reasonable **price** (Figure 8.8).

TABLE 8.2

Brief Outline on the Phases and the Steps Involved in EBD

Design Phase

Customer and Stakeholders Value

At the outset of the hospital design cycle, the **Customer and Stakeholders Values** are clearly set by the users of the system (defined earlier). This is vital input for planners. It avoids drastic changes midway in the hospital project and thus keeps the costs and time overruns under control. It concurs with the "initial stage" of the A3 tool.

Deterrent

Once the initial purpose of the hospital has been defined, EBD attempts to systematically analyze the **Deterrents** or constraints that need to be addressed to complete the setting up of the hospital. The activities in this stage are the analysis of constraints related to humans, methods, materials, money, and time. Through the various communicative channels available, issues are defined, researched, and resolved between the stakeholders and the hospital planners. The tools that may be used are Six-S, which **Sorts** values according to stratified customers and stakeholders; then further looks for commonality in benefits, **Sets** them in order of priorities, **Scrubs** away impractical values, analyzes **Safety** issues, **Standardizes** design and the processes that go with it, which it then **Sustains** in implementing. Data collected through **Spaghetti, Handout,** and **A3 approaches** provide a practical definition of the desires of the customers and stakeholders of the hospital. It concurs with the "gap analysis" phase of the A3 tool.

Hypothetical Design

An initial **Hypothetical Design** of the hospital consequently emerges and it reflects the values of the customers and the stakeholders as well as the various deterrents or constraints that exist within. It shows the physical space allocated for the resources and its utilization pertaining to humans, methods, materials, money, and time management. The objective, to avoid unevenness and overburdened processes, is achieved by removing waste. The hospital planner communicates the outcome for the proposed design to the stakeholders for feedback and course correction. It concurs with the "targeted" setting phase of the A3 tool.

Process Design

Concurrently, the **Processes** that are to be operationalized are taken up. They are deduced, defined, researched, analyzed, and incorporated into plans by the design team, leading to further refinement of the physical space in the hospital. It concurs with the "rapid action event" and "solution planning" phase of the A3 tool.

Service Design

With a well-conceived hypothetical design in hand, various vendors may be called into the hospital project. The values and deterrents of the hypothetical design and the remedial processes to be followed are communicated to them through documents. These activities lead to a detailed **Service Design** of the hospital from the vendors. It includes the MEP designs and the costs related to them. It also concurs with the "rapid action event" and "solution planning" phase of the A3 tool.

(*Continued*)

TABLE 8.2 (CONTINUED)

Brief Outline on the Phases and the Steps Involved in EBD

Design Phase

Empirical Design

The next step is the **Empirical Design** or the detail design, which is the culmination and coordination of all the previous ideas, design, and data; reflecting the customers and the stakeholders' vision, the analyzed deterrents in the project, the hypothetical design, and the details of the services within. The empirical plans include details regarding technical, financial as well as time-line or scheduling issues. It concurs with the "completion plan" phase in the A3 tool.

Implementation Phase

Execution

Vendors are called in for the **Execution** once the empirical design of the hospital emerges. The bidding tenders are in elaborate detail from data arising from the previous steps of the project. The vendors then put in a realistic cost quotation, which is then vetted by the management or owners of the hospital. A focused team of project managers then monitors the set cost and time schedules for the project. It concurs with the "confirmed phase" in the A3 tool.

Installation

The hospital projects involve a great degree of coordination among vendors supplying expensive medical and non-medical equipment and services. The culmination of all the earlier activities, including the empirical design and its execution, is the **Installation** step of the hospital. This is a concurrent exercise with the execution phase of the project. Simultaneous with the construction phase, various MEP are put in place as per the detailed plan. It concurs with the "confirmed phase" in the A3 tool.

Commissioning

The **Commissioning** of the hospital involves a rational plan for the key resource utilization of humans, methods, materials, money, time, and marketing strategies and its implementation. At this point, the services put in are taken to the end users, namely, the customers. It concurs with the "confirmed phase" in the A3 tool.

Hiccups

Any new or a retrofitted hospital will undergo **Hiccups**. These may be minimized if LA with EBD is followed. EBD ensures that possible hiccups are identified at the empirical planning phase through simulating various conditions of failure built upon data from past experiences. It concurs with the "in-sight phase" in the A3 tool.

Alteration

Finally, to fine-tune or correct mistakes, and to ramp up the project to its fullest potential, the **Alteration** step must inevitably be performed. It concurs with the "in-sight phase" in the A3 tool.

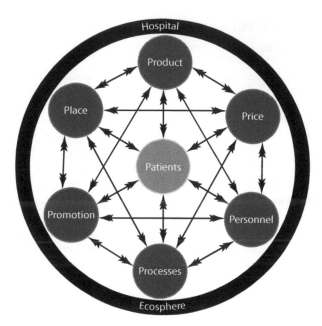

FIGURE 8.8
Interrelationship of a hospital's ecosphere.

A hospital has an enigmatic and dynamic ecosphere, where all the previously highlighted "**p**"s are intertwined. FMEA, a process analytic tool already in use in other industries—in aviation it is used to investigate aircraft crashes—was basic to inducting the culture, the design, the execution, and subsequently the operation of this hospital.

Today, patient safety is a burning issue. As the Institute of Medicine (IOM)[5] reported: the probability of a hospital preventable medical death will occur in the range of 3 to 6 per 1,000 admissions and that an adverse event will occur in the range of 3 to 4 per every 1,000 admissions.

Events relating to medication errors are common in India, but they generally go unreported. Such errors may be incurred from **methodology** (processes), such as in a hospital's laboratory, **machine** (equipment) in which calibration and maintenance is faulty, and finally, **humans** (hospital staff) who are meant to control all of the variables but fail to do so.

Reiling[6] and others tell us that Reason (1990) and Norman (1988) concluded from their studies that most daily activities are routine and completed with little or no higher-level thought processes. In these types of activities, errors known as slips or mistakes (lapses) can occur for multiple reasons, including distractions, interruptions, multitasking, or any deviation from the routine activity. Other behaviors require a conscious, knowledge-based thought process that often borrows from past experiences. Errors in these behaviors are referred to as mistakes and can result from a lack of knowledge, experience, communication, or even misjudgment.

Safety issues may be **Active** or **Latent**. At Iris Hospital, foremost on the minds of the design team were the active issues that had to be addressed, such as "medication error" and "nosocomial infection."

- **Medication error** was largely tackled by introducing computerized prescription order entry (CPOE) and medicine management system (MMS) as part of the process for ordering, processing, delivering, and validating medicine for the patient. The process was in sync with the billing and inventory management processes, and automatically archived data as part of the electronic medical record (EMR). The data generated correlated seamlessly with the hospital's financial reporting.
- At the design stage, **nosocomial infection** was tackled with active measures on contact and airborne infection routes. Alcohol spray handwash in all patient-related areas was incorporated to reduce infection via contact routes. Issues on susceptible hosts, modes of transmission, the source of infection, and the places of entry and exit were identified and analyzed, and appropriate processes were established. The design incorporated the necessary airflow direction and related ventilation parameters. *High-efficiency particulate air* (HEPA) filters and other measures were appropriated to avoid airborne infection. Protocols and surveillance systems were infused in the operation phase.

For **Latent** issues, fire safety and waste management were also resolved (Figure 8.9).
- **Fire Safety** includes fire control, firefighting, and evacuation systems.

    For **Fire Control**, mock-up drills are held regularly with the intention to sensitize all concerned to the factors responsible for starting a fire and the requisite steps to prevent its spread.

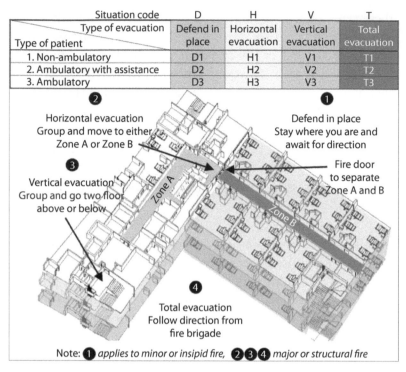

Situation code	D	H	V	T
Type of evacuation / Type of patient	Defend in place	Horizontal evacuation	Vertical evacuation	Total evacuation
1. Non-ambulatory	D1	H1	V1	T1
2. Ambulatory with assistance	D2	H2	V2	T2
3. Ambulatory	D3	H3	V3	T3

❷ Horizontal evacuation
Group and move to either
Zone A or Zone B

❸ Vertical evacuation
Group and go two floor
above or below

Zone A

Zone B

❶ Defend in place
Stay where you are and
await for direction

Fire door
to separate
Zone A and B

❹ Total evacuation
Follow direction from
fire brigade

Note: **❶** *applies to minor or insipid fire,* **❷❸❹** *major or structural fire*

FIGURE 8.9
Fire evacuation system at Iris Hospital.

Measures that were put in place to facilitate **Firefighting** included fire alarms, smoke detectors, sprinklers, fire hydrants, mechanical air exhaust systems, zoning, fire gas masks, fire-resistant doors, fire escape staircases, a refuge area between certain floors, enclosed service shafts, emergency lighting, closed-circuit television (CCTV), and communication systems such as fire signage for evacuation, public address systems, walkie-talkies, and so on.

For **Fire Evacuation**, Figure 8.9 shows the plan and actions put in place at Iris Hospital.

- **Waste Management** guidelines given by the Department of Environment, Government of West Bengal,[7] were strictly adhered to. The waste generated was collected at source, and segregated into variously sized color-coded bags. A specialist external agency was then engaged for their collection and appropriate disposal. Figure 8.10 gives an idea of the process that is followed at Iris Hospital (Figure 8.10).

Segregation ⟶ Storage ⟶ Disposal

Waste management at Iris Hospital

Yellow bag label	Blue bag label	Black bag label

Clinical waste for incineration	Clinical waste for autoclave	Clinical waste for landfill

Infected wasted (non-plastic)
Non plastic lab waste
Cotton, gauze, bandage, mask, cap, disposable drapes and gowns

Infected wasted (plastic)
Non plastic lab waste
Tubing, catheter, syringes without needles, gloves, empty blood bags

Sharp wasted
(In puncture proof container)
Needles and glass vials
broken glass bottles

Non hazardous waste: such as-paper, food items, and plastic water bottles—**Black bag with no label**

FIGURE 8.10
Waste management at Iris Hospital.

2. Standardized location of equipment, supplies, room layouts, and care processes

It became evident to the design team at the hypothetical design stage that non-value attributes were tantamount to WASTE. They cause an uneven delivering service and needlessly overburden scarce resources. Value stream analysis (VSA), the exercise explained earlier, gave the team a new design direction.

- Issues related to **equipment location** and its layout were analyzed and then standardized according to usefulness. Savings were made by negotiating bulk purchases whenever possible. This decision making at the design stage of the project helped cut down on the capital costs of the hospital project.
- Analyzing consumables and durable **supplies** in terms of physical location, effective movement from source (centralized storage) to destination (nurses' station complex) and finally to the end users (patients, doctors, etc.) is imperative from the operational perspective. After deliberations through the VSA, consensus was

arrived at and implemented by leveraging CPOE and MMS in the software.

- **Room layouts** were standardized to be as flexible as possible, maintaining space for future alteration in a service mix (Figure 8.17). This reduced construction time, shortened installation time, and eased monitoring of assets through the HIS.
- **Care processes** were standardized following a few aberrations in the care of acute and chronic patients. Like the combinations and recombinations of the 26 letters of the English alphabet making up words, then sentences, paragraphs, and finally, the meaningful content of this chapter, the finely tuned, choreographed sequences of activities between processes and personnel of any hospital are essential for the satisfactory outcome of care processes. At Iris Hospital, the moment a patient is admitted, standardized protocols and software modules kick in. An amalgamation of these, and with well-trained caregivers, satisfactory services may be delivered. Keeping in mind the example of a patient who, having been admitted with myocardial infarction, dies within the hour from cardiogenic shock, we can perhaps fathom the crucial structure of patient care. The hospital has ICT at its core. Service delivery is built upon protocols and processes.

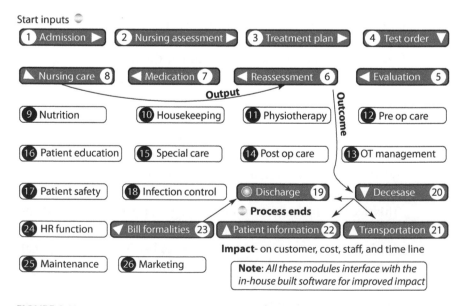

FIGURE 8.11
Protocols and modules for patient care at Iris Hospital.

These, embedded as algorithms in the software program, are called modules. The standard operating practice (SOP) synergizes with the software modules in the HIS developed in-house. The protocols and modules primarily involved in the care delivery system for the myocardial infraction patient are 1 through 8 and 19 through 23, as shown in Figure 8.11.

Care delivery is largely standardized and the software modules help to automatically record the EMR of the patient. Data capture allows accessibility, awareness, accountability, and analysis of the impact on the patient's care.

3. **Involve patient/families in the design process**

Patient-defined values are the most important determinant in the design process for a present-day hospital. What the customer does not value is waste, which must be eliminated. Why should any customer value or desire Iris Hospital? Primary and secondary research done in-house appears to provide an answer, namely:

  • **Ambience and Comfort**: Roger Ulrich et al.[8] at Texas A&M University and Georgia Tech undertook groundbreaking research and analysis on this topic. Their work set the standard guidelines for hospital design. It was backed up by empirical studies to evaluate the impact on clinical outcomes. The study scientifically analyzed the role played by natural light, the natural surroundings with bodies of water, trees, neutral colors, and

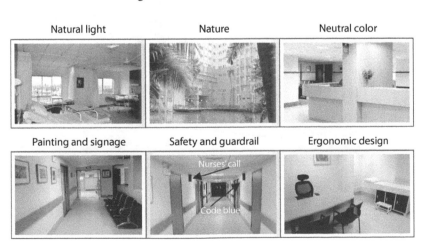

FIGURE 8.12
Effect of ambiance on patient's well-being.

paintings in rooms. All of these were found to be important in the healing process. Appropriate pathfinders, signage at important locations, the presence of guardrails for patients' safety, and better ergonomic intervention in the work environment were necessary to prevent emotional exhaustion and burnout. Iris Hospital complied with these findings to the extent possible, as shown in Figure 8.12.

- **Security and Assurance:** These were a focus for the design team, and became an important differentiator for Iris Hospital. The nurses' call system and code blue alert were put in each patient room with a visual display in the corridor, and at the nurses' station. Multiple CCTVs were strategically placed on each floor, and linked to a control center for surveillance and the safety of patients and staffs.
- **Communication with Staff:** In order to meet the goal set for shortened discharge time (discharge goal: 15 minutes), decentralized billing and cash collection were undertaken at the nurses' stations, shown in Figure 8.15. For transparency in billing, all protocols, processes, and personnel have to be in close

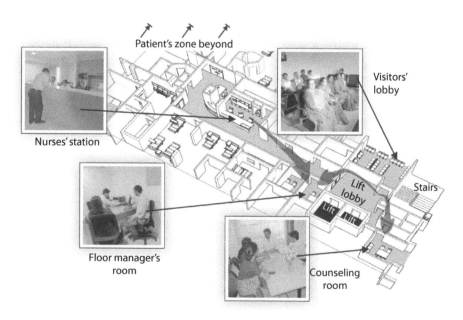

FIGURE 8.13
Importance of patient communication.

communication to gel seamlessly. The software at Iris Hospital ensures that this is a reality.

Other communications tools such as telephones, mobiles, SMSs, walkie-talkies, fax, intranet, Internet, and so on, are also used freely to augment communication.

- **Information on Patient Status:** This is vital to deliver service with a human touch. This was achieved by designing a floor manager's cabin on each floor as well as locating the nurses' station close to it. Besides these, a visitors' lobby and a counseling room were set up to deal with the human side of delivering care. Figure 8.13 shows the layout.

4. **Use an established checklist for current/future design**

Iris Hospital was designed using computer-aided design (CAD). Dynamic data exchange (DDE) between it and in-house developed software documented the attributes of entities created in CAD. This process helped to record, to generate a checklist, and to present it to the stakeholders for audit and course correction during the project stage. Now that the hospital is in operation, the key activities for patient care and safety and back-office tasks are supported by the HIS, which has been an in-house development. This, in turn, reflects the protocols and processes documented in the standard operating manual. As a result, all activities, current and future, are automatically backed up, and could be audited in the form of a checklist.

For example, patient discharge is an important milestone in care delivery. The Joint Commission on Accreditation of Healthcare Organizations (JCAHO)[9] has laid down the guidelines for this activity in "Standard IM.6.10,EP7." A patient's planned discharge activates a complex set of process coordination. Failure in these activities will affect the standard of the discharge report.

Normally, the report should reflect demographic details, reasons for hospitalization, and significant findings from diagnostic studies, as well as procedures done, medications given, discharge condition, and instructions or advice on the next course of action.

At Iris Hospital, all these activities are sentinel events, built into the software. The discharge documents are not generated unless the validated fields are filled and/or updated in the relevant modules, as shown in Figure 8.14. A spin-off of this process is quicker discharge and accountability all around.

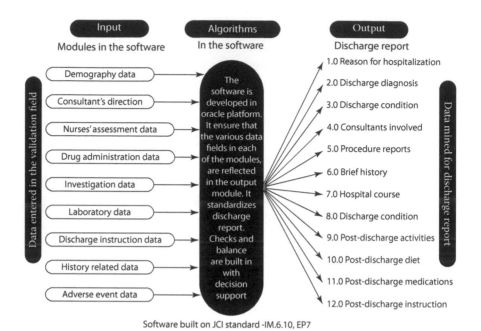

FIGURE 8.14
Basic logic flow in the hospital information system.

This is possible because data are entered in the software at each event, during the entire life cycle of the patient's stay. The software algorithm ensures that the rules set for the discharge process are followed. Thus, the checklist is automatic. On discharge, the software simply mines the relevant data and presents it as the discharge report. It then archives the data and the EMR is automatically generated.

This process has been successfully implemented in the hospital. Against a standard discharge timescale of 2–4 hours in other hospitals, Iris Hospital manages the same in 15–20 minutes.

5. **Bring critical information for decision making close to the patient**
   At Iris Hospital, the nurses' station on the medical/surgical floors is the focal point for both clinical and non-clinical information flow (Figure 8.15).
   • **Clinical information**: The early warning system (EWS) (Figure 8.18), an enabling software tool, records the vitals of the patient. Parameters such as systolic BP, pulse, temperature, respiration rate, Glasgow Coma Score (GCS), urine output, capillary refilling, oxygen saturation, and so on are uploaded to the software

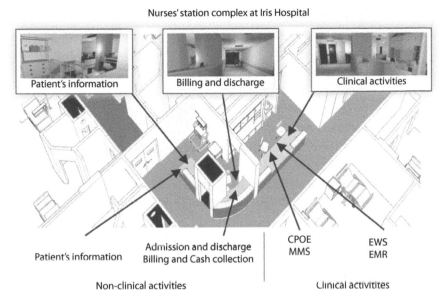

Nurses' station complex at Iris Hospital

Patient's information | Billing and discharge | Clinical activities

Patient's information | Admission and discharge
Billing and Cash collection | CPOE
MMS | EWS
EMR

Non-clinical activities | Clinical activitites

FIGURE 8.15
Bringing critical information to decision makers.

(Figure 8.18). Due to the algorithms built in, any aberration in the values alerts the caregivers to take action. The information flow on medication that goes through the medication management system (MMS), and is executed through CPOE, falls within its purview.

- **Non-clinical information**: Wireless networking of the system ensures that the admission and discharge processes can take place at the nurses' station or at any other location. The patient's family need not run to multiple locations in the hospital to complete the discharge process. The caregivers here are competent to address information and queries regarding billing and post-discharge follow-up instructions. The informational flow attempts to obviate medical error. Further, EMR can be scrutinized at a computer terminal, which enables the caregiver to take the appropriate decisions on patient care. Figure 8.15 shows all the processes followed at the nurses' station at Iris Hospital.

6. Reduce noise

Florence Nightingale said
...Unnecessary noise is the cruelest absence of care. [10]

Numerous studies have shown that noise leads to sleep deprivation, increased use of medicine, slow healing, and increased perceptions of pain. Noise is known to raise blood pressure and heart rate, to alter the respiratory rate, and it may cause vasoconstriction. Noise is a contributor to medical error.

The noise in a hospital has two sources:

- **Operational noise** is generated by loud conversations between the staff, medical professionals, and visitors, and from the equipment used. Staff, doctors, and visitors are made aware of this by putting up appropriate signage highlighting the adverse effects of noise on patients. Unnecessary noise from medical equipment is muted whenever possible.

- **Structural noise** is generated by the hospital building, by ventilation, the air-conditioning system, back up electrical generators, and squeaking doors. The design team grasped these factors at the planning stage. When they actually designed the hospital, they made proactive efforts to reduce the structural noise, for example, using sound-insulated electrical generators. Insulated false ceilings were used to reduce the noise from above the ceiling. To reduce external noise, a 10″ outer brick wall with an air gap joint was constructed. The windows were double glazed glass

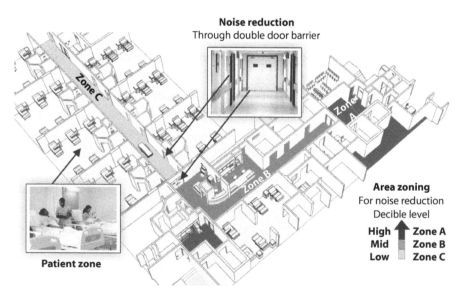

FIGURE 8.16
Layout design for noise reduction in patient's room.

with an air gap in between to both reduce noise and increase heat insulation. Another measure was to create a barrier between the patient's zone and the source of major noise generation, namely, the nurses' station, the hub of patient-care activities (Figure 8.16).

7. **Use adaptive systems that will allow function in the future**

The JCI[11] has stated that

- The lengthy cycle of design and construction is often overtaken by the rapid cycle of innovation in medicine and technology. As a result, some buildings are partially obsolete when they open, and nearly every healthcare structure will be obsolete in some way before it has completed its useful life.
- A hospital is constructed to operate for decades. In the current era, it should be designed to accommodate the ever-changing modes of care. To the extent possible, these should be represented as space with flexible interiors and adaptable utilities for mechanical, electrical, and plumbing (MEP) systems.

With the advent of ICT, which plays a pivotal role in hospital operations, what has changed most rapidly is the traditional outlook to delivering patient care. The focus today is on reducing average length of stay (ALOS), with moves toward daycare and homecare services. Advancements in optics and electronics have made medical equipment small and sleek, thereby requiring less space. The old school of thought may have outlived its utility in the current day and age.

Iris Hospital was built on a modular concept, with a standardized approach to the care delivery processes. The design team faced up to the challenge of ensuring a flexible and adaptive design, so that future changes would cause minimal disruptions to ongoing hospital operations.

At the outset, the structural grid layout was iterated, such that the structural columns did not interfere with functionality. The area demarcated for a doctor's chamber, when doubled, would be equivalent to a single- or double-bedded room. This area, when further doubled, could accommodate a ward with five beds or an operating theater or a catheterization laboratory. Additionally, the toilets throughout the hospital have a standardized layout with adequate measures to avoid accidents such as patient falls. The shafts have been positioned to work for multiple utilities including the active fire-smoke evacuation system. Figure 8.17 illustrates these points.

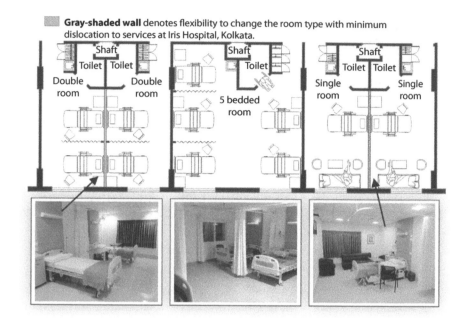

FIGURE 8.17
Adaptive systems with flexible design.

8. Articulate a set of principles by which everything is measured

At Iris Hospital, processes and systems have been developed to measure some of the important clinical and non-clinical outcomes. These are shared with the stakeholders and their impact reviewed by the strategic and tactical management teams.

- At the **Clinical level**, data collected from the EWS are analyzed for any sentinel events, shown in Figure 8.18.

In an episode, the anesthetist prescribed a morphine table, eight-hourly dosage for Day 1 of the post-operative period. But after the first dose, the patient's blood pressure and pulse rate fell alarmingly. The algorithm built into the HIS flashed the alarm for the criticality of the patient. The caregivers brought this to the notice of the anesthetist. The next dose of morphine tablet was stopped and appropriate measures were taken to stabilize the patient, who recovered gradually and was discharged in a satisfactory condition. Figure 8.18 shows the patient data output on the dashboard at the monitor. The caregiver, in this episode, the nurse in charge of that shift, raised the alarm to the concerned primary physician, who in turn, advised appropriate measures.

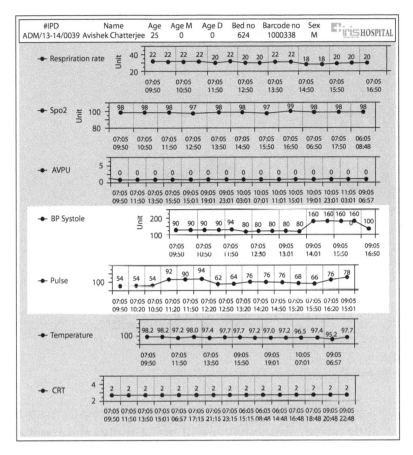

FIGURE 8.18
Measuring the clinical outcome through the early warning system (EWS).

The stereotypical method is to manually document the patient data in various care-related documents, in the hope that caregivers will consistently respond to any aberration or abnormal findings. This response is often lacking. Failure to react by the caregiver affects the clinical outcome. The documents can in no way prompt the caregivers to respond. A visual aid, such as the dashboard in the HIS at Iris Hospital, may fill in the information gaps toward better care.

• At the **Non-clinical level**, data are collated at the control center at Iris Hospital, as shown in Figure 8.19. There were three objectives for data collection: surveillance, control, and monitor or measure. The design, development, and implementation of the

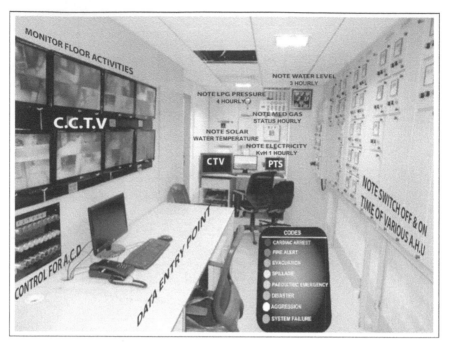

FIGURE 8.19
Measuring non-clinical outcomes at the control center.

software module were done in-house, and frugally, with very little capital. Two technical staff per shift man this room 24/7, noting the data displayed in the software module. Following data collection, the algorithm in the software displays the sentinel events and forewarns the operational staff and higher management of any deviation from the forecasted values. For example, a deviation from the forecasted electricity consumption, for any time range, can be viewed from the HIS and management can undertake proactive steps, before things get out of hand.

9. Begin equipment planning on Day 1

The Iris Hospital was developed in AutoCAD©™ for design with 3D Studio Max©™ for visualization. Templates for all the equipment were built with this software. The database software developed in-house was established to dynamically export the values of various attributes from AutoCAD©™ and to prepare the room data sheet (RDS) along with other financial matrixes. Summated values from the RDS reflected the capital cost of plant and machinery. This was

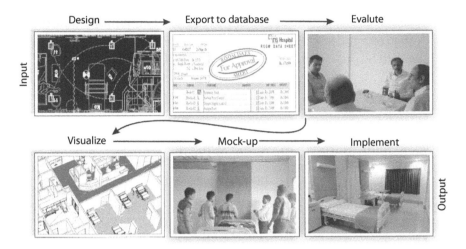

FIGURE 8.20
Equipment planning: Concept design to implementation.

the contemplated forecasted budget of the hospital. Subsequently, during the project execution stage, any deviation from the forecasted budget was analyzed and acted on. The information generated was shared with the owners, architects, vendors, and the project's commercial finance team to align the project with the budget and schedule. Figure 8.20 illustrates the process followed for a typical patient room.

10. Begin mock-ups on Day 1

Important milestones followed the detailed design stage visualized. Consensus was arrived at on the layouts and the processes of each of the functional areas of the hospital. Figure 8.21 illustrates the progress of the nurses' station complex at Iris Hospital. During the

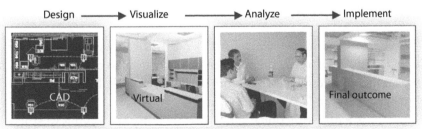

Emergence of nurses' station complex at Iris Hospital

FIGURE 8.21
Concept design to implementation.

operational stage, the approach helped to communicate and train caregivers and staff in the standardized processes and protocols that were to be maintained.

SUMMARY

Daring to think differently is the first step to innovation. This small step was indeed a giant leap for the management at Iris Hospital to risk the design and operation of the hospital with the Lean principles, and work toward the EBD outcome. The key objective was to curtail capital cost and yet deliver quality service.

Right at the start of the venture, Team Iris was aware that there were no clear-cut paths to a quintessential hospital. At the project phase, norms, rules, statutes, clearances, litigation, technological obsolescence, safety, socioeconomic dynamics, and political uncertainties were deterrents that had to be conquered. Again, at the operational phase, policies, protocols, processes, cultural variance, staff motivation, high attrition, waste, unevenness in process flow, and overburdened systems were the challenges that they had to address.

In conceiving the project, the design team kept in mind the mantra of Richard Sprow:[12]

> What is most important is to focus on a planning process leading to form, not on designing an architectural idea first. It was also critical to think in terms of an open system of planning, in which variables such as required services, anticipated volume, operational and staffing assumptions, and building system decisions could all be adjusted and tuned as needed while keeping in mind the basic goal of a high quality, low upkeep, flexible and expandable hospital concept which can be an expression of a new hospital type for world use.

The change in mind-set worked wonders. The LA became the appropriate way to move forward. The reliance on EBD enabled coming up with a hospital that differentiated itself from other hospitals in Kolkata and lived up to customers' and stakeholders' values.

Today, it is a fully functional multispecialty hospital, having weathered the pains of any start-up system. Differentiators such as CPOE, MMS, a control center for resource management, decentralized billing, and a discharge system have been successfully implemented. The software is fully integrated for automatic archiving of data including clinical data through EWS and MMS. Patients are successfully discharged based on the JCAHO's guidelines. The software automatically sends SMSs to the appropriate stakeholders for action on sentinel events such as admission, discharge, patient criticality, abnormal findings, and more besides.

But, the biggest challenges for the management are the stereotypical entrenchments. Many harbor the notion that the software system is a threat and will replace human jobs. The caregivers and staffs must be sensitive to the direction that Iris Hospital has embarked upon, and the environment that they hope to create. To allay threat perceptions and change the existing work culture, regular training and monitoring has been put in place based on the LA. The results are perceptible. There are slow and steady improvements toward delivering a quality service. The management too is learning new lessons every day to improve on the implementation of the processes.

Finally, Team Iris reflected on the Lean and EBD approach and realized that, had this methodology not been followed at the conceptual and execution phase, it could have led to pandemonium in the project. Some of the issues could have been:

- Communication and decision making could have been lackadaisical by all the stakeholders and this in turn would have resulted in an asymmetrical and incoherent information flow.
- Waste of resources was iterated during process mapping. This was done before the architectural drawings were taken up. By not following this approach, appropriate measures could not have been infused in the drawing and operational processes due to lack of awareness among the different stakeholders.
- Customer and stakeholder' needs could not be addressed unless the Lean and EBD logic was systematically pursued.
- The cliché **"Time is Money"** holds true in a project or process change. **Time** could have been lost while incorporating the needs of the customer and stakeholder at various stages, as the project or the process change went along. This, in turn, could have resulted in **Money** being lost while aligning and making and remaking different changes in the attributes of the project.

In hindsight, Iris Hospital could not have differentiated itself without the Lean and EBD approach.

REFERENCES

1. Churchill W. Famous Quotations and Stories. http://www.winstonchurchill.org/resources/quotations/famous-quotations-and-stories. (Accessed March 7, 2015.)
2. Joint Commission International. 2008. Health Care at the Crossroads: Guiding Principles for the Development of the Hospital of the Future. http://www.jointcommission.org/assets/1/18/hosptal_future.pdf, (p. 34). (Accessed March 29, 2012.)
3. Samuelson P.A., Nordhaus W.D. 1998. *Economics*. Boston, MA: Irwin/McGraw-Hill, 171–172.
4. Reiling J.G. 2005. Creating a Culture of Patient Safety through Innovative Hospital. http://www.ncbi.nlm.nih.gov/books/NBK20491/. (Accessed March 9, 2015.)
5. Kohn L.T., Corrigan J.M., Donaldson M.S. 2000. To Err Is Human: Building a Safer Health System. http://www.ncbi.nlm.nih.gov/books/NBK225187//. (Accessed March 21, 2015.)
6. Norman D.A. 1988. *The Psychology of Everyday Things*. New York: Basic Books.
7. West Bengal Pollution Control Board. April 2016, Municipal Solid Waste Management http://www.wbpcb.gov.in/pages/display/37-municipal-solid-waste-management (Accessed June 30, 2016.)
8. Ulrich R.S. et al. 2004. The Role of the Physical Environment in the Hospital of the 21st Century: A Once-in-a-Lifetime Opportunity (p. 2). https://www.healthdesign.org/sites/default/files/Role%20Physical%20Environ%20in%20the%2021st%20Century%20Hospital_0.pdf. (Accessed on March 5, 2015.)
9. JCAHO. Requirements for Discharge Summary, IM.6.10 EP7. http://www.touro.com/upload/assets/pdfs/pulsedec06.pdf. Accessed on March 3, 2015.
10. Nightingale F, Mazer S.E. 2008. Nursing, Noise, and Norms: Why Nightingale Is Still Right. http://healinghealth.com/images/uploads/files/NursingNoiseNorms.pdf. (Accessed March 13, 2015.)
11. JCI. 2008. Health Care at the Crossroad: Guiding Principles for the Development of the Hospital of the Future. http://www.jointcommission.org/assets/1/18/Hosptal_Future.pdf. (Accessed April 3, 2015.)
12. Sprow R. Planning Hospitals of the Future. http://www.perkinseastman.com/dynamic/document/week/asset/download/3411781/3411781.pdf. (Accessed May 9, 2015.)

9

Virtual Hospitals of the Future

Sachin Gaur

CONTENTS

INTRODUCTION

The science fiction writer William Gibson says that "the future is already here—it's just not evenly distributed." This chapter explores the possible near future, which can be perceived through existing technologies with potential not yet exploited, and innovative enterprises that have not yet become commonplace.

Some futures will never be evenly distributed; some potential will never become actual. New technologies do not determine a future; they enable several alternative futures. The diffusion of innovations is hampered, amplified, and directed by various issues, such as the cost of production and ownership, the ease of use, the perceived value, and regulatory issues. Some new technologies are disruptive, making old technologies and associated production systems obsolete. The guardians of the old will not go away without a fight. In some cases, the new is so overwhelming that the old stands no chance, such as mechanical typewriters against personal computers, or landlines against mobiles. In healthcare, there are cases where new technologies, such as electronic patient records, have struggled for decades to get traction.

There are technologies that have the potential to significantly change the ways that health services are produced, for example, the mobile Internet, the Internet of Things (IoT), wearable sensors, big data analytics, predictive analytics, cloud computing, and high speed networks.

For such technologies to find wide applications there are three basic requirements. The performance of technologies must fulfill certain standards. For example, the possibility of telemedicine was recognized several decades ago. However, for it to work in life-or-death situations, it must be reliable and offer sufficient accuracy. That is, there is a performance threshold that must be reached before an application can get broad acceptance. Second, in complex systems each component needs standard interfaces and common protocols for interoperability. The development of virtual hospitals is not possible without implementing e-Health standards to the core of each component. Otherwise, such systems will end up being non-standard implementation and the system developers must bear huge maintenance costs. In a non-standard environment, new technologies are more disruptive than in an environment with standards that allow the seamless addition of new modules. Third, cybersecurity and data privacy issues must be solved.

For a technology to be accepted, it must bring some clear benefits. The foremost are cost-effectiveness and new functionalities, which is the possibility to do something that was not possible before. These in turn are enabled by miniaturization, modularization, interoperability, speed, accurate reporting, prediction, forecasting, benchmarking, and the ability to match demand and supply.

When the potential of new technologies is assessed, the context, intervention, mechanism, outcome (CIMO) methodology of evaluation science can be employed. This poses the following questions:

- What is the *context* (C) where the technology is applied: which types of medical problems, patients, providers, and situations are affected?
- How does the technology translate into an *intervention* (I): what is changed, and how is it done?
- Through what kinds of *mechanisms* (M) does the intervention work: how does it affect cost, quality, and functionality?
- Which are the expected and actual *outcomes* (O) for different constituencies: patients, families, caregivers, insurers, and so on, in terms of money, time, convenience, therapeutic benefits, and quality of life?

VIRTUAL CLINICS

Visiting a clinic for the first time can be expensive and time-consuming. Today, there are emerging models of virtual clinics that offer appointments without the need for patients to be physically present. This requires good Internet connection and devices that can transmit patient data, such as blood pressure, to the doctor. Business Wire reports one such early success of a virtual clinic, VirtuWell.[1] It provides diagnosis and treatment for 50 common everyday illnesses in four midwestern states. Since its inauguration in 2010, it has completed more than 100,000 visits in four years. At a per visit cost of US$45, VirtuWell delivers an average savings of US$88 per visit compared to other places of care. One VirtuWell visit can save up to 2.5 hours of travel and waiting time, as indicated by customers. With 100,000 completed visits that sums up to 250,000 hours, or 28 years saved. The context (C) is nonurgent primary care where diagnosis and treatment do not require physical presence. The availability of high-speed Internet is required.

The intervention (I) enabled by technology is that patients communicate through the Internet instead of making visits.

The mechanism (M) at work is the reduction of transaction costs to both patients and providers; for patients this means less cost of travel and waiting; for provider this means reduced cost of facilities.

The reported outcome (O) is a US$85 saving per visit with 98% of customers satisfied and willing to recommend VirtuWell to friends and family.

WEARABLE TECHNOLOGY: MEDICAL-GRADE HEALTH TRACKING

Several manufacturers have introduced health-tracking gadgets. Most of these cover basic parameters such as steps walked and sleep and heart rate tracking. These are sold to users who are interested in monitoring their own health and progress through physical exercise. Most of these gadgets, however, do not produce the accuracy and the types of data that would be required for clinical use.

Google has recently announced a medical-grade health-tracking band, which will track pulse, heart rate, and skin temperature.[2] Google intends to position the device so that physicians should prescribe it to their patients.

The context (C) is patients who need regular monitoring of their medical condition, feedback on their progress, early warning in case their condition deteriorates, assisted self-help, and access to care in case of incidents.

The intervention (I) is to provide wearable sensors linked to a system of algorithmic feedback and access to live service providers in case of need.

The mechanisms (M) are more accurate continuous real-time data, feedback that enables lifestyle adjustment, and timely action in the case of incidents.

The expected outcomes (O) are reduced unnecessary visits, less anxiety, a sense of control, and timely contact with a caregiver.

HEALTHCARE AT HOME

There is a rising trend in healthcare delivery done in the style of e-commerce: on demand and delivery to the patient's home. In India there are already multiple players providing patients with the opportunity to hire medical staff for long-term care at home.[3] The service is targeting elderly patients. India has the second-largest geriatric population in the world.[4] So, the market for healthcare at home is only going to increase.

Before the advent of modern hospitals, most care was provided at home. Hospitals brought the advantages of regular monitoring, diagnostics, a controlled environment, and access to staff for regular therapies and incident management. Most homes could not offer such conditions and house the necessary equipment. This is about to change as housing standards improve and various devices become smaller and cheaper.

Another problem with home care is logistics, staffing, and scheduling. If patients do not need, or cannot afford, the continuous presence of professional staff, the caregiver needs to allocate his or her time between several patients at different locations. Thus, capacity utilization becomes a problem. If the need for care varies over time and there is the possibility of emergencies, staff scheduling and dispatching become an issue.

Smartphones with geostationary positioning (GPS) capability enable innovations in logistics, for example, to connect service customers and providers. To manage regular home care, various scheduling and routing applications can be used to reduce caregivers' travel time. For irregular or unscheduled care, dispatching applications can be used. A well-known application is the taxi company Uber,[5] which provides service delivery on demand through a mobile application. On-demand aggregation of service by using information technology (IT) and match-making between supply and demand is now commonly known as "uber-ifying" or "uber for x."

Home care is a way to utilize the abovementioned wearable technologies and smartphones to create a business model that can reduce costs and hospital congestion, while reducing the difficulties for patients, and offering care customized to their needs.

The context (C) is patients with adequate housing who require monitoring and regular therapies, and occasional unscheduled services.

The intervention (I) is to bring some hospital equipment to the patient's home (e.g., dialysis machines), easy access to unscheduled care through uberization.

The mechanism (M) works through reduced trips by the caregiver, less hospital congestion, and the possibility for family members to contribute.

Expected outcomes are (O) lower cost, more frequent therapies, and flexibility.

CONCEPTUAL DESIGN OF THE VIRTUAL HOSPITAL

There are already a few components that will lead to the making of virtual hospitals and a virtual healthcare service provider (VHSP). These are likely to evolve as new components and functionalities are added. Virtualization severs the time and location constraints of the traditional hospital system; the standard response to any health problem is no longer the obvious trip to a hospital. With the time–location constraints reduced, supply can more efficiently match demand.

VHSP is a network of dynamically linked components. Figure 9.1 shows six such components.

Starting from the patient's own house (Component 1), the patient might have access to wearable technology, recording his or her health data. It can be shared with a VHSP on demand through a mobile application. The VHSP might also provide the hardware components under an annual or monthly subscription plan, and secure storage of the patient's health data in the cloud (Component 4).

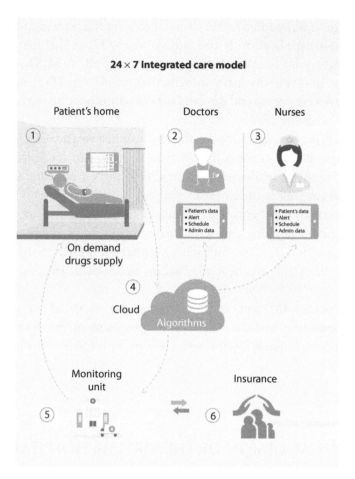

FIGURE 9.1
Conceptual flow diagram of a virtual hospital.

The family can access the health data of the patient from the cloud in real time from a remote location, thereby providing the patient's family with emotional comfort and trust in the service. Additionally, the service can provide various features related to billing, emergency alerts, and legal approvals to the patient's relatives and caretakers.

A contract of care stipulates the availability of permanent doctors (Component 2) and nurses (Component 3) for patient monitoring and treatment, as well as the possibility of on-demand services as needed.

Component 5 is a physically remote monitoring unit, ideally a hospital. It would provide the backup support for the patient with emergency services and transport. The monitoring unit would also make sure that the care staff meet their service level agreements and follow quality standards.

Component 6 is the insurance company, which provides health insurance to the patient. Such a care model, which is virtual hence digital, is ideal for an insurance company as it can provide full transparency about the patient's treatment.

NEW OUTCOMES WITH VIRTUAL HOSPITALS

The virtual hospital will not cover all needs. Traditional time–location constrained hospitals will be necessary for many problems, such as emergencies, trauma, elective procedures, childbirth, and complex cure processes. The context in which the virtual hospital most obviously applies consists of patients with long-term, low-intensity needs, such as the disease management of chronic conditions, general frailty that comes with old age, post-surgical rehabilitation, and palliative care at the end of life.

In such contexts, the virtual hospital is an intervention that can be assumed to work through the mechanisms shown in Figure 9.2. These are "lower transaction costs," "improved quality (benchmarking)," "increased accessibility," and "predictive analytics." The underlying assumption in each of the outcomes is that the mode of delivery would have a digital footprint; it should be possible to measure the transaction and create

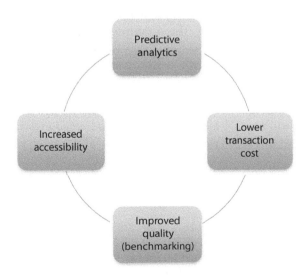

FIGURE 9.2
Possible outcomes with a virtual hospital approach.

important data points. Obviously, such mechanisms can also be applied at time–location constrained hospitals. However, it appears that the cutting-edge applications will first arrive in the virtual setting, as here the cost benefits tend to be more clear than in an environment with significant fixed costs.

The information and communication technology applied in virtual hospitals is a game changer in the competition in care markets. The digital footprints can be aggregated and analyzed to produce accurate data on quality, including the quality of clinical decision making, patient safety, and patient satisfaction. This allows public rating and benchmarking of competing providers.

The virtual hospital concept means that all the data at every stage is going to cloud storage. It will open new opportunities to run predictive analytics and make precise estimates of future demand.

SUMMARY

In the introduction, we talked about the future being unevenly distributed. We might wonder when and how virtual hospitals will become a reality. Not all at once, but over time. Experiments in new ways of healthcare delivery are taking place with cutting-edge technology in the defense sector[6] and in last mile rural areas.[7] The components that successfully emerge from these experiments will provide the building blocks of the virtual hospitals of the future. The outcomes of such a virtual and digital healthcare delivery would be lower cost of care, improved quality, and predictive analytics.

However, not all is good with a digital future. There are increasing attacks on healthcare facilities to extort money using computer viruses known as Ransomware.[8,9] Hence, we need a dedicated effort to safeguard patient data and infrastructure.

REFERENCES

1. Business Wire. (2015). Virtuwell case study. Study retrieved from: http://www.businesswire.com/news/home/20140617005116/en/virtuwell-surpasses-100000-cases-treated#.VbnRjlwwSGd. Accessed September 4, 2015.
2. Bloomberg. (2015). Google reveals health-tracking wristband. Details retrieved from: http://www.bloomberg.com/news/articles/2015-06-23/google-developing-health-tracking-wristband-for-health-research. Accessed September 4, 2015.

3. Wharton. (2015). Home health care in india: in search of the right business model. Study retrieved from: http://knowledge.wharton.upenn.edu/article/home-health-care-india-search-right-business-model/. Accessed September 4, 2015.
4. Livemint. (2015). 20% of population to be elderly by 2050: HelpAge India report. Details retrieved from: http://www.livemint.com/Politics/z6BacVOwf5SvmpD9P1BcaK/20-of-population-to-be-elderly-by-2050-HelpAge-India-repor.html. Accessed September 4, 2015.
5. Wikipedia. (2015). Uber Company. Details retrieved from: https://en.wikipedia.org/wiki/Uber_(company). Accessed September 4, 2015.
6. Health.mil. (2016). General Leonard Wood Army Community Hospital demonstrates new era of virtual army medicine. Details retrieved from: http://www.health.mil/News/Articles/2016/09/08/General-Leonard-Wood-Army-Community-Hospital-demonstrates-new-era-of-virtual-Army-Medicine. Accessed January 9, 2017.
7. Wish Foundation. (2017). http://www.wishfoundationindia.org. Accessed January 9, 2017.
8. InnovatioCuris Blog. (2016). Looming danger of Ransomware on Indian enterprises and health sector. Details retrieved from: http://innovatiocuris.com/looming-danger-of-ransomware/. Accessed January 9, 2017
9. CSO Online. (2016). The rise of Ransomware in healthcare. Details retrieved from: http://www.csoonline.com/article/3091080/security/the-rise-of-ransomware-in-healthcare.html. Accessed January 9, 2017.

10

Redefining Healthcare of Tomorrow in Smart City

V.K. Singh and Nimisha Singh

CONTENTS

INTRODUCTION

A smart city is a developed urban area that has integrated digital technologies such as information and communication technology (ICT) and Internet of Things (IoT) solutions embedded across city functions such as hospitals, transport, education, energy, and infrastructure to provide quality of life to its citizens and improve the efficiency of services. There is no universal definition of a smart city as it may mean different things to different societies. A smart city in India would be different from a smart city in the United States. Each city is different even in the same country and has unique attributes due to its local government, society, resources, and existing infrastructure. Several citations and a definition of smart cities can be viewed in Wikipedia, from which a few are listed as follows[1]:

- Caragliu and Nijkamp 2009: "A city can be defined as 'smart' when investments in human and social capital and traditional (transport) and modern (ICT) communication infrastructure fuel sustainable economic development and a high quality of life, with a wise management of natural resources, through participatory action and engagement."
- Frost and Sullivan 2014: "We identified eight key aspects that define a Smart City—smart governance, smart energy, smart building, smart mobility, smart infrastructure, smart technology, smart healthcare and smart citizen."
- Indian Government 2014: "Smart City offers sustainability in terms of economic activities and employment opportunities to a wide section of its residents, regardless of their level of education, skills or income levels."

To have a successful and sustainable smart city, local government should formulate its own concept, vision, mission, and road map. The government should consider the following steps when creating a smart city road map:

- Understand and study the business needs, the community needs and desires, the available resources, demographics, and so on.
- Create a vision in line with these needs.
- Develop policies and plans in alignment with the vision.
- Engage the community by welcoming their innovative ideas and be a part of the mission. Events, expos, hackathons, and competitions can be arranged for engaging the public.
- Build partnerships with various stakeholders of the ecosystem.

The three pillars of a smart city are people, process, and technology. Cities such as Amsterdam are a good example, showcasing the consortium between the three pillars and fostering a culture of citizen engagement. Amsterdam organizes the Amsterdam Smart City Challenge annually and accepts proposals for development from citizens. Other smart cities that have illustrated this kind of accord are Barcelona, Stockholm, and Singapore. Market research firm Juniper Research ranked Singapore the smartest city globally for 2016, followed by Barcelona, London, San Francisco, and Oslo.[2]

INDIA SMART CITIES MISSION

The Smart Cities Mission of India under the leadership of Honorable Prime Minister Narendra Modi is a great initiative toward urbanization in India. It is estimated that 40% of India's population will live in cities by 2030, an increase from 340 million people in 2008 to 590 million by 2030.[3] The mission is a renewal and retrofitting program of 109 cities. In January 2016, the government announced the first group of 20 cities. The government of India (GOI) has allocated an estimated $7.5 billion to the mission. The core infrastructure elements in a smart city would include:[4]

- Adequate water supply
- Assured electricity supply
- Sanitation, including solid waste management
- Efficient urban mobility and public transport
- Affordable housing, especially for the poor
- Robust information technology (IT) connectivity and digitalization
- Good governance, especially e-governance and citizen participation
- Sustainable environment
- Safety and security of citizens, particularly women, children, and the elderly
- Health and education

The smart solutions specified by the GOI are illustrated in Figure 10.1.[5] The GOI does not impose the list on local governments. Since each city has its own unique attributes, they can add or choose from the list.

Not only are Indian companies investing in this mission, but the United Kingdom is also working closely with India. The two countries have a bilateral agreement to strengthen collaboration in healthcare in Indian smart cities. The UK and Indian governments have set up a taskforce to ensure the collaboration of various universities, organizations, and national health services (NHS) in the implementation of smart healthcare in these cities. The Indo UK Institutes of Health project now has King's College Hospital as a strategic partner for the first of the planned 11 institutes.

e-Governance and citizen services

Public information, grievance redressal
Electronic service delivery
Citizen engagement
Citizens—city's eyes and ears
Video crime monitoring

 Waste management

Waste to energy and fuel
Waste to compost
Waste water to be treated
Recycling and reduction of C and D waste

 Water management

Smart meters and management
Leakage identification, preventive
  maintenance
Water quality monitoring

Smart solutions

Urban mobility

Smart parking
Intelligent traffic management
Integrated multimodal transport

 Energy management

Smart meters and management
Renewable sources of energy
Energy efficient and green buildings

  Others

Tele-medicine and tele-education
Incubation/trade facilitation centers
Skill development center

FIGURE 10.1
Smart solutions listed by the government of India.

SMART HEALTHCARE

Advancements in digital technology such as e-Health, m-Health, tele-medicine, and the IoT are making healthcare delivery smarter. The concept of smart healthcare refers to deploying computing, information, and networking technologies to analyze data in a predictive manner to aid in disease prevention and to deliver quality care at a lower cost. Smart healthcare solutions include telemedicine, real-time monitoring, population health, personalized medicine, computer-aided surgery, decision support systems, health 2.0, and ubiquitous computing.[6] *Health 2.0* is a term that refers to social media and mobile and cloud technology in connecting patients and clinicians. According to a Business Wire research and markets report, global smart healthcare market is expected to grow at a compound annual growth rate (CAGR) of 24.55% during 2016–2020.[7]

The healthcare ecosystem is now focusing on smart healthcare in smart cities. Access to quality healthcare is one of the core components of smart cities, hence it should be carefully considered when planning smart healthcare in a city. One such example of smart health in a smart city is Saensuk Smart City in Thailand. Launched in 2014, the initiative is a three-year pilot by the municipality in collaboration with technology partners Dell, Intel, and the IoT City Innovation Center (ICIC). The pilot project, which began in January 2016, aims to monitor elderly patients with IoT applications in health monitoring, emergency notification, environment sensing, home monitoring, and tracking for safety.[8]

SMART HEALTHCARE FRAMEWORK

There has been significant uptake of ICT by healthcare organizations over the last few decades. Few organizations have excelled in adopting technology and a few have failed even after spending huge amounts of money. Smart cities should learn from the failures of these healthcare organizations when implementing a smart healthcare solution. The healthcare stakeholders should consider the following framework when designing and implementing smart healthcare across smart cities:

- Selecting smart healthcare solutions: The stakeholders should decide on the smart healthcare solutions to be implemented in line with the smart city vision. An illustrative list of the solutions is provided in the next section. The infrastructure, local resources, and needs of the population should be kept in mind when selecting the solutions for a smart city.
- Study and retrofit the existing infrastructure: Facility and IT infrastructure should be studied in detail and retrofitted according to the vision of the smart city and the smart solution selected. Smart cities should consider and coordinate with all of the various systems of infrastructure such as water, energy, and so on, to have a holistic approach while planning. Cross-sectoral health promotion should be encouraged across the city. This means that each sector, such as education, traffic, waste, and so on, should promote the health and safety of citizens by including it as one of their objectives in their smart city planning. Cities should involve local innovators such as start-ups, universities, and research centers in developing existing city infrastructure. One of the intrinsic parts of infrastructure is

connectivity, which should be planned and implemented effectively such that citizens, especially those at the bottom of the pyramid, can communicate with their healthcare provider.

- Study and redesign the processes: In a smart city there is a paradigm shift in the way that communication and care is delivered. This shift needs to be streamlined to avoid confusions and delays. This means redesigning end-to-end healthcare processes, for example, the process of data collection and analyzing, so that stakeholders can plan and predict the future health needs of an increasing population. Sharing health data will also make citizens smarter as they will have access to health information that will help them to make informed decisions and be engaged in their health. The amount of complex data that will come with smart cities represents huge opportunities in reshaping and innovating healthcare delivery. Therefore, stakeholders should work toward creating step-by-step processes and strategies so that smart healthcare solutions can be integrated into the existing system without any glitches.

- Capacity building: The implementation of smart solutions requires smart people in order to fully leverage digitalization in a smart city. Issues such as a shortage of skilled labor are obvious in a smart city due to changes in processes, technology, and infrastructure. An assessment of the skills gap should be performed to tackle these issues. Management and technology skills should be addressed and designed across the ecosystem to manage the smart healthcare model. Also, multidisciplinary learning should be promoted to foster innovation in cities. All universities should reform their curriculum for skill development and allow students to engage in multidisciplinary work. Public–private partnership (PPP) models in skills training can be a win-win situation.

- Citizens' awareness and collaboration: Awareness and collaboration among citizens is another factor that is responsible for the success of sustainable smart healthcare in a smart city. Citizens can be reticent in accepting the transformation occurring around them. Therefore, change management for all should be laid down as early as possible. Citizens should be made aware of the new infrastructure and healthcare solutions that are being used so that they can engage in their health. Citizens should also be made aware of the importance of data collection and sharing for preventive medicine. Health literacy should also be focused on to achieve smarter citizens in the city. As has been found, there is always a lack of health information understanding. Citizens need to share innovative ideas and their feedback with the government at all stages to ensure that the smart city vision is in line with the citizens' needs and aspirations.

• Develop a self-sustaining business model: The creation of smart healthcare in a smart city is a very cost-intensive initiative; therefore, after the initial investment, it needs be developed as a self-sustaining business model as the government cannot afford the huge cost burden year after year.

SMART HEALTHCARE SOLUTIONS IN SMART CITIES

Smart healthcare consists of various solutions and systems such as

• Population health analytics: This can be defined as an iterative process of population health data aggregation across disparate health IT resources and analyses to proactively improve clinical, operational, and financial outcomes. Retrospective analytic tools help in risk stratification by analyzing resources such as health records, claims data, and so on to lower costs by better coordination and management. Moving on to the next level of predictive analytics of the population can help healthcare stakeholders focus on preventive care and patient engagement. To improve health outcomes in a smart city, population health analytics is key. Effective population health analytics requires PPP and data standards for integration. The government should invest in this solution on a phase-wise basis as they need to do a better job at collecting data and should focus on data literacy.

• Smart hospital design: The smart hospital infrastructure optimizes resources, lowers costs, and increases patient satisfaction. A smart hospital integrates the use of various wireless technologies and sensors to create an efficient, accessible, coordinated, and safer environment for patients and providers. With the advent and rapid rise of the IoT, layers of smartness are being added to hospitals. The various applications of IoT range from remote monitoring, chronic disease management, medication management, patient self-management, and workflow or operations management. It has proved to be useful not only in managing health but also in disease prevention and wellness promotion. A healthcare ecosystem can benefit from IoT application in terms of improved medical outcomes, better quality of life, and lower health costs. The IoT is a network connecting diverse sets of smart devices, wearables, sensors, robotic devices, radio-frequency identification (RFID), and so on, over the Internet for communication and information exchange. The sensors enable the hospital infrastructure to monitor environmental parameters such as temperature, humidity, light, sound, and so on in real time and provide real-time alerts. They help in automating and improving clinical workflows by eliminating waste. Improved workflows and robotic devices result in safer treatment. RFID technology can be used for tracking and identification in the hospital setup. Unraveling the tremendous potential of the IoT lies within analyzing the huge amount of data generated in this kind of smart infrastructure and using it to enhance healthcare delivery. The latest traction worldwide is Chatbots in the communications industry, which can act as an interface to communicate and manage IoT devices. Chatbots are automated agents that stimulate conversation using machine learning and artificial intelligence mobile messaging apps. It is not a new concept; in 1966, ELIZA was designed to interact with patients. Chatbots have the edge on mobile apps as no download is required and it consumes less space. An example of a healthcare Chatbot is Florence from Viget, which aids in improving medication adherence. Chatbots with IoT integration could be the next big thing to happen. Cost and time can be a challenge while implementing it in a smart hospital as it requires much planning and a strong ICT infrastructure. Cities should think of innovative ideas to keep costs and time to a minimum while designing smart hospitals. Chapter 8 of this book details the various solutions that hospitals should adopt to reduce costs and improve efficiency. Cities should think of innovative ideas to keep the costs and time to a minimum while designing smart hospitals.

- Smart emergency and ambulatory care: Countries such as India need to revamp their emergency and ambulatory care services as they still lack standardization. A single emergency number at the national level, such as 911 in the United States, is yet to be implemented in India. Challenges related to the shortfall of skilled labor and reaching patients on time even in difficult terrains can be addressed by smart emergency response systems encompassing technologies such as global positioning systems (GPS), IoT, and big data analytics.

- Automated quality and performance management of healthcare delivery: Performance management means monitoring, measuring, and improving organizational performance. Advancements in IT have led to automation in health system performance management, such as business intelligence platforms, data warehousing, dashboards solutions, and so on. Business intelligence solutions can help in streamlining processes, cutting down costs, improving decision making, and identifying new opportunities within smart cities by extracting and analyzing data.

- Smart healthcare delivery services including remote monitoring such as Telehealth, m-Health: Enable patients to access care anywhere and anytime. This solution helps in effectively managing chronic patients. It is imperative that remote monitoring is an integral part of the smart cities of a country such as India to reach the bottom of the pyramid as these people do not have access to healthcare. Smart health services may include remote patient monitoring (RPM), telemedicine, and mobile health. Telemedicine has been part of India for the last 16 years but has gained momentum in recent years. The key drivers for telemedicine and RPM are the lack of healthcare facilities, the shortage of healthcare professionals, and the urban–rural divide. m-Health, on the other hand, focuses more on monitoring, diagnostics, booking doctor appointments, medical services search, and preventive care. Telemedicine helps in expanding reach with limited resources, while mobile health aids in engaging the population and improving adherence. The key drivers for m-Health are the increase in mobile penetration, the need for healthcare workers, and its accessibility on the go. The recent demonetization of the 500 and 1000 Indian rupees note has sparked the use of Internet and mobile banking in India. People who hesitated to use mobile apps are now becoming aware and educated about the benefits of transacting using digitalization. India's first digital and cashless village, Akodara in Gujarat, is a great example of digitalization for upcoming smart cities in India.

- Clinical decision support system (CDSS): Can be a perfect fit for improving the quality of healthcare in smart cities as it allows a provider to better and more quickly make a diagnosis, thereby reducing misdiagnoses and unnecessary test/procedures. CDSS is a software that has been designed as a direct aid to clinical decision making in which the characteristics of an individual patient are matched to a computerized clinical knowledge base (KB), and patient-specific assessments or recommendations are then presented to the clinician and/or the patient for a decision.[9] The primary objective of the CDSS is to help in promptly deriving reliable clinical conclusions for the healthcare professional.

- Smart healthcare education and training systems: Smart healthcare education is a paradigm shift in the medical education field. It is basically learning in the digital age, which enables learning on the go. Technologies such as cloud computing, big data analytics, and the IoT can help in producing and analyzing the behavioral data of learners, which in turn builds a data-enriched and personalized learner-centric environment. Healthcare professionals need to continuously update their information regarding the latest drug, technology, and disease so as to solve patients' problems. The medical field is increasingly relying on mobile devices as a source of communication, medical education, and information gathering. There are myriad mobile apps in the marketplace for medical professionals to access medical information, continuing medical education (CME) updates, knowledge assessment for medical students, medical calculators, log cases, and discussions. Healthcare simulation and gamification can be another component of the smart education ecosystem. All these technologies in smart education can help providers make quick decisions, increase the quality of care, and improve knowledge.
- Twenty-first-century clinical services (e.g., personalized care services): Personalized healthcare is a broader platform that includes not only genetics and genomics but also any other biologic information that helps predict risk for disease or how a patient will respond to treatments.[10] Technologies such as data analytics, including machine learning and predictive modeling, can help in understanding the cause and effect of treatment. An important part of personalized healthcare is engaging the patient and providing personalized care to meet the individual's specific health needs. This could be done with the help of self-monitoring digital tools/solutions such as mobile apps, wearables, home healthcare, and so on. Self-monitoring apps/wearables help people track their own health in real time and provide suggestions on diets and exercise regimes based on the user's pattern. To improve the health-related behavior of the user, connected devices with a smartphone provide intelligent advice such as detecting a nearby staircase and recommending the user take it

instead of an elevator, having a glass of water, and so on. The data from these tools helps providers in predicting future health issues and creating awareness about prevention among patients. It is also helpful in managing chronic cases more effectively. Home healthcare is also a growing trend and is gaining a lot of traction with entrepreneurs. Home healthcare can help the aging and disabled population to receive quality care. Home healthcare can reduce healthcare costs, reduce the average length of stay (ALOS) in hospital, and improve health outcomes. Smart cities should have an innovative business model for home healthcare to address the growing needs of the aged especially in a country such as India, which has the second-largest geriatric population in the world. Technologies such as smart homes and assisted-living robots can also act as enablers for the aging-in-place concept.

SMART HEALTHCARE LANDSCAPE

Healthcare in smart cities means having a proactive relationship between patient and provider to prevent illness and promote wellness. It refers to the use of data and information for the delivery of connected and tailored healthcare on the move. All stakeholders coordinate to reduce waste, be transparent, and increase productivity and quality.

Let's understand Figure 10.1 on smart healthcare landscape with a scenario. In a smart city, a citizen with a chronic condition feels unwell. The wearable worn by the person continuously monitors and analyzes his or her vitals and activity. On showing signs of variation, the centralized emergency care center is alerted. The smart emergency system detects the location of the patient with GPS and, with the help of intelligent traffic management, transfers the patient to hospital. The smart hospital, using various technologies such as e-health, CDSS, and IoT, helps in delivering high-quality care to the patient. Once the patient is discharged, he or she gets medication reminders and his or her medication adherence pattern is continuously streamed by a smart pill bottle to his or her provider for real-time analysis. This data helps the provider to be better informed about his or her patient's health and discuss the same during the follow-up tele-consultation. During the consultation, the doctor orders a few tests. The patient looks for the test, laboratory, and cost details with the help of the smart kiosk/m-app. Upon completion of the tests, the patient receives the result on his or her smart device, which is also shared by his or her provider. The patient's health record and laboratory, medication, and claims data help the stakeholders in a predictive analysis of the citizen's health, thereby reducing readmission in this case.

Another example could be an asthma patient who gets an alert on his or her smartphone regarding changes in the pollution levels. The smart home of the patient senses the air quality and intelligently adjusts the humidity level and filtration process to achieve purer air. This would mitigate the symptoms and risk of severe attacks. The wearable worn by the patient keeps a track of the air quality as well as the patient's vitals. If there is any variation in the patient's breathing pattern, a notification is sent to the physician for a tele-consultation. The patient's spirometer is connected to a smart inhaler that adjusts the dosage according to the spirometer reading.

CHALLENGES OF SMART HEALTHCARE

Smart city implementation needs a consortium of various stakeholders to bring about innovation in urban governance. This consortium would also bring challenges and issues. Challenges relating to finances, stakeholder management, technology, and political alignment need to be addressed for a self-sustainable city for the whole population. The following list contains some of the key challenges that governments/healthcare stakeholders face while implementing their smart city projects. The government should consider these challenges during the planning phase. Each country will have their own set of challenges according to the local resources, people, location, and technology.

- Retrofitting existing infrastructure to make it a smart city is more expensive than building a new smart city. Renovation and retrofitting leads to disturbance of the infrastructure and inconvenience to the citizens. Also, the integration of existing isolated legacy systems can be a big challenge.
- Collaboration among different stakeholders in smart cities is always an issue. The challenge lies in getting rid of the silos in which the stakeholders work and bringing them together. Every stakeholder has their own style of working and different perspectives/interests

that could lead to conflict. The standardization of processes and coordination on issues related to financials, sharing information, and service delivery processes are required between the stakeholders.

- Financial costs and funding a smart city project are important challenges to be considered. Business and cash flow models need to be clear and self-sustaining as huge amounts of money are involved in retrofitting or building a smart city. The involvement of government and private stakeholders in a PPP model should be clearly defined. Most of the time, the government controls and sanctions the funds, which may lead to delays due to clearance processes.

- Change in the behavior of the population and healthcare professionals is important to achieve the goals of sustainable smart health in a city. A smart city aims at improving quality of life by engaging all stakeholders of an ecosystem in decision making. This means that citizens and healthcare professionals can make the smart city a failure or a success by their attitude and behavior. A change in attitude toward technology, privacy, confidentiality, transparency, and energy conservation is needed.

- Technology challenges related to privacy, security, data storage, cost, and interoperability should be considered while planning smart healthcare. Data privacy and security is a primary concern in healthcare as confidential health data is involved. In a smart city, there is an exponential growth of digital patient data flowing in from electronic health records (EHRs), sensors, mobiles, and so on, which makes it easier for any data breach activity. Smart cities will also need to expand the existing infrastructure for better data storage and management. For a more connected healthcare in smart cities, the interoperability of networks needs to be considered. IT standardization should be the primary focus to have a sustainable technology model. Robust standards should be adopted for easy data sharing and communication. In developing countries such as India, the digital divide and challenges related to technology literacy and awareness need to be addressed.

- Cybersecurity is yet to filter into the health sector, more so in developing economies such as India. Ransomware attacks on hospitals are well known around the world; they have been reported in one of the states of the India Maharashtra secretariat where 150 personal computers were attacked.[11] The hospitals of tomorrow in smart cities will have big data with very sensitive details about patients' treatments causing privacy issues; any corruption to this data would create havoc in patient care. There is an urgent need to educate and train the hospital community in cybersecurity. As per the latest Symantec report,[12] India ranks third in Asia for the number of Ransomware attacks taking place. It is estimated that India experiences 170 attacks per day, out of which the majority are Ransomware. We are seeing an increasing number of instances where US hospitals are being impacted by Ransomware and huge ransoms are being demanded.[13] The criminals are aware of the high value of hospital data because of its sensitivity and criticality, hence the risk. Given the early signal from the US market, India and other countries should be prepared to tackle this looming challenge in the healthcare sector.

- Capability building is a herculean task in smart city implementation. A lack of quality and technology-savvy healthcare professionals can delay the implementation of a smart city. Training and skill development budgets are the least generous in every implementation. So, training and up-skilling a huge workforce resistant to change with limited resources is always a challenge.

SUMMARY

The future of urbanization lies in the successful implementation of a smart city. The smart city project aims at improving the quality of life of citizens and revolutionizing a city's infrastructure. For better health and quality of life of the citizens, healthcare needs to be the prime focus in a smart city implementation. Smart healthcare in smart cities entails strengthening IT to empower people to create new and innovative ideas to achieve sustainable and quality healthcare. The government and healthcare stakeholders need to address the challenges during the planning phase with remediation measures and involve citizens to create a safe and self-sustaining model.

REFERENCES

1. Smart City. https://en.wikipedia.org/wiki/Smart_city. Accessed on December 20, 2016.
2. Juniper Research. https://www.juniperresearch.com/press/press-releases/singapore-named-global-smart-city-2016. Accessed on December 20, 2016.
3. Bloomberg Philanthropies. https://www.bloomberg.org/program/government-innovation/india-smart-cities-mission/. Accessed on December 20, 2016.

4. Smart Cities Mission. http://smartcities.gov.in/content/innerpage/guidelines.php. Accessed on December 20, 2016.
5. Smart Cities Mission. http://smartcities.gov.in/content/innerpage/guidelines.php. Accessed on December 20, 2016.
6. Smart Health and Wellbeing. http://archive2.cra.org/ccc/files/docs/Natl_Priorities/web_health_spring.pdf. Accessed on December 20, 2016.
7. Business Wire. http://www.businesswire.com/news/home/20170109005849/en/Global-Smart-Healthcare-Market-Grow-24-2016-2020. Accessed on January 10, 2017.
8. Dell. http://www.dell.com/learn/us/en/uscorp1/press-releases/2016-07-26-saensuk-smart-city-pilots-first-healthcare-iot-project-with-dell-intel. Accessed on January 10, 2017.
9. Sim I, Gorman P, Greenes RA, Haynes RB, Kaplan B, Lehmann H, and Tang PC. Clinical decision support systems for the practice of evidence-based medicine. *J Am Med Inform Assoc* 2001;8(6):527–34.
10. Healthessentials. https://health.clevelandclinic.org/2012/05/what-is-personalized-healthcare/. Accessed on December 20, 2016.
11. *The Times of India*. http://timesofindia.indiatimes.com/india/Ransomware-hits-150-PCs-at-Maha-Mantralaya/articleshow/52441113.cms. Accessed on December 20, 2016.
12. Gadgets 360. http://gadgets.ndtv.com/internet/news/india-ranks-third-in-asia-for-ransomware-attacks-symantec-77785. Accessed on December 20, 2016.
13. Bitcoin. https://en.wikipedia.org/wiki/Bitcoin. Accessed on December 20, 2016.

11

Delivering Inclusive Intelligent Healthcare by Innovative and Comprehensive e-Health System

Kuo Shou-Jen and Lai Chien-Wen

CONTENTS

INTRODUCTION

This chapter is based on a case study of Changhua Christian Hospital (CCH), Taiwan, established by English missionaries Rev. C. Campbell Moody and Dr. David Landsborough III, who opened a church that doubled as a clinic in 1896. For over a century, CCH's commitment to serve and to give has received numerous honors. In pursuit of medical quality, CCH continually strives for excellence. It established the nation's first department of medical quality and demonstrated exceptional results of quality improvement at international and national conventions. The healthcare system includes five regional hospitals (Erhlin, Lukang, Lu-Tung, Yunlin, and Yuanlin Christian Hospitals), two affiliated hospitals (Nantou and Yuming Hospitals), and one children's hospital. There are about 8500 employees and 3500 beds within the CCH system. By integrating with the whole healthcare system, CCH provides the highest-quality medical care.

As a patient-centric hospital, CCH provides five whole cares—comprehensive healthcare consists of whole person, whole team, whole family, whole process, and whole community. Patients are referred to other specialists following a doctor's evaluation when multispecialty care is needed. Interprofessional meetings are held to formulate a comprehensive medical care plan according to the patient's needs. This plan integrates the patient's physical, mental, and spiritual care and family members' support of medical treatments. The Community Health Center and the Hospice Home Care Unit provide a safe, attentive service when patients are discharged. This comprehensive healthcare provides patients with seamless care from admission to discharge and back into the community.

In 2005, CCH officially launched its overseas medical service and missionary with the core value of "SHARE" (spiritual, health, alliance, resource, and education). Over the years, CCH has partnered with public and private organizations and national and international non-governmental organizations (NGOs) to conduct voluntary medical services and provide spiritual care in developing countries to match the millenarian development goals. The footprint of CCH's overseas medical missions covers Africa, Asia, the South Pacific, and Caribbean regions. In order to strengthen healthcare technologies and related knowledge, CCH has hosted short-term advanced training courses for medical personnel from diplomatic relations countries. Up to 2015, over 500 medical volunteers had been dispatched to developing countries and over 100 medical personnel from around the world had visited CCH for advanced training. Furthermore, CCH has mobilized the resources of university and academic institutions to promote public health education, improve childhood malnutrition, and set up an ecosystem of safe water in communities to achieve the global health sustainability goal.

STRENGTH OF TAIWAN'S HEALTHCARE SYSTEM

Taiwan has a population of approximately 23.1 million. Virtually all of Taiwan is covered by national health insurance. Universal access has enabled investment in healthcare resources. The number of hospital beds per 10,000 persons is 68.61, and the number of physicians per 10,000 persons is 16.79, excluding traditional Chinese medicine practitioners and dentists.

The area of Taiwan is 36,200 km^2 and there are 19 medical centers. Access is easy and people are free to choose their caregiver. Besides medical treatment, the main functions of the medical centers are education, research, and training. Laboratories have been established to manage clinics, science research, and animal trials, such as teaching wards and objective structure clinical examination (OSCE).

INTRODUCTION TO HOSPITAL LEADERSHIP AND MANAGEMENT

Dr. Garth Saloner, dean of Stanford Graduate School of Business (GSB), defined leadership as "softer skill sets, the real leadership, the ability to work with others and through others, to execute...."[1] The role of leadership is to increase personnel efficiency, the essence and goal of management. Under successful management, all employees unite toward the organization's visions and missions. The objective of hospital management is to empower teamwork through defining a hospital's strategy, the organization's goal-setting process, and integrating and focusing all members' objectives. The golden rule is to ensure patient safety and healthcare quality.

Changhua Christian Hospital is a Presbyterian-affiliated organization. In 1928, Dr. Landsborough took four pieces of skin from his wife Marjorie who readily volunteered without hesitation, and grafted them onto the wounds of a child, Chou Kin-Yao, to save his life. The story touched many, and is known as "Skin Graft of Love." In his book, Robert Greenleaf mentioned, "A new moral principle is emerging, which holds that the only authority deserving one's allegiance is that which is freely and knowingly granted by the led to the leader in response to, and in proportion to, the clearly evident servant stature of the leader."[2]

If a person acquires considerable knowledge and professional skills but lacks love, there will be little sense of mission. The following are the purpose, missions, values, spirit, and visions of CCHS:

> Purpose: *In the spirit of love of Jesus Christ, preaching the Gospel, serving the world.*
> Our missions: *Medical care, evangelism, service, education, research.*
> Our values: *Selfless dedication, humble service.*
> Our spirit: *Love God, love the land, love the people, and love oneself.*
> Visions: *Medical care—to establish a solid, comprehensive, and safe healthcare system.*
> Evangelism: *To become a medical missionary for holistic care.*
> Service: *To provide patient-centered services to care for communities and the underprivileged.*
> Education: *To be a benchmark hospital for education and training medical practitioners.*
> Research: *To become a medical research center adopting advanced medical technologies.*

iHOSPITAL PLANNING PROGRESS

With globalization, medical applications have evolved from basic medical treatment to modern patient-centered services. One of the key capabilities is knowing how to build a smart hospital to meet a future standard. The issues include safer treatment, user-friendly design, staff and patient engagement and teamwork, high standards of security and quality requirements, simplified circulations, process integration, sustainable buildings, safety requirements, accessibility, and green environments. All these issues must be planned.

Before building, a formula needs to be followed: performing a needs analysis, selecting a team, collecting data, creating a facility program, finalizing the plan, obtaining a certificate of need, phasing, creating a schedule, making a budget, documenting the plan, and balancing the budget.

Purposes of Planning Medical Building

A modern hospital places high requirements on the construction site, the construction equipment, the medical equipment, and hospital hygiene conditions. Hence, the general purposes are listed as following:

1. A patient-centered administration and innovation to systemize medical quality control and minimize expenditure.
2. To meet the requirement of green including energy saving, resource recycling, litter disposal, building materials, disaster prevention, and interior environment.
3. User-friendly design including the functional design of hospital buildings, decor, building facilities, medical facilities, and furniture.
4. To construct an intelligent building including information technology (IT), office automation (OA), a building automation system (BAS), and the most important item, a medical/healthcare equipment automation system.

Floor and Circulation Plans

After determining the overall plan, followed by short-term, mid-term, and long-term planning and integration of the programs from medical, medical technology, nursing, administration, logistics, IT, and so on, the floor and circulation plans can be established.

1. Planning building circulation

   Overall building circulation planning is used to determine the space allocation according to the space requirements summary table and to manage the floor plans, such as floor configuration, vertical circulation, and horizontal circulation. Vertical circulation considers vertical transportation equipment and vertical pipes for electrical equipment. Horizontal circulation considers the space needed for current circulation and responds to future capacity needs.
2. Planning for emergency department

   An emergency department (ER) is a miniature hospital. It runs 24/7, dealing with victims from a variety of accidents and injuries, intoxication, mental disorders, domestic violence, emerging infectious diseases, chemical poisoning disasters, food poisoning, and man-made disasters. The ER space plans need to consider medical treatment and equipment, and transport to operating rooms (OR) and other units.

3. The workflow and circulation of outpatient and inpatient clinics

Outpatient clinics are the first stop for contact between hospital staff and patients, and are also the most frequently used areas. These clinic spaces provide registration, waiting, treatment, and pharmacy, which are the primary environments for delivering a hospital's image. The planning of a patient room is the start of a hospital's internal plan. It will determine the column positions of a hospital's main structure and appearance. Usually, the nurses' station will be located with a clear view of the patient rooms and adjacent to elevators in order to be aware of patient flows and to provide efficient assistance within the shortest time. A general ward floor plan contains the healthcare facility, lounge, pantry, laundry room, accessible toilet, phone, and Internet to meet the daily living needs. A special patient room such as a positive/negative pressure isolation room should be located at a site with a suitable circulation design. Patient room floor plans for the intensive care unit should focus on efficiency, safety, and comfort. All this is relatively complex when building a hospital, and the space required for medical treatment and services should be discussed prior to planning the floor layout and circulation to provide a comfortable and safe healthcare environment.

4 Facility management

Facility management and safety (FMS) is an important section of the Joint Commission International Accreditation (JCIA) guidelines. They contain distinct requirements about legal regulations, risk presentation, emergency response, fire safety, hazardous substances, medical equipment, and public facility under one goal, which is the safety of patients, families, and staff. CCH has been accredited by the JCI since 2008.

Solution-Ready Package of iHospital: Introduction to Yuanlin Christian Hospital (YCH)

A hospital solution-ready package (SRP) includes an intelligent counter, an intelligent outpatient system, an intelligent television system, an intelligent LAB, an intelligent ward system, and other customized application systems. Each can be integrated with the hospital information system (HIS). Utilizing the intelligent counter, the intelligent outpatient system, and the intelligent television system improves clinic or number calling, public information announcing, cashier and registration counter, admission and discharge services, outpatient clinic, physiological examination, medical imaging, radiology, blood collection counter, health education, and the health examination center.

Satisfaction survey applications are installed on the counters collecting outpatient clinic feedback. It is helpful to analyze the feedback to optimize the clinic process and adjust the configuration. An intelligent LAB provides automatic processes such as registration, number calling, preparation and collection of tubes, classification, and so on. Automation of the LAB resolves the problems that large, medium, and small-sized hospitals in Taiwan have encountered. Bedside information provides the patient with necessary services, such as an introduction to the medical campus and its environment, a shuttle timetable, health education, medication, a satisfaction survey, television, entertainment, e-books, and so on, and can be integrated with an e-whiteboard at the nurses' station, a mobile cart (a personal computer [PC] mounted on a stroller used by the nurse), and smartphone as a cross-platform communication system, assisting nursing staff to provide for patients' needs in real time. YCH also facilitates an interactive kiosk and a light-emitting diode (LED) video wall, intelligent television, indoor air quality detection, and energy management to provide a user-friendly, smart, and high-quality healthcare service.

The iHospital facilities of YCH contain the following:

1. Intelligent multimedia monitoring center: This center supervises and runs the public broadcast system, outpatient information, counter information, ward information, an interactive kiosk, backup servers, and other functions that can be extended for future needs.

2. Intelligent multimedia broadcast system: The iHospital receives the information sent from a monitoring center and dispatches it to the terminal displays. The dispatched contents contain scheduled video programs, outpatient calling information, healthcare education, bulletins, texted information, e-posters, Microsoft PowerPoint (PPT or PPS) slide presentations, photographs, flash files, cable television, webpages, and date/time and weather information (when connected

to the Internet). The terminal display can be divided into 15 windows to convey different information.

3. Intelligent counter system: This system includes a self-ticket machine, LED displays, satisfaction surveys, and self-registration machines. It is a highly integrated turnkey solution. The counter provides a number to call for cashier or registration counter services. The LED display shows information such as a list of services, service provider's name, current intake number, and the number of people waiting. Meanwhile, the counter also provides the function of real-time feedback and can be accessed by the touchscreen. For instance, a five-scale satisfaction survey from "very satisfied" to "very unsatisfied" can be done on the go.

4. Intelligent outpatient system: This system displays the department, clinic number, contact number, doctor's name, nurse's name, waiting list, hospital information (video, photos, or texts), and so on. The patient's identity is protected as only the last name and one character of the forename (normally Chinese names have two Chinese characters) are given. Statistical data can be exported from the system as an index for average waiting time and average time to see a doctor. An intelligent physiological measurement is established in the outpatient clinic, which will record the blood pressure, weight, and height of the patient and transfer these data to the clinic by inserting the patient's insurance health card.

5. Intelligent LAB: YCH intends to be a high-end quality medical service with efficient and friendly processes especially using the LAB system. This system offers autoregistration, auto number calling, auto tubes preparation and collection, autoclassification, information automation, and remote management. Not only does the intelligent LAB significantly reduce patient waiting times, reduce the time spent conducting outpatient inspections, and reduce the risk of taking wrong bloods, but it also increases productivity and enhances the work environment. LAB has been applied in practical management by showing the advantages of a comfortable, secure, efficient, swift, and high-quality healthcare environment.

6. Intelligent ward system: This system is located at the nurses' station with a bedside Infocomm terminal (BIT) and a patient Infocomm terminal (PIT) as the service end points, providing the nurses' station with the ability to monitor a patient's status, such as name, vital signs, nurse bell, intravenous (IV) bell, and so on. The BIT

provides patients with medical information such as the name of the visiting doctor, nurse, and head nurse; reminders about inspections, operations, scheduled treatments, and prescriptions. The PIT offers hospital information such as instructions on hospitalization and discharge, introduction to the hospital environment and wards, meal orders, health education, satisfaction surveys, and personal entertainment. In brief, the system consists of four subsystems: control center at nurses' station, PIT, BIT, and a cross-platform communications system.

7. Intelligent precision medical services: The next generation of medical services will be involved with the precision medicine (PM). YCH has been designed to offer patients precise and intelligent medical services, which, of course, also extend to the ORs. We have developed a multifunctional OR, called a *hybrid OR*. "Hybrid" refers to integrated services. We have installed image scanners in the OR to assist doctors with judging preoperation, operation, and post-operation conditions, as well as to help them determine whether to end the operation, so they will be provided with good imaging support. The hybrid OR is a pioneering project in Taiwan, as well as one of the leading projects in the world. This innovative design is a major breakthrough for surgeons as it allows the entire process, including consultation around the engineering aspects and coordination of the medical equipment and devices, to be properly integrated with our main project. With the self-designed system at YCH, a ground rail allows a computed tomography (CT) scanner to travel on demand to a patient without introducing additional risks of moving the patient against OR protocol. The CT scanner is able to move into or out of the OR in less than 30 seconds, enabling scanning, diagnosis, and intervention in one room without moving the patient or equipment. This hybrid OR is a representation of all of our hard work. What does the introduction of advanced technology into a hospital signify to a surgeon? The accessibility to a greater amount of more advanced equipment and facilities increases the likelihood that operations will be successful and reduces the patients' pain and discomfort. Furthermore, such technology will allow us to confirm operation results, both during and after surgery, which is good news for surgeons, patients, and patients' families. Most operations have certain blind spots so the use of imaging offers a serious advantage. Thanks to these devices, the surgeons can perform more precise operations to achieve the goals of the operation and produce better

results. The devices can also confirm the results by providing clear imaging. These advantages will change surgeons' operating methods for the better and benefit the patients.

YCH integrates acute care over three floors comprising a medical intensive care unit, a surgical intensive care unit, and a cardiac catheterization room, where intensive units support each other to maximize the effectiveness of care (Figures 11.1 through 11.3). Another integration is OR and CT rooms, which is the hybrid OR. It is focused on providing enhanced visualization at the point of therapy delivery (Figures 11.4 through 11.6).

YCH provides a medical center–level service in a regional hospital by strengthening acute critical care in neurology, a 24-hour emergency room for major trauma, acute stroke and cardiovascular emergency treatment, and

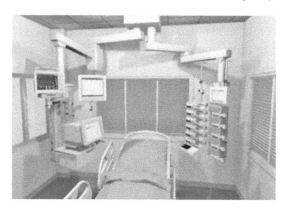

FIGURE 11.1
ICU cantilever at YCH.

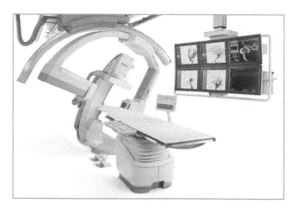

FIGURE 11.2
Digital cardiac catheterization x-ray machine at YCH.

FIGURE 11.3
ICU, 24 single beds at YCH.

FIGURE 11.4
Hybrid operating room at YCH.

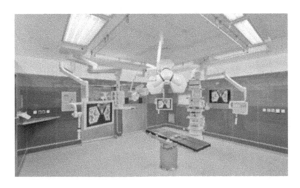

FIGURE 11.5
Hybrid operating room at YCH.

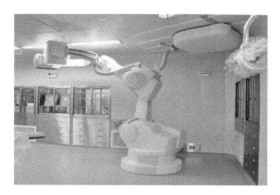

FIGURE 11.6
Hybrid operating room at YCH.

perinatal care for patients with high-risk pregnancies. To develop YCH as a real iHospital, intelligent systems such as intelligent counter, intelligent outpatient systems, intelligent LAB systems, patient infotainment systems, and an interactive kiosk and video wall have been adopted (Figures 11.7 and 11.8).

Intelligent Logistics Management System

Hospital logistics include property and infrastructure maintenance, mechanical and electrical operations, boiler room, canteen, laundry room, green cleaning, security, materials warehouse, and fleet management. Intelligent logistics management plays an important role in cutting cost, enhancing safety management and infection control risk, and indirectly

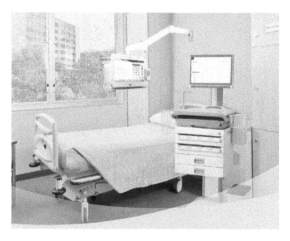

FIGURE 11.7
Patient infotainment system at YCH.

FIGURE 11.8
Lobby and counter at YCH.

minimizing expenditure. Hospitals may distinguish departments accord-ing to their functions.

In general, three systems can be recognized as follows:

1. Medical system: Pharmaceuticals, medical supplies, and equipment.
2. General system: Plumbing, electricity, gas, air conditioning, boilers, elevators, security, mortuary, parking, medical waste, cloth clothing, furniture, vehicles, fuel, equipment maintenance, and other accessories.
3. System of life: Appliances, food and oil, ingredients, cooking utensils, and so on. The intelligent logistics at CCH include the eBed turnaround system (eBTS), formerly known as the eHousekeeper's intelligent man-agement system (eHIMS); eInspection (the application in the eMo-bileCare suite that is designed for the quality control department); eFeedback (this system allows companies to capture customer feedback in a proactive method and it helps in playing a part in eco-friendliness as no paper is used while gathering the feedback); eCall (vehicles book-ing management); eTracking (waste management), and so on.

The targets of intelligent logistics are

1. Integration: Each logistics system can be combined to improve the service-oriented quality.
2. Flexibility: The system can adjust or modify job satisfaction with the collection of information.
3. Instant: Through the integration of processes and systems, any abnor-mal warning can be immediately notified to maintenance units.

4. Action: Each manager with portable communication equipment can deal with all logistic jobs.

The contents and results are divided into three parts as follows:

1. Environment service: The three main systems are bed cleaning management, action patrol, and waste management.
2. Customer service: Includes wheelchair rental, environment satisfaction survey, maintenance and management of public facilities, and transportation.
3. Quality management: Includes outsourcing staff management and quality of service indicators.

FUTURE CHALLENGES

Intelligentization will drive change over the next few decades. Based on current processes, we can predict the future. Change is difficult, but not to change would be disastrous.

The 4.0 industrial revolution has the potential to change all walks of life. The revolutionary impact of the iRobot and intelligent technology will have a surge impact just like steam, electricity, and the PC did in past centuries.

Facing difficulties and challenges, the beauty is having a dream and making that dream come true. I will finish with a quote from Leonardo da Vinci,[3] "I have been impressed with the urgency of doing. Knowing is not enough, we must apply. Being willing is not enough, we must do."

SUMMARY

Changhua Christian Hospital was founded by Dr. Landsborough III, and he and his son Dr. Landsborough IV served the Taiwanese people for nearly 70 years. The spirit they showed—*selfless dedication and humble service*—has become our values and lives on into the present. Although technology is constantly changing and hospital hardware continues to progress, even in the era of the intelligent hospital, the purpose, missions, values, and spirit won't change. We promote the spirit of humble service as the philosophy of "servant leadership," exporting our know-how westward to Mainland China, helping its hospitals and reversing the operating disadvantage, which became the early westward hospital in Taiwan. This is the spirit of "sharing common good," which means to share and help each other. No matter if it is to help hospitals in Mainland China or enterprises in Taiwan, CCH reveals the same attitude. For we know that once people put their own interests first, things will not progress. We share our experiences and profits without giving a thought to personal gain, because this will produce trust in each other, and hence more opportunities, which is the spirit of "to lose is to win."

An intelligent hospital applies new technologies helping patients in their medical treatments and processes. It will raise the quality of healthcare and further enhance the medical relationship between doctors and patients. Perhaps artificial intelligence (AI), virtual reality (VR), and augmented reality (AR) will enrich the function of the intelligent hospital. However, one must understand the most critical thing—the "human." Patients are human, as are doctors, nurses, and paramedical personnel (at least for now). The pattern of people-oriented medical services should be preserved. Technology is only the bridge between humans, patients, and healthcare providers.

Improvements in hospital management, medical technology, clinical processes, and more mature intelligent applications will certainly be very helpful for clinical needs and the combination of professional knowledge. In particular, the recent examples of intelligent healthcare with medical robots, which is the last mile of digital healthcare. The innovative experience of building an intelligent hospital could help such development. Challenges and difficulties will certainly arise during the innovative phase; however, only through the idea of innovation will the world change. In response to the fast pace of technological development, one can first apply the changes, and second, take action. Thus, history will be written in the future, observing the value of the existence of human beings.

REFERENCES

1. GSB Dean Garth Saloner Explains Why I'm at Stanford (2010, April 16), Ed Bastista, *Harvard Business Review*. Retrieved from http://www.edbatista.com/2010/04/stanford.html.
2. Robert K. Greenleaf, (2002). *The Servant as a Leader, Servant Leadership: A Journey Into the Nature of Legitimate Power and Greatness*. Paulist Press, Mahwah, NJ. USA.
3. Leonardo da Vinci Quotes. Retrieved from http://www.brainyquote.com/quotes/quotes/l/leonardoda120052.html.

12

Planning Safe Hospitals

Sushma Guleria

CONTENTS

INTRODUCTION

Vast diversities and dynamic geo-climatic conditions across the globe have made many nations highly vulnerable to different natural hazards. Over the past two decades, disasters have almost doubled. Furthermore, vulnerability is growing manifold with inadequate attention to changing risk patterns, placing more and more people in risk-prone zones. Medical care varies for each exigency as it depends on the hazard and vulnerable elements at risk, making it very dynamic, corroborating the fact that a disaster response *still* needs better "preparedness." Hence, stakeholders persist in talking about the need for a systematic approach and the safeguarding of our lifeline resources, which play a crucial role in an efficient response.

Never has the challenge "to substantially reduce the impact of disasters and to make risk reduction an essential component of development policies and programmes," as spelled out in the Hyogo Framework for Action 2005–2015 (HFA), been more compelling. Protecting people's health and lives from the risk of disasters is both a social and an economic necessity. From 2004 to 2013, more than 110,000 deaths were recorded annually on average due to natural and technological hazards, while 1.7 billion people were affected by disasters in the same period. A review of 94 assessments in Latin America and the Caribbean alone (from 1972 to 2011) estimated the damage to health infrastructure from disasters at $7.82 billion.[1] The 168 countries that adopted the HFA put forth the following priority for action in the health sector[2]:

> *Integrate disaster risk reduction planning into the health sector; promote the goal of "hospitals safe from disasters" by ensuring that all new hospitals are built with a level of resilience that strengthens their capacity to remain functional in disaster situations and implement mitigation measures to reinforce existing health facilities.*

Yet, despite this significant step by nations, it has been observed with alarm that a number of health facilities are still being built in highly hazard-prone areas, in addition to the fact that expenditure on hospitals may represent up to 70% of any national health budget.[3] Moreover, crises continue to leave behind non-functional health facilities, depriving affected communities of health benefits. Some 187 countries including India are signatories to the Sendai Framework (2015–2030), which is the successor instrument to the HFA that was adopted at the Third UN World Conference in Sendai, Japan, 2015. It encouraged the adoption and practice of a number of innovations with a strong emphasis on disaster risk reduction (DRR) and enhancing resilience with explicit focus on people, their health and livelihoods. Important global targets with respect to the protection of lives were[4]

1. *Substantially reduce the number of affected people globally by 2030, aiming to lower the average global figure per 100,000 in the decade 2020–2030 compared to the period 2005–2015.*
2. *Substantially reduce disaster damage to critical infrastructure and disruption of basic services, among them health and educational facilities, including through developing their resilience by 2030.*

IMPORTANCE OF HOSPITAL SAFETY

Hospitals are considered a critical lifeline infrastructure in the context of disasters and otherwise. A safe and resilient hospital not only ensures an effective healthcare response during disasters, but it also ensures the safety of those patients who are already being treated in the hospital. This calls for a high order of preparedness in a hospital to deal with disaster-related emergencies, mass causalities, and the resultant need for hospital space, staff, and resources, on-site safety from the spread of infections, epidemics, and even pandemics. Needless to say, these also include various nuclear, biological, and chemical (NBC) emergencies that need attention too. NBC concerns are addressed in Chapter 13 separately.

Risk reduction in the health sector needs special attention due to the high levels of occupancy in health facilities and the critical role that they are expected to play in a post-disaster scenario. Past experiences of various hazards have underscored the poor performance of critical care facilities, with some of these becoming victims themselves rather than saviors of the community. Hospitals are considered the strongest *capacities* and a useful resource for post-disaster response and its efficient management. However, we focus little on the thought that our capacities are equally our vulnerabilities.

When health facilities fail during disasters, whether for structural or functional reasons, they become unavailable for those affected at precisely the time they are most needed. Health sector damage can cause devastating secondary and tertiary impacts. The December 2004 Indian Ocean tsunami affected entire healthcare systems and very many beneficiaries, particularly the poor, at an untold cost. It damaged 61% of health facilities in Northern Aceh Province, and killed approximately 7% of its health workers and 30% of its midwives. As a consequence, Aceh's healthcare sector went into crisis and its recovery required intensive investment.[5] Likewise, the original Olive View Hospital in Los Angeles, California, was destroyed in the 1971 San Fernando earthquake and when it was rebuilt, the authorities took extreme care to build the facility as per new performance standards to maintain its functionality. This helped the building and the infrastructure to sustain the Northridge earthquake of 1994 without significant damage.[5] However, the building's fire sprinkler system broke, causing a flood-like situation and the evacuation of patients instead of taking in people injured in the earthquake. The hospital was closed for repairs for 4 weeks, which was essentially the golden period for caring for earthquake victims.

Another case in point is the Shizugawa Public Hospital in Miyagi, Japan. The hospital had devised preparedness plans, drawing lessons from earlier tsunamis in the area (2.8 m high), and had put all critical patient accommodation from the third floor upward considering tsunami heights double that (5.6 m) experienced in the region. Unfortunately, the tsunami on March 11, 2011, reached unprecedented heights and several patients and healthcare professionals from the lower floors of the hospital perished. It is significant that despite the precautions taken by the hospital, the location of power generators on the lower levels did not allow them to provide backup power that would have helped maintain life support to many critical patients.[6]

The 2005 earthquake of South Asia engulfed wide regions, affecting parts of Afghanistan, India, and Northern Pakistan. Strong aftershocks threatened structures already damaged by the initial quake. More than 73,000 people lost their lives and at least 150,000 others were injured. Needless to say, the demand for emergency medical care was overwhelming. The earthquake left an estimated 3.2 million people homeless. In Pakistan alone, 388 out of 796 health facilities ranging from well-equipped hospitals to rural clinics were destroyed. Additionally, 106 primary clinics and 50 dispensaries were also destroyed, often the only source of healthcare for neighboring rural communities, thereby overwhelming the remaining functional healthcare systems available. Because of this, nearly 14,000 persons had to be airlifted to Islamabad for treatment in the first month alone.[5]

Besides the physical damage to health facilities, the health sector itself was adversely affected, as many health professionals lost their lives. After the 2003 Algerian earthquake, 50% of the health facilities in the affected region were no longer functional due to damage.[5] These examples corroborate the need to identify critical gaps in a hospital disaster preparedness plan, thereby providing succor to the community at a time when it is most needed.

EXPECTATION

If vulnerability assessments are systematically carried out, if hospital disaster plans are better prepared, placed, tested, and widely disseminated, along with preparedness for mass casualty management, many lives can be saved and health facilities might function better despite the damage. Overall, from a humanitarian perspective, the gap between building an (un)safe hospital can be made negligible. But this tiny mitigation investment can create the difference between life and death, or between a community's impoverishment and its sustainable development. All this makes it imperative for countries and stakeholders to commit to the establishment of the Safe Hospitals Initiative and the 2015 *Hospital Safety Index* (HSI), which is a rapid diagnostic tool for assessing the safety and preparedness of hospitals, which need to incorporate various components of any hospital safety program, as in Figure 12.1.

As of now, 130 countries have reported to the World Health Organization (WHO) that they have "emergency preparedness and response programmes" in place. Seventy-seven countries have implemented activities

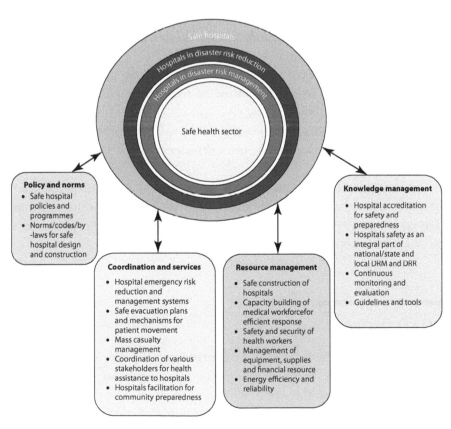

FIGURE 12.1
Components of a hospital safety program.

to make their hospitals safe and operational during emergencies. Building on this momentum, countries are called on to support the implementation of the Safe Hospitals Initiative and scale up actions to[1]

1. *Enable hospitals to continue to function and provide appropriate and sustained levels of healthcare during and following emergencies and disasters.*
2. *Protect health workers, patients, and families.*
3. *Protect the physical integrity of hospital buildings, equipment, and critical hospital systems.*
4. *Make hospitals safe and resilient to future risks, including climate variations.*

Proposed Targets Related to Building Safe Hospitals

1. *By 2030, all new hospitals and 80% of other new health facilities will be built to withstand hazards, in accordance with the safety and building codes of the country.*
2. *By 2030, 50% of existing hospitals and healthcare facilities requiring improved safety will be retrofitted in accordance with the safety and building codes of the country.*
3. *By 2030, all hospitals and health facilities will have emergency response plans for continuing healthcare in disasters.*

The basic intention behind the whole concept of advocating for safer hospitals is to enhance resilience and have better-prepared health facilities that are constructed more safely and are protected too. Safe hospitals must be designed to cope with future risks.[3]

CHALLENGES

Disaster scenarios have become a disturbing reality. For some hazards, hospitals are likely to receive advance warnings and activate their disaster plan before the approaching hazard. Most human-induced hazards are sudden in nature without giving sufficient reaction time, which can become a key ingredient in a mass casualty incident (MCI).

All these pose challenging implications for the hospital's preparedness and response, thereby making hospital disaster preparedness important at local, state, and national levels. Again, hospitals in the United States are mandated to have disaster response plans that are accredited by the Joint Commission on Accreditation of Healthcare Organizations (JCAHO); however, in India and probably in many other countries, there is no statutory body to regulate and accredit this requirement.

Many countries prone to hazards and vulnerable to disasters have tried, tested, and implemented actions on the assessment of healthcare facilities, conducting rapid visual assessments to undertake retrofitting of key hospitals with a **Build Back Better** approach, upgrading capacities, enhancing their levels of resilience, implementing hospital safety plans, incorporating training and capacity-building components in the plans, and carrying out drills for building a more resilient healthcare infrastructure. However, these efforts are more often sporadic and insufficiently integrated into developmental programs. Focusing on this need, many challenges remain, especially for developing countries with limited resources and facing high risks and threats from various hazards, necessitating them to construct facilities to withstand future hazards (including those from the risk of climate change), empowering staff to address safety issues, and ensuring that they are well prepared for the aftermath of a hazard. Although the measures necessary to prevent a functional collapse (contingency planning, drills, and staff training) require a significantly smaller financial investment, they nonetheless remain a major challenge to implementation.

A lackluster attitude toward safety, corruption, and cost-cutting actions by companies increases the threat of disasters in hospitals. The healthcare industry is under tremendous pressure to respond to new regulatory requirements. From endemics to pandemics, violence, healthcare-acquired infections, and contamination from pollutants, healthcare organizations are called on to be better prepared in times to come. Failure to adequately address these issues may heighten liabilities and increase compensation claims, fines, penalties, and more, damaging an organization's reputation. Therefore, hospitals should have a comprehensive risk reduction and management program that addresses these concerns. As part of this strategy, healthcare organizations should work with insurers covering the healthcare sector that understand the unique challenges facing the industry.[7]

SAFETY IS COST-EFFECTIVE

Building safe hospitals or protecting existing hospitals from the aftermath of a hazard can be surprisingly cheap. Small investments in structural and non-structural mitigation components are nothing compared to the risk of partial or complete destruction during a disaster, the death and injuries so caused that cannot be monetarily evaluated, and the equally high health, economic, and development impacts. It is estimated that the cost of a safe health facility is negligible when integrated early in design considerations. For new health facilities, incorporating comprehensive DRR measures from natural or human-induced hazards into designs from the beginning will only add 4% to the total construction cost.[5] Planning this investment into the processes for new hospitals can be easily targeted by advocacy, and should be given priority or mandated through bye-laws. To quote an example—in 2004, retrofitted health centers in the Cayman Islands were virtually undamaged during Hurricane Ivan. If they had not been retrofitted, specialists estimate that the hurricane would have caused 20% worth of damage to structures and 40% worth of damage to facilities.[5] The cost of retrofitting existing health facilities varies greatly; however, prioritizing the protection of critical care and hospital functionality reduces potential costs and provides excellent examples of cost-effectiveness. Not to forget that damage to non-structural elements often renders a hospital inoperable during a disaster and retrofitting non-structural elements only costs about 1% while protecting up to 90% of the value of a hospital.[5]

A SAFE HOSPITAL...

Disasters, depending on their type, intensity, and magnitude result in various levels of morbidity and mortality. The demand for curative care is highest during the acute emergency and initial response phase, when the affected population is most vulnerable to the newly exposed environment and before basic public health measures such as water, sanitation, and shelter have been implemented. Afterward, the priority shifts to preventive measures that can improve the overall health of the displaced population, which therefore calls for coordinated and in-sync efforts between curative and preventive health services, thereby targeting a reduction in mortality and morbidity rates. Safe hospitals are health facilities whose services remain accessible during and immediately following any emergency or crises *and*...[8]

> ...*will not collapse in disasters, killing patients and staff*
> ...*will be able to continue to function and provide critical services in emergencies*
> ...*have contingency plans in place, trained personnel to keep the network operational*

Various sectors such as planning, finance, public services, architecture, and engineering should be involved, and include[3]:

1. *Ensuring adequate risk reduction measures in the design and construction*
2. *Improving the non-structural and functional vulnerability of existing health facilities.*
3. *Adopting legislative and financial measures to select and retrofit the most critical facilities to increase levels of protection.*

After the January 26, 2001, Gujarat (India) earthquake, which razed most parts of Bhuj, what emerged from the rubble was a model city with new buildings no more than a storey high, a network of wide roads, and a mesh of seismographs spread across the district. As Nepal faces its biggest challenge, that is, rebuilding after the April 25, 2015, earthquake, it could look to Bhuj for solutions. With over 38,000 homes destroyed, killing 2,370 people, Bhuj continued to grow after the quake. The only multistorey structures in the city are the 70-odd buildings that survived the quake. *Plus, one exception: the three-storey G K General Hospital.* The Rs 100-crore hospital, which was completely rebuilt, is a model earthquake-resistant structure. The technology applied was the use of base-isolation, where lead-rubber bearings are used to isolate and protect structures during earthquakes.[9] These bearings act as shock absorbers and are built to withstand a quake of 8.5–9 magnitude. Likewise, during a 1990 earthquake in Costa Rica, five major hospitals were in the midst of being retrofitted. The retrofitted areas came through the quake in excellent condition and saved lives, while the incomplete areas suffered extensive damage. The preventive savings far exceeded the cost of the retrofitting.[5]

It's an established fact that there are no universal design guidelines to protect buildings from various natural hazards. Different hazards pose different challenges, and each hazard requires a different approach and recommendations. For instance, flooding is a more site-specific hazard; therefore, the preferred approach for new facilities is to select a site that is not subject to flooding, if not, site modifications or other site-specific building design features that mitigate anticipated floods will reduce the potential for damage.[10] When it comes to seismic and high-wind events, however, in addition to careful site selection, it becomes imperative to design resistant buildings including both structural and non-structural components. Emphasis can also be placed on having hospital-based ambulatory care departments that can easily be converted for post-disaster care during any emergency. Clinic space can be used for triage or emergency treatment rooms, and ambulatory diagnostic equipment is suitable for use during emergency. The key to having hospital-based ambulatory capacity available in the aftermath of major disasters can indeed be thoughtful planning. Further, new and emerging technologies ranging from electronic devices, such as nanoscale sensors and wireless communication networks, are rapidly changing patient treatment practices and administration practices. These innovative medical advances empower hospitals with tools that enable faster diagnosis and better treatment even when disasters impair the functioning of electronic equipment, making them an indispensable backbone of hospitals.[10]

Hospitals usually have mid to high levels of occupancy, with patients, staff, and many visitors present 24/7. Many patients require constant attention and at times continuous specialized care. Operations also depend on a steady supply of medical and other equipment. In addition, a hospital's vulnerability is aggravated by the presence of hazardous substances that may be spilled or released during a hazard event, which calls for facilities to be available to monitor their functioning on a continuous basis. A well-established emergency operation center (EOC) as a component of a hospital's administration could serve this purpose. This would help not only to check on workers but also to monitor equipment functioning and any unwanted incident could be immediately contained. Hospitals are extremely complex systems that depend on an extensive network of mechanical, electrical, and piping installations. Isolation rooms usually have negative pressure to avoid harmful airborne organisms migrating outside. Likewise, wards housing patients with immune system deficiencies require a positive pressure differential, so that harmful organisms do not enter patients' rooms and needlessly infect them. A malfunction in any one part of this ventilation system could create a risk of infection to patients and staff. This system is extremely vulnerable to disruption as a result of indirect building damage especially from winds and collapse in earthquakes and needs attention during design considerations.[10]

Also, hospitals depend on several essential piping systems. Medical gasses are among the most important, along with water, steam, and fire sprinkler systems, oxygen and other gasses required for patient care. Unless properly secured and braced, these installations can be easily dislodged or broken, causing dangerous leakage and potential additional damage. The sewer system may be disrupted during floods or earthquakes and may overflow or break down. Waste disposal is another essential, because when toilets back up, or sterilizers, dishwashers, and other automated cleaning equipment cannot be discharged, this immediately affects the patients' needs. Retention ponds or holding tanks coupled with backflow and diversion valves can be employed to solve this problem.[10]

Elevator service is another vulnerable element of power failures and damage to their installation. An emergency power supply system is another very critical element. This system enables hospital installations and equipment that have not sustained direct physical damage to function normally in any disaster along with catering to fuel supply and storage needs. Therefore, for uninterrupted operation during a power outage, adequate electrical wiring must be installed in all areas that require an uninterrupted power supply.[10] Since all this calls for an increase in construction costs, the decision lies in a thorough evaluation of the relative vulnerability of various functions that may be hampered due to a power outage. The established fact remains that as patients become more critically ill and diagnosis and treatment become more dependent on computers, monitors, and other electrical equipment, the need for emergency power will continue to grow.

Many types of falling hazards can occur as a result of a disaster. In the past, bottles in clinical laboratories have fallen and started fires. Earthquakes have the potential to cause considerable injury to personnel and can become a potential source of fire, although fire protection measures have been present in building codes for a long time, in the form of approved materials, fire-resistant assemblies, exiting requirements, emergency exit routes, and many other specifications. An evident practice in India is that hospitals must not make the basement a dumping and storage ground and ensure easy access to hospitals so that fire tenders can enter the building in a timely manner during an emergency. Hospitals in India have now also been instructed to review the status of fire safety norms at regular intervals and appoint nodal officers who will be responsible for any lapse in compliance of safety norms.

Security is another major and at times grave concern for any public institution and especially hospitals. Beyond the ethical responsibility to keep patients and staff safe, there is an abundance of expensive medical equipment and potentially harmful drugs that also puts medical facilities at heightened risk. In this regard, real-time locating systems (RTLS) have been steadily gaining attention as a method of tracking hospital equipment. RTLS use wireless signals to transmit the object's location to a server-based software application, and can be monitored in real time. Other innovations making their way into hospitals include high-definition integrated camera/playback systems, lone-worker protection devices, and weapons screening.[11] Thus, advocates for the need to embrace a multihazard approach when designing or retrofitting a hospital are essential for its protection. This can help to avoid aggravating the vulnerability of many hospital building components and systems.

BASIC FACTS FOR SAFE HOSPITALS[5]

Many factors put hospitals and health facilities at risk:

- *Buildings:* Their vulnerable location, design specifications, and the quality of the materials used, all contribute to a hospital's ability to withstand different hazards.
- *Patients:* During emergencies, damage to hospitals can compound patients' vulnerability, as well as increasing their number.
- *Health workforce:* Loss or unavailability of health workers compromises care for the injured. Emergent hiring from outside to sustain the response adds to the overall economic burden.
- *Equipment:* Damage to non-structural elements often surpasses the cost of overall building damage.
- *Components:* Structural essential elements responsible for overall safety such as beams, columns, slabs, load-bearing walls, braces, or foundations as well as non-structural elements such as water heaters or storage tanks, mechanical equipment, cabinets, and lifelines.

- *Functional collapse:* These include storage spaces and laboratories or operating theaters, medical records and services, logistic and administrative processes (such as contracting, procurement, and maintenance routines).
- *Field hospitals:* These may be successful alternative arrangements, but are found to be extremely expensive solutions and not satisfactorily cost-effective.
- *Building codes:* Strict enforcement of building codes and severe penalties for failing to follow them need utmost priority.[5]

HOSPITAL DISASTER MANAGEMENT PLAN (DMP)

1. Conducting a hazard, vulnerability, and capacity (HVC) assessment: Responding to the urgent societal call to change the paradigm from the traditional practice of giving relief, administration's primary role should also be toward integrating adequate preparedness. Though, as mandated by the Disaster Management (DM) Act 2005 of India, every hospital is required to *have an emergency plan in place*, experiences from the Indian Ocean tsunami of 2004; the Kashmir earthquake of 2005, particularly when the children's hospital in Jammu collapsed; the city of Bhuj, Gujarat, in 2001, when the civil hospital was reduced to rubble; and more recently the incidents of fire in the states of Kolkata (2011) and Odisha (2016) raise the question of the effectiveness of these plans.[8] To include such measures in a holistic plan for hospitals, it is necessary to conduct an extensive HVC assessment within the hospital compound. Hazard identification via checking on background events is essential to determine the events that are most likely to affect the hospital premises and to take subsequent decisions. Likewise, vulnerability analysis captures people's inability to protect themselves against possible damage or to recover from the consequences of natural phenomena without outside help. Vulnerability is about "not having" while capacities are about "having." These include various resources (manpower, equipment, etc.) that can resist the impact of a hazard and aid quick recovery.[6]
2. Developing a HSI: A HSI is one of a variety of tools developed by the Pan American Health Organization and a group of Caribbean and Latin American experts that is being widely used by hospitals to gather

information they need for sound decision making during the response phase.[12] It provides a snapshot of the probability that a health facility will continue to function during a crisis based on structural, non-structural, and functional factors, including the environment and health services. Also, as it is relatively inexpensive and easy to apply, it becomes an important first step toward prioritizing investments in hospital safety.

A HSI classifies a hospital's safety level into **categories A, B, or C** according to a numerical ranking.[12] Applying the index is not time-consuming and gives an accurate although general idea of which safety level the facility falls into and improvement measures recommended, as mentioned in Figure 12.2. Variables or elements are grouped into submodules, and a group of submodules constitutes one module. The value of each variable is multiplied by its relative weight in a submodule. The sum of the values of all the variables in a submodule gives 100% of that submodule. The module for structural safety has a weighted value of 50% of the index, the non-structural module has a weighted value of 30%, and functional capacity is weighted at 20%. The sum of the weighted results of the three modules gives a hospital safety rating expressed as the probability (percentage). Each component's safety is ranked as **high, medium, or low**, following a series of predetermined standards.

Safety index	Classification	Action points
0–0.35	C	Urgent intervention measures required. The hospital's current safety levels can either be inadequate or insufficient to protect the lives of patients and hospital staff during and after a disaster.
0.36–0.65	B	Intervention measures are needed in the short term, as the health facility's current level of safety could potentially put patients, staff, and hospitals' functioning at risk during or after a disaster.
0.66–1	A	It is quite likely that the hospital will continue to function post a disaster. Nevertheless, it is recommended to continue with measures to improve response capacity and to carry out relief in the medium and preventive long-term measures to reduce risk especially to improve structural safety.

FIGURE 12.2
HSI suggestions for intervention.

These scores are weighted according to the importance of the aspect that is being evaluated. The HSI has a maximum value of 1 and a minimum of 0. Not to forget, it may be neither feasible nor easy to take into account the fact that it will always be difficult for a hospital to remain perfectly operational, hence, it is rare for a facility to be given a safety index of "1."[12]

3. Checklist: (a) **Geographic location of the health facility:** Includes a description of the hazards or threats and the geotechnical properties of soils at the site of the health facility.[12] (b) **Structural safety:** Evaluating structural safety involves an assessment of the type of structure, materials, and previous exposure to hazards. The objective is to determine if the structure meets standards for providing services during eventualities or whether it would compromise structural integrity and its functional capacity. It is imperative to identify potential risks in terms of the type of design, structure, construction materials, and critical components of the structure.[12] (c) **Non-structural safety:** Failure of non-structural elements does not usually put the stability of a building at risk, but it can endanger people and the contents of the building. These elements could separate, fall, or tip, which can have a detrimental impact on important structural elements necessitating provisions for supports, anchors, and secure storage, and whether equipment/resources can withstand hazards and remain functional during and after a disaster. This analysis includes the safety of critical networks such as the water system, power, communications, ventilation, air-conditioning systems, and medical diagnostic and treatment equipment. Architectural elements such as facings, doors, windows, and so on must also be evaluated to determine their vulnerability to hazards. Safety of access to the facility and internal and external traffic need consideration along with lighting systems, fire protection systems, false ceilings, and other components.[12] (d) **Safety based on functional capacity:** This includes aspects such as general hospital management, implementation of disaster plans including contingency and evacuation plans, availability and usage of resources for disaster preparedness and response, level of training of the staff including safety of the priority services that allow the hospital to remain operational.[12]

4. Components of a hospital DMP: The hospital DMP should essentially be built through conducting a thorough risk assessment. It must be a multi-hazard holistic plan that assists and equips the hospital

administration to organize its preparedness for pre, during, and post disaster. In addition to having a well-documented plan, it would be prudent to have regular drills to test these plans. Hospital plans should consider the possibility that a hospital might need to evacuate partially or wholly, quarantine, or divert incoming patients. For example, in the event of flooding, the ground floor services may need to shift to higher floors or a makeshift operating theater may be needed. Spare capacities for such contingencies should be included too.

Hospitals may like to form their own internal disaster management committee. Such a committee could be chaired by the medical superintendent (MS) and include members from administration, representatives from various departments, the chief security officer (CSO), the chief nursing officer (CNO), the sanitation officer (SO), engineering services, and so on. The final plan is required to fulfill the following objectives[13]:

- To facilitate HVC assessment and develop a HIS
- To define and promote the development of standard operating procedures (SOPs)
- To have in place a contingency plan for an effective internal/external response, as in Figures 12.3 and 12.4
- To document the disaster activation and deactivation plan
- To promote, enhance, and sustain training and capacity building

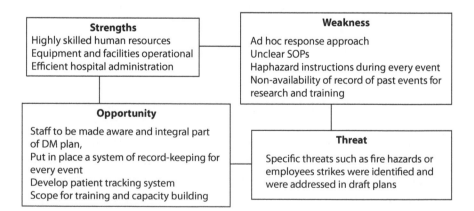

FIGURE 12.3
Roles and responsibilities during external disasters. (From EKU Online, Natural disasters and hospital safety. Retrieved from http://safetymanagement.eku.edu/resources/infographics/natural-disasters-and-hospital-safety/. Accessed 25 November 2016.)

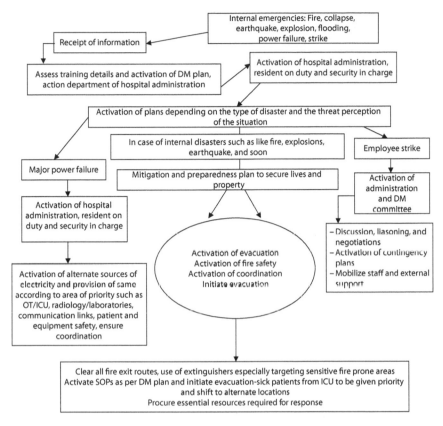

FIGURE 12.4
Roles and responsibilities during internal disasters. (From EKU Online, Natural disasters and hospital safety. Retrieved from http://safetymanagement.eku.edu/resources/info-graphics/natural-disasters-and-hospital-safety/. Accessed 25th November 2016.)

- To control media and crowd management
- To set up triage, resuscitation, and treatment teams
- To have a separate plan of action for dealing with epidemics/infections, as in Figure 12.5
- To maintain and update a directory of key contacts and a list of vital equipment
- To plan for conduct, analysis, and documentation of disaster mock drills

Additionally, while making design decisions for hospital spaces, particular attention should be paid to the movement of patients, transfers, and visibility. Vulnerable patients should typically have limited movement and exposure with others in the hospital, location of elevators, and earmarked "patient corridors."[14]

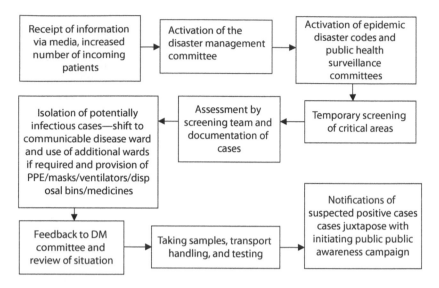

FIGURE 12.5
Roles and responsibilities during epidemics–infections. (From EKU Online, Natural disasters and hospital safety. Retrieved from http://safetymanagement.eku.edu/resources/ infographics/natural-disasters-and-hospital-safety/. Accessed 25th November 2016.)

SUMMARY

Health services have a unique moral imperative to provide hospitals and health facilities with adequate protection. They carry with them the social implications that if they fail it may become an addendum to an already devastated state and carry immense risk. Death of the most vulnerable among the social groups, that is, the sick, the elderly, and children, in hospitals during disasters can have a crippling effect on community morale. However, an effective response and a functional health service following a disaster can reinforce a sense of stability and social cohesiveness. Functioning hospitals can prove to be powerful symbols of social progress, and are prerequisites for stability and developmental growth. Latent conditions and failures in the healthcare sector can be minimized through strategic improvements in the design of the facilities and a focus on patient safety.[14] While globally the health sector has placed great emphasis on the eradication of various diseases, it has unknowingly neglected adequate emphasis on maintaining the functionality of health facilities post any disaster and how mitigation and preparedness planning can help these facilities remain functional. Utmost priority must be placed on raising the level of performance of hospitals to operate at more than their carrying capacity to serve the dependent community post the aftermath of a major disaster; thereby, corroborating the need for decision makers in the health sector to have a vision and a commitment to build safe hospitals by adequately integrating prevention, mitigation, preparedness, and response strategies in place.

REFERENCES

1. Concept Note-Working Session on Disaster Risk Management for Healthy Societies. UN World Conference on Disaster Risk Reduction; Sendai, Japan, March 2015.
2. World Health Organization. *Hospital Safety Index: Guide for Evaluators* (Second Edition), 2015. Retrieved from http://www.who.int/hac/techguidance/hospital_safety_index_evaluators.pdf. Accessed 12 November 2016.
3. Comprehensive Safe Hospital Framework, 2015. Retrieved from http://www.who.int/hac/techguidance/comprehensive_safe_hospital_framework.pdf. Accessed 10 November 2016.
4. United Nations Sendai Framework for Disaster Risk Reduction, 2015–2030. UNISDR/GE/2015-ICLUX; EN 5000, 1st edition, 2015.
5. World Disaster Reduction Campaign: Hospitals Safe from Disasters, Reduce Risk, Protect Health Facilities, Save Lives. Joint Report of the International Strategy for Disaster Reduction (ISDR), World Health Organization (WHO) and World Bank (WB), 2008–2009. Retrieved from https://www.unisdr.org/2009/campaign/pdf/wdrc-2008-2009-information-kit.pdf. Accessed 15 November 2016.
6. Workshops on Hospital Preparedness for Disasters in India: A Geo-Hazards Society (GHS). World Health Organization (WHO) India Initiative, New Delhi, India, January 2012.
7. Doherty D, and Carino R. Critical Risks Facing the Healthcare Industry, April 2015. Retrieved from http://www.acegroupe.com/us-en/businesses/medical-risk_critical-risk_wp.aspx.html. Accessed 27 June 2017.
8. National Disaster Management Guidelines: Hospital Safety. National Disaster Management Authority, Government of India, December 2013.
9. The Kutch Earthquake 2001: recollections, lessons and Insights. Pramod K. Mishra. Published by the National Institute of Disaster Management, Ministry of Home Affairs, Government of India, 2004.
10. FEMA 577: Chapter 1: Hospital Design Considerations. Retrieved from https://www.fema.gov/media-library-data/20130726-1610-20490-3588/577_ch1.pdf. Accessed 22 November 2016.
11. EKU Online. Natural Disasters and Hospital Safety. Retrieved from http://safetymanagement.eku.edu/resources/infographics/natural-disasters-and-hospital-safety/. Accessed 25 November 2016.
12. Other Pan American Health Organization. *Hospital Safety Index: Guide for Evaluators* (Series: Safe Hospitals from Disasters, No. 1). Washington DC: Regional Office of the World Health Organization, 2008. Retrieved from http://www.preventionweb.net/files/8974_SafeHosEvaluatorGuideEngl.pdf. Accessed 15 November 2016.

13. Talati S, Bhatia P, Kumar A, Gupta AK, and Ojha D. Strategic Planning and Designing of a Hospital Disaster Manual in a Tertiary Care, Teaching, Research and Referral Institute in India. *World J Emerg Med*. 2014; 5(1): 35–41. Retrieved from https://www.ncbi.nlm.nih.gov/pmc/articles/PMC4129869/. Accessed 21 November 2016.
14. Reiling J. Safe Design of Healthcare Facilities. *Qual Saf Health Care*. 2006; 15(1): i34–i40. Retrieved from https://www.ncbi.nlm.nih.gov/pmc/articles/PMC2464867/. Accessed 20 November 2016.

13

Designing Innovative Facilities: Contamination and Security Hazards at Hospitals

Raman Chawla and V.K. Singh

CONTENTS

INTRODUCTION

The grave danger of chemical, biological, radiological, nuclear, and explosive (CBRNE)-related terrorism poses an imminent contamination threat to all healthcare institutions across the world. In another scenario, patients coming from an area attacked by CBRNE require special decontamination facilities at a healthcare facility. This calls for an integrated approach that is initiated from the inception of the facility through its design stage until completion. According to Interpol, the CBRNE risk is evolving as the terrorist groups are intent on using this type of technological attack. Though biological agents are cheaper, they have not, as yet, been used frequently; however, even a hoax event can trigger mass panic and fear. On the other hand, the probability that radiological and nuclear devices will be used with malicious intent is significantly high due to advancements in information technology, financial globalization, and the increased number of theft possibilities as large number of radiological devices are available in unprotected medical sector. The risk is also due to non-removal of a nuclear source from obsolete radiotherapy equipment and others, which would be enough to make a dirty bomb. This can happen in countries where there is lax implementation of regulations. It occurred in India when equipment with a nuclear source from a teaching institution was disposed of as scrap. The workers handling the scrap material suffered nuclear burns. Real-time incidences such as the bombings in Abuja, Boston, London, Madrid, Moscow, Mumbai, and Oklahoma, or the chemical attacks on the Tokyo subway and in Syria are glaring examples of the use of chemical and explosive devices for terrorism.[1] The common element of response required for all such incidences is advanced and immediate healthcare provision both at the site of the incident and in healthcare establishments. The critical deciding factor of the efficacy of such a response procedure is the "mitigation of contamination hazard."

There are more than 1400 listed human pathogens of which more than half are zoonotic in nature. However, only a small proportion of these pathogens can cause human epidemics/pandemics.[2] The recent episodes of the Ebola virus, classified as a category A priority pathogen by the World Health Organization (WHO), showed the highest fatality rate of 50%–90% in the remote villages of Central and West Africa. Among its five species, the Zaire Ebola virus is the most aggressive, exhibiting a 90% mortality rate. Currently, no antiviral therapy or approved vaccine is available to mitigate its impact.[3] Thus, the contamination management and containment of the source by trace analysis at the field level requires trained and equipped personnel with courage, self-motivation, and more importantly, common sense developed from experience. To understand this aspect, one has to visualize the scenario, and a question regarding the operational response comes to mind, which is how a responder wearing complete protective clothing (masks and a breathing apparatus) can boost the confidence of a probable sick person about his or her isolation especially in remote villages where there is no awareness of this kind.[4] In addition, the spread of disease resulting in a massive death toll can easily be believed to be an act of evil leading to public congregations to calm the spirits (superstitious beliefs). Such congregations will spread the causative agent more easily, increasing the mortality rate. Thus, the health response to a biological event on the one hand is a dynamic process of prepared-ness–response–repreparedness, while also being an act of rapid reaction to contain the spread and severity at multiple sites in the affected zones.

Among all these CBRNE incidences, the management of contamina-tion gets priority. This chapter describes how creating an innovative and resilient design from the inception of the structure can provide long-term and effective solutions to this global challenge. The implementation of innovative ideas at the conceptual, design, and developmental stages of a healthcare establishment provides a rigorous framework that can acceler-ate the process of adaptation and the ability to recover (resilience) from any known and unknown contamination "security and safety" hazards. Some of the contamination-related factors that have emerged from newly developed healthcare establishments include:

1. Robustness of the structure against natural disasters
2. New inbuilt facilities within the structure to enhance contamination resilience
3. Lean hospital designing toward contamination mitigation
4. Resource networking for enhanced surge
5. Cost-effective innovations for healthcare establishment

Earthquake-resistant infrastructure build up, the location of isolation and quarantine wards, and the ability to adapt to manage the flow of con-taminated victims while isolating them from the non-contaminated pop-ulation at the hospital itself, are some of the features of CBRN-designated healthcare facilities. Some of the critical infrastructural requirements that can transform a newly developing hospital into a "contaminant-resilient" hospital are hot operating theaters (OTs) that can manage contaminated victims directly; upgradation of district level fire and emergency services toward inclusion of hospital decontamination system; wide area network-ing (WAN)-based security system allowing businesses in residential areas to continue; detection system alerts for the activation of various evacua-tion plans; antidote surge and critical storage in accessible corridors and security vaults; highly contaminated items/clothing disposal/incineration/

decomposition system; diagnostic networks and sample collection, dispense, and recovery systems; specialized tertiary care facility such as bone marrow transplantation; beta radiation–induced burn surgery management, and so on. Such innovative ideas adopted from industry need to be customized to fulfill these requirements. The ensuing subsections describe infrastructural innovation that can be designed and integrated into evolving health management strategies to support the dynamicity of the process of establishing a healthcare institution with intrinsic resilience toward contamination hazards.

INFRASTRUCTURAL RESILIENCE: EARTHQUAKE-RESISTANT HEALTHCARE ESTABLISHMENTS

Structural resilience refers to the capacity of a system to tolerate perturbation or disturbances without collapsing into a qualitatively different state, to withstand shock and rebuild whenever necessary. Hospitals and other healthcare facilities are top-priority lifeline buildings among the more than 120 million buildings in seismic zones III, IV, and V of the Indian subcontinent. Seismic retrofitting of structural foundations as well as non-structural components such as building finishes and contents based on rapid visual screening and detailed vulnerability assessment (DVA) are required for all existing healthcare facilities. India has adopted a quality accreditation procedure that requires these buildings to be resilient against natural phenomena. Preconstructed buildings or those under construction should fulfill the requirement of earthquake-resistant design and construction-related Bureau of Indian Standards (BIS) codes IS: 4326; IS:13920, and IS: 13935.[5]

SUPERIMPOSING LEAN HOSPITAL DESIGN PRINCIPLES FOR "CONTAMINATION MITIGATION"

The Lean hospital design sequentially focuses first on designing waste-free processes followed by the actual design of the facility accommodating these processes. The current contamination hazard management model has been adapted from the Lean hospital design process described by Chris Lloyd.[6] The intrinsic principle of initiation of any design is linked to the voice of the customer or the client's perspective and safety. In accordance with the client's preferences, one of which is "special needs," a service needs to be rendered through an agreement process. The aim of this model is to reduce waiting time or time wasted during an irrelevant process while also converting this time into a quality period of certain utility. However, contamination management should start even before entering the hospital. Fear and panic will continue until everyone admitted to the hospital has been decontaminated. In order to reduce the long waiting time until decontamination, the scale of the emergency defines the need of the victim in relation to the surge capacity of the hospital. The process becomes extremely cost-effective as the integral design structure of the hospital will allow a greatly enhanced surge capacity. The next step would be to test CBRN decontamination scenarios using simulation modeling. In 2010, CBRN emergency management wards were developed at critical sites while preparing for any eventuality expected during the Commonwealth Games in New Delhi, India.

The next step is to freeze the design, which requires multiple expertise to advise upon the efficiency of various decontamination agents, their probable efficacy, the cost of stockpiling and linked shelf life, the available industrial suppliers, matching the material supply unit size with respect to the structural design to reduce efforts in extending capacity, and an integrated design to maintain privacy/use during peacetime. Thus, it should be a team-enabled process. First, the macro layout is defined followed by the micro layout for each step supported by infrastructure and the requisite supplies to be built within. The design will be finalized for the commissioning process. The commissioning process starts with exploring the steps of preplanning to identify needs and capabilities as well to design multiple solutions to a query proposed in order to critically analyze and identify the best possible solution. A detailed design using these solutions will be developed and implemented in the establishment of the facility. Figure 13.1 describes the various innovative technological/infrastructural requirements needed to support a typical decontamination setup.

The fixed decontamination facility contains an automated decontamination (decon) chamber with a minimum of five separate divisions for entry by male, female/child (both walking and non-walking), and responder, respectively; built-in detectors to check the level of contamination after washing with decon agent(s); a cassette-based system to install a CBRN agent–specific decon system; a microprocessor to regulate the threshold limits decided for the decontamination level (based on the level of the

Macro Layout of Decon Cycle	Structural Resilience Attributes	Functional Resilience Attributes
Secondary Triage	— Multiple route patterns with associated flexibility from ambulance/evacuation vehicle to point of entry — Detection (automated) gates or hand hand equipment — Medical First Responder's (MFRs) Suits should be available	— Skilled staff able to perform secondary triage and collect data/transfer the ambulatory patient to the point of entry — Trained to use the detection equipment effectively — Tagging cards for victims to designate their point of entry and bags to collect jewels
De-clothing	— Closed/covered section to maintain privacy — Instructions layout in English, Hindi and regional language — Provided with specific clothe/jewellery cutter for ambulatory victims support — Adequate number of small bags with tags to collect costly items — Eco-pots linked with hoses to dispose off the clothes in black bags	— Trained staff to manage psychology of victims especially females to remove their jewelry especially marriage related jewels — Able to remove the clothes of ambulatory victims without delay while preventing aggravation of trauma or spread of contamination — Decontamination suits are preferableat this site
Decontamination	— Automated station able to screen the load and conduct decon cycles accordingly — Distant load of different cassettes of decon material — Automated waste collection and drying system without human interference — Powerful suction and air based touch free drying	— Digital info system to count the tag (waterproof) for quality check of decon level achieved; able to change threshold limits based on mass casualty incidence — Auxiliary technical support in adjacent support facility so that automation remained functional at all times — Fuel backup to restore the power at any time
Re-clothing	— Medicated aprons so that any micro-flora is dosen't to grow — Able to manage ambient temperature of body — Tag drier facility so that number of victim remained intact	— Supported trained staff essential for ambulatory victims and vulnerable victims — Able to provide directions to some victims who appears to be fine and tough after such decontamination procedures, but they might feel itchy
Frisking	— Automated/semi-automated/gated/fully man-based facility to detect levels of contamination left prior to entering into clean zone	— Trained staff to conduct frisking, tertiary triage to direct the outflow of the victims towords designated locations
Parallel Supportive Flow	— Parallel movement of staff through frisking doors at tech support, supply/power support and data management system sections	— Trained staff essential to provide these supportive systems in place to ensure continuous operations

FIGURE 13.1
Macro-layout design of typical decontamination set up

incidence); a linked one side open valve hatch to dispose of contaminated clothes; a waste collection chamber to collect the contaminated water that is linked to a bigger chamber with highly absorbing sacs, which converts the waste into dried matter that is transportable to an isolated dumping location. Figure 13.2 describes the built-in decontamination unit in the layout of a multistorey tertiary care facility. The deployable decon units possess the same design; however, they are self-operable and expandable

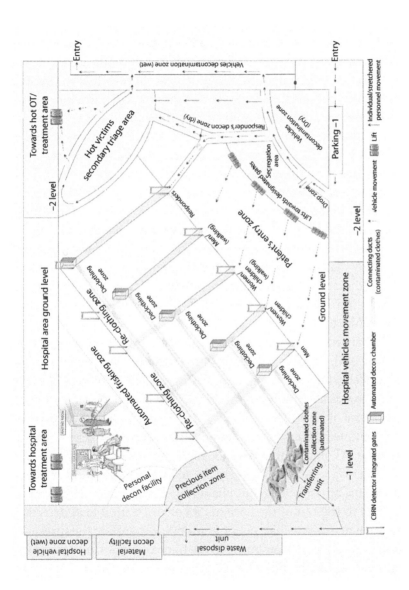

FIGURE 13.2
Hospital-based decontamination facility.

to manage mass casualty events at a preidentified location in the open area of the hospital to enhance the surge capacity of the designated hospital.

Identifying Critical Sites for Hot Operation Theater(s)

During a mass casualty event involving contamination, casualties with the highest triage category, transported from the hot zones at the incident site, undergo localized medical decontamination procedures while en route in the emergency evacuation vehicle. Such victims might require immediate surgical intervention, thus they need to be allowed into the OTs despite being partially contaminated. The OTs designated for such purposes are referred as Hot OTs. These Hot OTs require innovative features to be built into the structure to ensure its immediate transition. These include marking out an isolated route (from point of entry) duly modifiable to cut off from the rest of the hospital to reach the Hot OT; structural modification at the entry point, a hot air high pressure flow chamber to remove surface contamination; provision of protective clothing for surgeons and associated staff that can resist cross-contamination; modified eco-waste pots that can digest the contaminated waste into a disposable biomass at preidentified disposal sites; and chemical/UV/gas-based material decontamination cabinets.

The facility should be designed to be linked such that the airflow and the water flow of these OTs go directly to the contaminated air/water collection chamber while delinking it from the rest of the hospital's waste management system. Air ducts should be installed with dedicated masks for surgeons and staff within the OT so that they can breathe clean air. Staff trained in medical decontamination should accompany the surgical team; reusable OT positioning devices; high-range monitoring cameras for non-interfering monitoring to help the team during unwanted emergency situations; an airlock clothes changing chamber so that its flow is not connected to the rest of the hospital; a contamination load detection system to warn of any possible contamination hazard above the threshold value; control access time monitoring to estimate the exposure time of the operating team, which should be linked internally to the normal OTs with different internal dual-gated procedures with hot air pressure flow so that once the major surgery and decontamination are completed, the victim can be transferred to a normal OT for completion of the final procedures. Such OTs will enhance the surge capacity to deal with hot victims requiring surgical interventions.

Cost-Effective Transition of Specialized Divisions

The use of an existing specialized facility for CBRN emergency management would be a cost-effective solution to mitigate the impact of such emergencies at hospitals. Some transitions and their relative economic impact are given in Table 13.1

Locating Isolation and Quarantine Wards

Isolation and quarantine wards are useful for (a) isolating chemical or radioactive elemental exposed/contaminated victims to prevent them from catching infections from others; and (b) quarantining victims who have been exposed to biothreat agents and who can infect others. However, in the former case, isolating the air supply is not essential while in the latter case, it is always recommended to have an isolated supply to ensure that an agent is not spreading through the air ducts. In both cases, human excreta and biomedical waste should be segregated from the other biological waste of the hospital. Such wards should be equipped with advanced facilities for continuous monitoring of vital patterns; oxygen duct supply; and double-door entry points with a pressurized airflow. The relative humidity of such wards should be controlled and bath/toilet units should be built within the structural facility having a separate waste collecting storage unit. They should be airlock units to ensure complete isolation. The route patterns of entry and exit from the area, the protocol of visits by managing staff including experts' visits, and double-walled mirror separation with an auditory unit to meet the relatives while maintaining isolation are essential elements of such wards/facility.

SURGE AND RELATIVE ECONOMIC IMPACT

Surge is a relative term as it is a factor that defines resilience in terms of the extended coping ability of the healthcare facility with respect to its existing capacity. It is not a simple ratio of capacities, but a culmination of (1) the resources that can be utilized optimally by material triage along with a pre-identified vendor-based emergency supply system; (2) the structural advantages/limitations of the facility; (3) the manpower expertise and maximum extensible utility; and (4) the hospital's network-based augmentative surge.

TABLE 13.1

Reorientation of Some Hospital Facilities toward Contamination Mitigation

Existing Facility[a]	Reorientation toward Additional Responsibilities	Relative Economic Impact with Respect to Development of New Facility
Bone Marrow Transplantation	To manage hematopoietic syndrome in gamma radiation–exposed individuals.	No significant economic impact.
Testing/ Diagnostic Facility	Reorientation to add other biomarker tests to understand the effect of drugs.	Structural development of contaminated sample treatment zones; basic equipment; and specific chemicals for such bioassays are required—little impact.
Gamma Camera Facility	Reorient to use for radio-isotopic distribution and therapeutic effects of decorporation drugs over a period of time.	Nil; however, confirmed diagnostics can be achieved by linking it with high-resolution sector field inductive coupled plasma mass spectroscopy facilities. This will require standardization of sample collection and safe dispatch.
Hospital Pharmacy	Reorient hospital pharmacy to develop ties with antidotes/ vaccines/prophylactics/ immunomodulators/anti-toxins/empirically evident trial drugs/drugs under Phase II trials/third- and fourth-line antimicrobials/contaminated wound care ointments/ supportive care growth regulators, cytokines, etc., useful for the mitigation of the deleterious impact of CBRN agents on the human body.	Hospital-level surge planning will decipher their quantities and turnover cycle contributing toward the economic impact. However, no new structure or staff will be required. The extended storage areas within designs can save a lot.
Gastroenterology and Neurology	Reorient to manage acute radiation multiorgan dysfunction syndrome and nerve agents poisoning, etc.	Only training doctors/staff will have little impact. Structural design to include isolation wards is necessary.

(Continued)

TABLE 13.1 (CONTINUED)

Reorientation of Some Hospital Facilities toward Contamination Mitigation

Existing Facility[a]	Reorientation toward Additional Responsibilities	Relative Economic Impact with Respect to Development of New Facility
Clinical Microbiology	Upgradation to include multi-drug-resistant reemerging pathogens and biological warfare agents.	Significant impact if hospital is designated to manage all types of biological warfare agents, as complete cyclic process of management needs biosafety level to complement the respective agents. Separately deployable facility near hospital is a more economically viable choice with respect to safety consideration.
Reconstructive Plastic Surgery	Skin lesions during an attack of blister agents or beta burns, etc., will be additionally managed.	Nil, except cost factor to manage such victims as long-term hospital stay will be a critical limitation.
Respiratory Care	Lung asphyxiates and the microbial induction of lung infections, etc., requires such facility.	Nil.
Other Departments	Reorient to include the needs of CBRN agent-induced bodily harm.	Minimal.
AYUSH Facility	Ayurveda, yoga, unani, siddha, and homeopathy facility needs to be reoriented to include various probable Natural Plant Products (NPP) or other modalities for efficient and faster recovery, utilizing both scientific and empirical evidence-based research/ requisite approvals of competent regulatory bodies.	Both an unknown agent attack (not detected earlier) and palliative care require such modalities. Significant impact as such departments are currently non-existent or if they do exist, are not backed up by significant pharma-based research and development.

[a] List is not exhaustive and is limited to selected departments only.

In the case of acute contamination by CBRN agents, these factor(s) do not vary with the exception of the psychological impact on manpower and the vendor-based supply system. However, in the case of a Level 2/3 biological emergency, panic might lead to social disruption and the continuous absenteeism of critical manpower, worsening the situation. Thus, defining an absolute surge is not a "value" but a dynamic estimate. In general, the minimum surge for a 200-bedded hospital should be two times with respect to a mass casualty event provided the facility has a significant open area.

Lean Design to Augment Surge of Medical Countermeasures

The U.S. Strategic National Stockpile (SNS) Program is responsible for the management and delivery of life-saving medicines and other essential commodities during an emergency affecting the community. The Centre for Disease Control in the United States claims that using the SNS,

> *"it can provide emergency medicine to protect the nation against highest-risk threats for under $2 per person, per year."*

The prime health preparedness spectral arenas identified by the CDC to manage a bioterrorism threat include biosurveillance, community resilience, countermeasures and mitigation, incident management, information management, and surge management.[7] The Iris Medication Management System as described by Biswas S.K. and Singh V.K. (2015)[8] provides details about use of lean operation in hospital planning and design. The ensuing section describes how this system can be integrated with respect to changed needs to manage internal contamination due to radioactive chemicals, chemical warfare agents, and biological agents. The important aspects linked to such superimposition include:

- Industry-based inventory system to stockpile the products at designated locations as extra storage units other than at hospitals (along with their turnover time, etc.).
- Optimization model to utilize existing dosages at hospitals for the first 48 hours until the network approach–based dosages are unavailable.
- Specific diagnostic support (not available within hospital limits) should also be linked to such network support.

The prime principles of Lean design are to eliminate waste by reducing or removing defects, transportation, overproduction, inventory, waiting, motion, non-utilization of staff, excess processing, categorization and prioritization with respect to the risk/hazard, and available time lines. The proposed changes in the system to manage contamination hazard include:

- The patient unique identifier and the tertiary triage card number (bar coded) should be the same to ensure that "decontaminated victims" are designated to the right arena to prevent waste of resources.
- The expected ratio of worried well category to extremely affected victims can be significantly high, thus a tertiary triage–linked reception zone should be designed to manage fear, equipped with trained staff; regular medications available at hospitals are used to manage the worried well category who get filtered at this stage.

The antidotes for all CBRN agents need to be stockpiled at designated hospitals; however, this appears to be detrimental with respect to the economic impact. An antimicrobial stewardship program with the cooperation of pharmacists, infectious disease specialists, and clinical microbiologists under able leadership can reduce selective pressure-induced resistance patterns.[9] However, such a program requires a complete structure that should support awareness campaigns in its outreach to the community.

The question arises which antidotes/countermeasures/vaccines should be stored and which should be available through a networking approach. The antidotes/essential medical countermeasures to manage the health effects of contamination agents should consider the following factors:

- Requirement of countermeasure—prophylactic, immediately after exposure/delayed administration (after complete diagnostics)
- Lifesaving or supportive countermeasure
- Shelf life and storage conditions
- Dosage requirement/adult in first 48 hours
- Available commercially in the market or its analog or only from specific manufacturers
- Efficacy pattern with respect to time of administration
- Route of drug administrable should be preferably oral or self injectable through auto injectors.
- Does it need medical supervision while being administered?
- Possible side effects of dosing if the victim is not contaminated and mistakenly administered
- Cost imperatives and probable threat to utility by terrorist groups
- Whether linked to any existing national or international stockpiling policy

- If available through other policies, the minimum time to reach the hospital site during worst-case scenarios

The abovementioned indicators direct the design of a waste-free process with effective time lines to manage casualties in the first 48 hours based on the expected scenario. The process needs to be supported by corridor walls and various quality designs to accommodate storage at various temperature ranges/other conditions while simultaneously authorizing access to ensure optimal usage during emergencies.

SECURITY AGAINST SECONDARY ATTACKS

Terrorist attacks on soft and vulnerable targets such as schools, hospitals, and so on are an emerging trend. Sequential bomb attacks also show a similar pattern that after an interval during which time casualties have reached hospitals, secondary bomb attacks at hospital sites have been observed. In 2008, in Ahmedabad, Gujarat, India, 21 bomb blasts hit the city within a span of 70 minutes in which 56 people died and more than 200 were injured.[10] Of these 21 blasts, 2 blasts occurred on the premises of different hospitals 40 minutes later when the injured were being admitted to these hospitals.[11,12] This act of brutality shows that the terrorist's strategy of secondary attacks can trigger much more panic, fear, and chaos. Considering the possibility that such attacks might contain CBRN material, then dirty attacks will further aggravate the situation. The prehospital care, the secondary healthcare at the hospital reception including decontamination, and eventually the tertiary lifesaving care will be significantly affected. The deployment of physical security measures at hospitals is essential. The Joint Commission standard EC.2.10 requires a hospital to identify its own security risks:

> *"It is essential that a hospital manages the physical and personal security of patients, staff (including the potential for violence to patients and staff in the workplace) and individuals coming to the hospital's buildings".*[13]

Security should be multilayered and the design of a hospital should support the mitigation of security threats. It should include security systems, motion detectors, surveillance cameras, bullet-resistant windows, and key-lock systems at hospital pharmacies[14] as well as at other critical sites. A terrorism response plan should be in place with each functional section connected as part of a primary, supportive, and contingency plan to be executed with the support of emergency responders.[15] A trend in shooter incidences has also increased at the hospital level. A study suggests that between 2000 and 2012, there were 154 shooter incidences in American hospitals, raising security concerns to have gun lockers at each entrance and enhanced surveillance measures in place.[16]

Security measures to prevent dirty bomb attacks should include gates that have metal and radiation detectors, physical security to frisk any chemical warfare agents, and unlabeled fluids or dry mass should be checked in every suspicious cases. Microbial load counters for the surveillance of any biological threat along with sensitive areas with a radiation monitoring system should be the second layer of the design. The movement of patients, to identify anything suspicious, requires design-supported invisible cameras. An interlocking mechanism between the various sensitive areas is essential to ensure that the area under attack can be isolated. An evacuation plan for hospitals should be developed prior to the finalization of the hospital design as there would be mixed populations of ambulatory, support staff, or relatives to ambulatory and non-ambulatory victims, and so on. The plans need to define priority and thus a structural plan should support this functional aspect. To manage dirty bomb mitigation while escaping from the contaminated dust, necessary handheld respiratory apparatus are necessary along with other safety equipment and antidotes, and the corridor walls should be designed with storage to make these accessible so that they can be made available immediately with the help of an emergency evacuation team. This is a similar approach to a fire hazard plan with pipes, hammers, and mist sprays to manage fire. In terms of airborne infections preventive care against both accidental and intentional attacks, it has been observed that the most cost-effective strategy to achieve high levels of air disinfection is germicidal irradiation of a room as compared to other mechanical modes.[17] These security measures, though appearing costly as a first line of investment, act as an insurance cover against attacks, thus they cannot be ignored.

Business Continuity System against Security Hazards

The business continuity operation planning of a healthcare establishment refers to the presence of critical staff and resources to manage basic to advanced operations. During the spread of unknown biological agents, the panic caused might lead to the evacuation of hospitals for normal healthcare.

In such cases, the nearby residential areas with resident doctors/staff need to have a security system and a procedural system to utilize their services in the most effective manner. Some of the key elements include: (1) telemedicine concept with household connectivity to advise regular outbound patients that they are not allowed to visit the hospital during such periods; (2) special advisory panel video conference meeting to discuss critical cases and the dynamics of procedures through such in-house built systems; (3) dynamic panels that can be controlled at a few identified control centers to change the access and non-access pathways; (4) vendor-based resource management and digitally enabled decision-making tools provisions to enhance resource inventory for such periods; (5) monitoring of isolation and quarantine wards staffed with critical personnel from the household locations; (6) movement of advisory designs compatible with structural facility designs to accommodate such changes for a long period so that the spread can be contained while providing effective tertiary care. It is important to understand that in such cases, the microorganism could affect numerous bodily functions including the neural system. On the other hand, the worried well category, that is, their relatives, might pose a serious security threat to such facilities. Numerous IT service providers can provide robust, cost-effective WAN/cloud-based security and an information exchange system in such areas if integrated at the design stage. Lean hospital design calls for the development of these procedures prior to designing such structural facilities able to support business continuity operations.

CONTAMINATED WASTE MANAGEMENT SYSTEM

Waste management practices to keep hospitals safe during mass casualty events involving contamination require numerous structural features to be built in to the design format. According to the Lean design concept: the staff requirement, its directional movement, specific doors with restricted access; separate lifts for the transfer of contaminated waste; and training and awareness to remove fear/myths are important practices to be established first. The design should accommodate wastebins lined with lead as a radioactive shield; however, soil-casted disposable bins can also be used as these are cost-effective, though their thickness might lead to an increase in weight. The empirical scientific evidence states that soil or concrete with appropriate thickness can shield against radioactivity exposure though this is yet to be proven via scientific studies.

A collection site with cemented inbound walled pits should be included at the design stage of the preidentified site to prevent the spread of contamination to the ecosystem. The micro-floral species that will be used for decomposing such waste should be identified. Chemical and biological waste should be managed as per the general precautions laid down by the infection control committee of the hospital. It is pertinent to understand that in the case of Category A/B biological warfare agents, biosafety and biosecurity plans need to be activated. Such measures require designs with least human interference to prevent cross-contamination.

The networking of hospitals with nodal departments for CBRN waste management and preparedness plans is required to be laid down accordingly. A separate area for the transit of carriers that will carry this waste needs to be defined. The "dilute, delay, and decay" concept, neutralization, and antimicrobials concept design need to be incorporated to manage radioactive chemicals, chemical warfare agents, and biological waste management, respectively. The bulk storage areas for these chemicals and delay tanks are also a critical structural requirement.

INDUSTRIAL INDOVATIONS

The India Innovative Growth Program saw a tremendous increase in the number of applications of innovative processes: 110 in 2007 to 819 in 2012.[18] An analysis of end-user industrial classification of the technologies in this program showed that the growth share of pharmaceutical and healthcare technologies (averaged on an annual basis) based on the data was 7% in 2007 and had reached nearly 60% in 2012.[19,20] Table 13.2 lists the selected technologies of pharmaceuticals and healthcare. These Indovations (Innovations of India)[21] are indicators that the efforts to provide comfort and care to patients are increasing day by day. Knowledge of these technologies to upgrade the design of a healthcare facility to match these requirements should also be incorporated as part of the strategy. Global innovations should also be explored while finalizing a waste-free process in a Lean hospital design.

TABLE 13.2

Pharmaceutical and Health Sector Indovations under IGIP (2007–2015)

Healthcare	Indovations[a]
Diagnostic Care	X-ray to 3-D; serum-based kit for the diagnosis of visceral leishmaniasis (Kala-Azar) and PKDL; efficient cost-effective detection kits for banana viruses; low-cost point-of-care diagnostic device for blood cell counting; SES-molecular diagnostic services; beta-thalassemia carrier detection kit; LAMP-based diagnostics; sensory array–based wideframe digital diagnostic x-ray imager; complete indigenous technology to spin hemodialysis-grade hollow fiber membranes; low-cost portable and safe digital x-ray for use in orthopedics and pediatrics clinics; development of x-ray visible polymers for non-invasive imaging applications; ENT multiscope and recorder plastic biochip–based disposable electrochemical immunosensor; and MEMS sensor.
Decision-Making Aid Tools and Biomedical Devices	Physician-Assisted Artificial Intelligence System (PAIRS)—logical medical systems; an apparatus for automating pathological procedures; biomedical instrument compatible with telemedicine system automated microscopic investigations.
Pregnancy and Infant Child Care	MiraCradle—neonate cooler; smartphone-integrated non-invasive fetal ECG monitor to detect fetal distress; emergency labor cot for child delivery at remote access; ICT intervention to empower maternal healthcare (Chetna); CareMother—mobile pre- and high-risk care—digital sensors–based pregnancy care.
Orthopedic and Trauma Care	Bioadhesives—protein-based adhesive material replaces stitches, staples, and screws used in repairing damaged tissues; a versatile and intelligent biomechanical medical device for regenerating new bone in the human body; bionic arms; bone grafts designed via a biomimetic approach from natural origin materials; innovative and cost-effective knee-ankle-foot orthosis.
Cardiac Care	Mobile-based heart disease and stroke detection system; nanopolymer coating on coronary stent systems and; CardioTrack—remote ECG diagnostics.
Cancer Care	Recombinant protein with serological and cancer diagnostic application; non-invasive oral cancer detection device; biomimetic smart aerosols for lung cancer, tuberculosis, and other pulmonary diseases; a novel therapy for colon cancer.
Visually Challenged and Ophthalmic Care	Electronic pen aiding visually impaired in reading and understanding textual contents; 3nethra—an intelligent prescreening ophthalmology device; handheld digital retinal imaging system; visually challenged ergonomic behavior.

(Continued)

TABLE 13.2 (CONTINUED)

Pharmaceutical and Health Sector Indovations under IGIP (2007–2015)

Healthcare	Indovations[a]
Diabetic Care	A continuous non-invasive blood glucose monitoring system based on photoacoustic spectroscopy; companion diagnostics for diabetes management—simple test to detect anti-insulin antibodies allows switching of insulin analogs; diabetes complication diagnosis and guidance; making natural sugar diabetic friendly; a new method for detecting diabetic neuropathy and predicting foot ulcer development.
Dental Care	Broad spectrum root canal filling composition for endodontic usage; 2 in1 self-secured orthodontic spring separator for dental patients; automatic dental x-ray processor.
Pharmaceuticals	A novel antibiotic adjuvant entity for lowering antimicrobial resistance; drug discovery/drug target identification technology; screening tools for the detection of DNA damaging agents; novel herbal formulation for arthritis and related conditions; novel topical microemulsion formulations for the treatment of rheumatic disorders and related infections; Asthma Cure, a herbal product for curing asthma and bronchitis/allergy; natural formulation for chronic wound healing; oral sustained-release nanodrug for the treatment of tuberculosis; natural product–based formulations for Capccin (arthritic pain relief); and natural product–based formulation for aseptic.
Clinical and Follow-Up Care	Photodynamic therapy laser system—destroys cancerous cells; an improved method and system for ventricular defibrillation; fabric-based heating elements for warmth/fomentation in medical applications; dance aid for deaf; genetic diagnosis and personalized medicine for maximum healthcare; mobility solution for patients with neurological disorder/spinal cord injury; home-based devices for speech and language problems; technology platform for producing proteins and viral therapies; safety medical device to safeguard medical professionals from needle stick injuries and blood-borne infections during needle withdrawal and disposal.

[a] Technologies identified under the India Innovative Growth Program (2007–2015) under the Pharmaceuticals and Healthcare Sector.[19,20]

SUMMARY

Contamination threats are pertinent and require the integration of innovative ideas at the conceptualization, design, and development stages of the healthcare establishment itself. A rigorous framework evolved will accelerate the (surge) process of adaptation and the ability to recover

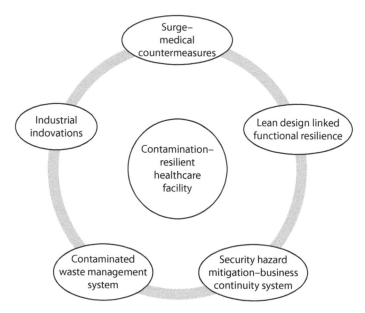

FIGURE 13.3
Contamination-resilient healthcare design.

(resilience) from any known and unknown contamination "security and safety" hazards. The design of a healthcare facility accommodating such provisions leads to and escalates cost imperatives. However, during a mass casualty event involving contamination hazards, the lack of such provisions will either cripple the system or lead to its complete closure/functional non-performance for a very long period.

Structural resilience targeting cost-effective strategies and its integration with dynamic management practices can transform newly developing hospitals into "contaminant resilient." The balanced approach is to include structural-based provisions at the design and development stages while functional-based requirements can be fulfilled in a phased manner. Such an optimal strategy can provide long-term benefits with respect to a relatively less-significant short-term economic impact. Figure 13.3 illustrates the conceptual design to accommodate critical features that summarize the contamination-resilient design of a healthcare facility.

The intrinsic resilience is linked to orient industrial attention toward such needs and its relative impact on the manufacturing sector in an evolutionary manner. An inbuilt process able to envision long-term benefits with respect to short-term economic impacts is a formidable challenge.

The culmination of cost-effective strategies to reduce the economic impact is the only viable choice that will create a platform to mitigate this challenge. In addition, a strategy to create awareness, train doctors and other staff, and use mock exercises to test the hospital emergency management plans can further contribute toward "contamination resilience."

"A thought or idea is the beginning of innovation and small but continuous steps can provide an effective and implementable solution in the long term".

REFERENCES

1. Comscore. (2015). Preventing CBRNE Terrorism. http://www.interpol.int/Crime-areas/Terrorism/CBRNE/Preventing-CBRNE-terrorism. (Accessed 25 June, 2015.)
2. Taylor L.H., Latham S.M., and Woolhouse M.E. (2001). Risk factors for human disease emergence. *Philos Trans R Soc Lond B Biol Sci* Vol. 356, pp. 983–989. Archived in http://wwwnc.cdc.gov/eid/article/11/12/05-0997_article.
3. Passi D., Sharma S., Dutta S.R., Dudeja P., and Sharma V. (2015). Ebola virus disease (the killer virus): Another threat to humans and bioterrorism: Brief review and recent updates. *J Clin Diagn Res* Vol. 9, No. 6, pp. 1–8.
4. Comscore. (2014). Wael Daddous, Inside the Ebola Outbreak. Frontline Documentary filmed at Sierra Leone released by pbs.org. http://www.pbs.org/wgbh/pages/frontline/ebola-outbreak. (Accessed 21 June, 2015.)
5. Comscore. (2007). National Disaster Management Guidelines on Earthquakes. www.ndma.gov.in. (Accessed 31 July, 2015.)
6. Lloyd C. (2014). Innovative approaches to build health care facilities. In Singh V.K. and Lillrank P (eds). *Innovations in Healthcare Management: Cost Effective and Sustainable Solutions* (pp. 93–106). CRC Press, Boca Raton, Florida.
7. Comscore. (2015). National Snapshot of Public Health Preparedness. https://www.cdc.gov/phpr/pubs-links/2015/index.html. (Accessed 14 August, 2015.)
8. Biswas S.K., and Singh V.K. (2014). Hospital planning and design innovation for lean operations. In Singh V.K. and Lillrank P. *Innovations in Healthcare Management: Cost Effective and Sustainable Solutions* (pp. 93–106). CRC Press, Boca Raton, Florida.
9. Kim J., Craft D.W., and Katzman M. (2015). Building an antimicrobial stewardship program: Cooperative roles for pharmacists, infectious diseases specialists, and clinical microbiologists. *Lab Med* Vol. 46, No. 2, pp. e65–71.
10. Comscore. (2008). Gujarat police release three sketches. The Hindu. Kasturi & Sons Ltd. 6 August 2008. Archived in Wikipedia. (Reference No.3: https://en.wikipedia.org/wiki/2008_Ahmedabad_bombings.)
11. Comscore. (2008). Death toll in Ahmedabad serial blasts rises to 55. Khabrein.info. 1 August 2008. Archived in Wikipedia. (Reference No.4: https://en.wikipedia.org/wiki/2008_Ahmedabad_bombings).
12. Comscore. (2008). Indian cities on high alert after blasts. CNN (Turner Broadcasting System). 27 July 2008. Archived in Wikipedia. (Reference No.13: https://en.wikipedia.org/wiki/2008_Ahmedabad_bombings.)

13. Comscore. (2015). Joint Commission Requirements. http://www.hcpro.com/HOM-73140-5577/Joint-Commission-Requirements.html. (Accessed 14 August, 2015.)
14. Smolarek R.T., Roffe B.D., and Solomon D.K. (1984). Types of selected security devices for hospital pharmacies. *Hosp Pharm* Vol. 19, No. 12, pp. 795–797.
15. White D.E. (2002). A terrorism response plan for hospital security and safety officers. *J Healthc Prot Manage* Vol. 18, No. 1, pp. 15–23.
16. No Authors Listed. (2014). Experts advise hospitals to heed warning signs, leverage security to prepare against shootings. *ED Manage* Vol. 26, No. 9, pp. 97–101.
17. Nardell E.A. (2015). Indoor environmental control of TB and other airborne infections. *Indoor Air* Vol. 26, pp. 79–87. doi: 10.1111/ina.12232.
18. Conscore. (2012). Compendium of Selected Technologies: DST-Lockheed Martin India Innovative Growth Programme (2007–2012). http://www.indiainnovates.in/pdfs/DST-Innovation-Growth-Report-2012.pdf. (Accessed 15 July, 2015.)
19. Conscore. (2013). DST-Lockheed Programme—Brochure. http://www.indiainnovates.in/pdfs/DST-Lockheed-Programme-Brochure2013.pdf. (Accessed 15 July, 2015.)
20. Conscore. (2015). India Innovative Growth Programme—Results. http://www.indiainnovates.in/images/iigp2015results.pdf. (Accessed 30 July, 2015.)
21. Bhalla S., and Verma N.S. (2014). Indovations: Frugal innovations in Indian health care. In Singh V.K. and Lillrank P (eds). *Innovations in Healthcare Management: Cost Effective and Sustainable Solutions* (pp. 319–360). CRC Press, Boca Raton, Florida.

14

Adapt or Obsolesce: The Evolution of Singapore Health System

Matthew Saunders

CONTENTS

BACKGROUND: HOW THE SINGAPORE HEALTH SYSTEM WAS BORN

> It is not the strongest of the species that survives or the most intelligent but the one most responsive to change.
>
> **Charles Darwin, 1809**

This chapter looks at Singapore's healthcare facilities from the outside in, examining the influences that are shaping their new, leaner future. But to glimpse their future, we must understand their origins. South East Asia is undergoing a significant healthcare evolution reflecting its rapid economic growth. However, health inequalities across the countries of the region reflect the contrasts in their differing rates of growth and their response to change. Singapore has been on its own meteoric trajectory since its expulsion from the Federation of Malaysia and an economically and politically challenging start to its independence in 1965. Per capita income was then US$516 compared with US$1851 in the United Kingdom, which was also emerging from the devastation of the Second World War.[1] Fifty years later, Singapore's per capita income has overtaken that of both the United Kingdom and the United States.[1] However, World Bank Data in 2013 shows that Singapore has managed to limit its expenditure on health to just 4.6% of gross domestic product (GDP) compared with 9.1% in the United Kingdom and an eye-popping 17.1% in the United States.[2] This has not been at the expense of health outcomes. In 2013, Singaporeans could expect to live to an average age of 82, compared with 81 years in the United Kingdom and 79 years in the United States.[3] Similarly, between 2010 and 2014, infant mortality rates in Singapore were 2 per 1000 live births compared to 4 in the United Kingdom and 6 in the United States.[4] So, what has characterized Singapore's response to the challenges and has led to this divergence of outcomes?

Making Quantum Leaps

Singapore is interesting because its small size and single-party-dominated political system have made it agile and able to respond quickly to changing circumstances. It continues to learn from the experiences of developed economies and avoids the same pitfalls. Singapore recognized the prime determinants of health early on, investing in sanitation, clean water supplies, public transport infrastructure, education, good public housing (82% of Singaporeans live in public housing development board [HDB] accommodation),[5] and of course healthcare. However, Singapore's social welfare policies have tended to favor the development of the young and working population over the elderly and disabled in its drive to develop its economy.

A Policy of Self-Reliance

Lee Kuan Yew, prime minister of Singapore from its independence in 1965 until stepping down as minister mentor in 1990, guided Singapore's policy with a single-minded determination to vest an individual's own interest in his or her health. Educated as a lawyer at Cambridge in the United Kingdom and called to the Bar in London, he benefited from and admired Aneurin Bevan's National Health Service (NHS) but also observed the problems it faced. In a free healthcare system, where supply is finite, demand is ultimately controlled by waiting times and limitations on service, no matter how much waste and inefficiency are cut out. There is also little incentive to avoid the need to use the system. For those who can afford it, the private sector makes up any shortcomings in the public system.

Singapore inherited its own version of the UK NHS when it was still a British colony; however, faced with extreme economic challenges after independence, Lee Kuan Yew determined that individuals should share the responsibility for their own health and opted for a co-pay system in Singapore. The intention has always been to make people save into government schemes to cover their medical costs. For those on low incomes, a sliding scale of government subsidies was created.

In *Hard Truths To Keep Singapore Going*, Lee Kuan Yew explained that he was mainly concerned in the early days that:

> *...nobody derails the idea of having individual accounts for CPF (Central Provident Fund) and Medisave. Whatever you earn, it's yours. Because once you have that individual account, any suggestion that you put it into a common pool and everybody takes out from it (as with other welfare systems) is bound to lose you votes.*[6]

Lee went on to ask:

> *Are you prepared to put your money into a common pool, having slogged and built up your CPF nest egg? It's yours and if you don't use it, you can leave it*

to your children or your relatives or whoever you like. Why should you put it into a common pool and everybody draws out at your expense, which is what's happening in some Western countries?[6]

In a cautionary note to public servants, Lee Kuan Yew warned:

Subsidies on consumption are wrong and ruinous.....for however wealthy a nation, it cannot carry health, unemployment and pension benefits without massive taxation and overloading the system, reducing the incentives to work and to save and to care for one's family - when all can look to the state for welfare. Social and health benefits are like opium or heroin. People get addicted and the withdrawal of welfare benefits is very painful.[7]

The share of government expenditure on healthcare was quickly reversed. Singapore set up an enduring foundation of a universal healthcare coverage system for its citizens with a financing system based on the twin philosophies of individual responsibility and affordable healthcare for all. To ensure that no Singaporean was denied access to basic affordable healthcare, a multilayer system of protection was evolved. The first tier of cover provides for up to 80% government subsidy based on ability to pay.[8] In 1984, Medisave, the second tier of cover, was introduced.[8] This is a mandatory personal savings scheme for Singaporeans and permanent residents to cover personal and immediate family hospitalization, day surgery, and certain outpatient costs.[8] Contributions range from 8.5% to 10.5% of wages depending on the age group.[8] On December 31, 2010, the average amount in each Medisave account stood at S$16,900, which at the time was enough to pay for between 9 and10 subsidized acute hospital episodes.[8]

In 1990, Medishield, the third tier of protection, was introduced.[8] It is an optional, low-cost, top-up insurance scheme to help contribute to large hospital bills and avoid wiping out an individual's Medisave account.[8] This covers only the cheapest B2/C wards.[8] The government has further risk-pooled a limited amount of the financial risks of severe or catastrophic illnesses or disability with a suit of optional insurance plans: Eldershield and Eldershield Supplement Plans. For middle- and higher-income Singaporeans, they can further supplement their basic cover with private Integrated Shield Plans insurance for treatment in the private sector.[8] To avoid overconsumption, there is still a co-pay element to these insurance schemes. To avoid private insurers "cherry picking" the healthiest clients, the government-run Medishield cover has to be in place as a precondition of offering any top-up insurance.

The fourth and final level of protection is Medifund, a government endowment fund for needy Singaporeans who cannot pay their hospital bills despite the subsidies in place.[8] The Medisave and Medishield insurance system is operated by the government's central provident fund (CPF) board.[8]

These schemes have helped maintain the Singapore government's spending to about 39.8% of healthcare expenditure in Singapore, while in the United Kingdom, 83.5% is covered by the government.[9]

This emphasis on self-reliance, a regulatory framework that controls what doctors charge in the public sector, and subsidies for dormitory-style inpatient wards of 6–12 beds, has largely helped to control cost, minimize bureaucracy, and put money into higher-quality care.

PARADIGM SHIFT: CAUSES OF THIS SHIFT

Despite this effort to contain costs within an affordable universally accessible health system, there are three key factors undermining this structure:

Rising Cost of Healthcare

In recent years, cost inflation of healthcare in Singapore has been running at more than twice the increase in average salaries, which only increased by 2.0% between 2009 and 2014.[10][10,11] This is due in part to advances in medical technology, pharmaceuticals, and specialist procedures. The other major contributor is people living longer into old age and with comorbidities of non-communicable diseases (NCDs) caused by poor lifestyle choices along the way. The cost of healthcare rises exponentially with age. The struggle to cope with the cost of care is exacerbated by the increasingly uneven share of wealth, with the rich getting richer relative to the poor.

In an article, "Reforming Health Care in Singapore," Jeremy Lim highlights the developing inequalities in the system that threaten the social fabric in Singapore:

> *A survey last year revealed that 72 per cent of Singaporeans believed they "cannot afford to get sick these days due to high medical costs." The Singapore Conversation process led by Education Minister Heng Swee Keat also*

identified health-care affordability as a major concern of citizens. This year, the Government Parliamentary Committee for Health issued an unprecedented report recommending changes to improve affordability.[12]

Current subsidies are increasingly proving to be inadequate for many of those least able to pay and most vulnerable in society, who rely on voluntary welfare organizations to bridge the gap. The Singapore government is introducing policies to increase the number of claimable chronic conditions. Since June 1, 2015, epilepsy, osteoporosis, psoriasis, and rheumatoid arthritis are covered under the new community health assist scheme (CHAS) and Medisave.[13] This means that CHAS and Medisave cover most of the common chronic conditions. But is this too little too late? Does it sufficiently relieve the burden on the poor?

Since 2003, the Ministry of Health (MOH) has published a table comparing the total hospital costs at each of its hospitals, extending it to include private hospitals in an effort to create transparency and competition. By 2014, 65 procedures were included in their Table of Surgical Procedures.[14] At the same time, both Malaysia and Thailand have been extending their health tourism programs to provide cheaper alternatives for Singaporeans seeking treatment. Medisave may be used at selected hospitals in Malaysia. This policy has helped to ease the bed crisis experienced in Singapore.

Aging Society

The system worked well for a generation of young, driven Singaporeans who were developing a nation. There was even concern at one stage that the population was growing too fast. In the 1960s, a policy was introduced to restrict the number of children that parents were allowed. That policy was reversed, but to no avail. That generation, now referred to as the Pioneer Generation, is aging and the population is not replacing itself fast enough. Despite policies and financial incentives to reverse the decline, the reproductive rate in 2015 was only 1.2, well below the replacement rate of 2.1 per family.[15] Singapore government statistics predict that by 2030, approximately one in five of the population will be over 65 (Figure 14.1).[16] On average, each person over the retirement age of 65 will be supported by only two working adults compared with around five today.[17] This is placing the cost burden on fewer and fewer shoulders of the working-age population. The baby boomers are the new cohort of elderly who, as they live longer, will consume around 50% of their lifetime healthcare costs

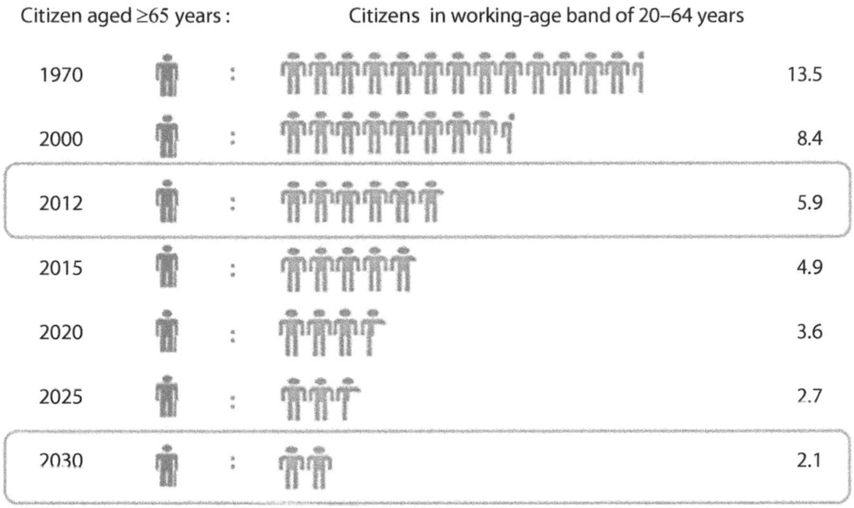

Citizen aged ≥65 years :		Citizens in working-age band of 20–64 years	
1970	👤 :	👥👥👥👥👥👥👥	13.5
2000	👤 :	👥👥👥👥	8.4
2012	👤 :	👥👥👥	5.9
2015	👤 :	👥👥👥	4.9
2020	👤 :	👥👥	3.6
2025	👤 :	👥👥	2.7
2030	👤 :	👥	2.1

FIGURE 14.1

Declining old-age support ratio. (From A Sustainable Population for a Dynamic Singapore [Internet]. Singapore: National Population and Talent Division [cited 2015 August 16]. Chart 1.5: Declining Old-Age Support Ratio (p. 13). Available from: http://population.sg/whitepaper/resource-files/population-white-paper.pdf.)

during their senior years. For those over 85, it is estimated that they will consume one-third of the total.[18]

Rise of Non-Communicable Diseases

NCDs stemming from conditions such as hyperlipidemia, hypertension, and hypoglycemia are leading to chronic conditions such as diabetes, chronic obstructive pulmonary disorder, cardiovascular disease, strokes, and cancers. The incidence of these NCDs is rising, not only among the elderly but also the younger working-age population. For the first time in history, children are less healthy than their parents' generation and are not projected to live as long if nothing is done about it.

Medicine has been passive, where people don't participate in their well-being and doctors are incentivized to diagnose and fix the problem rather than prevent it in the first place. People are still not being offered enough information to make informed healthy choices about nutrition, exercise, or behavioral changes that help prevent the abovementioned conditions and contribute to a happier, stress-reduced life. While there has been a move toward providing nutritional information on food packaging, including percentage contribution to average daily requirements, the food industry has consistently lobbied against it and avoided providing a simple traffic light labeling system to alert people to foodstuffs high in sugar or unhealthy low-density lipoprotein (LDL) cholesterol. Regulators have tended to be slow in taking the initiative. Consider the case of tobacco, where tax revenues are weighed against public health costs and political popularity. There are calls to treat sugar in a similar way to tobacco, but part of the problem is the confused message. For years, people were told to avoid fat, associating it with obesity, but within a generation we are now being told that sugar is the real villain. It is estimated that up to 80% of cases of type 2 diabetes can be delayed or prevented by changes in lifestyle and diet.[20] Similar figures apply to strokes and heart attacks.[21]

This potent cocktail of increasing costs, an aging society, and NCDs is not unique to Singapore. It is an unsustainable situation for any economy. Before we look at how Singapore is responding, let's take a look at the paradigm shift that is beginning to take shape in the developed world.

PARADIGM SHIFT: HOW HEALTHCARE DELIVERY IS RESPONDING

The disruption that is taking place is the combined effect of the aforementioned key factors conspiring to undermine healthcare systems, while colliding with new technologies, the global sharing of data analytics, and models of care that better utilize finite resources. The result is a recognition that it is time for a radical change in how we approach healthcare and that we have many of the tools necessary to effect this change. Possibly the biggest obstacle is winning hearts and minds.

Singapore is adapting as it learns from developed countries who are finding that there is poor utilization of healthcare facilities. In an article entitled "Hospitals May be Disappearing in the Era of Health Care Reform," Robert Pearl explains:

> *A century ago, traveling even moderate distances was incredibly slow and expensive compared to the cost of hospital care. Therefore, building a hospital in every town made sense. Hospitals became a source of great civic pride for community leaders who comprised the governing boards. And so the "community hospital" was born.*

Founded by physicians, religious groups and public municipalities, the number of U.S. hospitals grew exponentially from 178 in 1873 to 4,300 in 1909 to 6,000 in 1946. The passage of the Hill-Burton Act in 1946 helped further expand that number to 7,200 by 1970.

With the introduction of the publicly funded Medicare and Medicaid programs in 1966, the number of individuals with health insurance skyrocketed – as did the demand for inpatient services, as did hospital costs.

By the 1990s, high-margin procedures such as heart bypass surgery and total joint replacement were performed in (and advertised by) nearly every hospital. But the demand for inpatient services sharply declined in the 1990s with the introduction of managed care, the expansion of outpatient alternatives, and the mounting costs of a hospital stay. During that decade, some hospitals were forced to merge or shut down.[22]

What we are seeing is a shift toward facilities that focus on specialist and day procedures. The practitioners are well-practiced at what they do so they tend to get better outcomes than the low-volume facilities; this, in turn, increases the popularity of the specialist centers and increases volumes in a virtuous cycle. Travel is now not an issue. People are prepared to travel to get the best treatment. Low-volume facilities cease to be competitive while they maintain underutilized equipment and staff who are on fixed salaries. Singapore is small, so travel is less of an issue, but attracting health tourism or avoiding Singaporeans going abroad for cheaper healthcare is another matter.

In the United Kingdom, regions are streamlining and integrating services, reducing bed numbers, redistributing accident and emergency (A&E) departments, and repurposing or even closing hospitals to increase efficiency and reduce rising costs to the NHS.

There is also a trend toward having stand-alone urgent care centers, strategically located between communities for ease of access and with very efficient means of transferring complex cases to tertiary and quaternary facilities. The facilities have multidisciplinary teams that meet twice a day to coordinate anything from psychological, medical, surgical, and physical comorbidities. They have specialists in trauma, geriatricians for the frail elderly, rapid assessment units, ambulatory care, operating theaters, and beds for stays of up to 72 hours. Being a newer model of care, it will take time to change the habits of patients. Singapore is developing a similar model with its new, much larger polyclinics that have elder care day services, urgent care centers, and multidisciplinary team practices offering more services previously only available in hospitals.

How Singapore Is Having to Catch Up and Adapt at the Same Time

Integrated Intermediate Care Hubs and the Role of Primary Care

While developed healthcare systems have been looking at reducing the number of expensive acute hospital beds in their system as they transition toward day-care facilities and primary care settings closer to home, Singapore has been suffering an acute shortage of beds. According to World Bank statistics, in 2011, Singapore had only 2.0 hospital beds per 1000 head of population compared to 2.9 in the United Kingdom.[23] Singapore has had some catching up to do. After a period of 12 years of not building any hospitals prior to the opening of the 590 bed Khoo Teck Puat acute public hospital in Yishun in 2010, the Singapore MOH plans to expand the number of acute beds to 30% by 2020 to meet a population growth of around 25% over that period.[24] It is also working with the private sector to utilize its spare capacity.

However, Singapore has had the benefit of hindsight from the experience of the United States and Northern Europe to help moderate the increase and prepare a more robust healthcare model comparable with where the United States and Northern Europe are heading. In order to reduce the demand on acute hospital beds, the number of intermediate long-term care (ILTC) beds, which are cheaper to build and operate, is projected to double within that period. Among these ILTC beds there will be integrated intermediate care hubs (IICH) adjacent to major acute hospitals, such as the 500 bed IICH at Novena next to Tan Tock Seng Hospital and the 550 bed community hospital at Singapore General Hospital Outram Campus. These will provide an integrated model of care for step-down patients after an acute episode such as hip replacements or strokes and provide on-ward rehabilitation therapies. They include apartments fitted out to match the HDB standard designs to help patients and family members properly prepare for the challenges that a patient with long-term disabilities will face when he or she returns home. This integrated approach provides outreach nursing services, social workers, and therapists to help with the transition to home and monitor the patient's progress once at home. It also helps to transition the patient into new multidisciplinary primary care teams in new polyclinics that now have dedicated elder day-care centers to maintain the continuity of integrated care at a local level once discharged. All this aims to reduce the number of unnecessary readmissions to hospital that have been contributing to bed blocking and congestion in A&E departments.

This vertical and horizontal integration of services involves group general practices offering a wider range of services not previously available in the primary care setting. Efforts are being made to encourage individual private general practitioners to come together to form group practices to give them the critical mass to offer a wider range of services. This trend uses facilities that are less expensive to run, brings care closer to home, and better utilizes expensive health infrastructure.

Singapore is doubling the number of nursing homes to cater for those unable to age in place and providing nurses to do periodic home visits.[25] Companies such as Active Global Specialized Caregivers are finding increasing demand for full-time home nursing from qualified nurses from countries such as India, Sri Lanka, Indonesia, and the Philippines.[25] They are employed on the same work permits as domestic helpers.[25] However, as they live in and get food and lodgings their pay may be one-sixth to one-quarter of what would be paid to a locally registered nurse doing 12-hour shifts and living out, who might cost S$6000.[25] It is also about half the cost of a place in a nursing home, which can cost anything from S$1200 to S$3500 after government subsidies.[25] The job scope may include taking patients through exercises, dressing wounds, monitoring vital signs, and bathing and feeding.[25]

Apart from the cost benefits, this model offers families the support they need to enable their loved ones to age in place with dignity.

Advance Medical Directives

As in life, there should be dignity and self-determination in death. Singapore has introduced the advance medical directive (AMD). This is a legal document you sign in advance to inform your doctor that you do not want any life-sustaining treatment to be used to prolong your life in the event that you become terminally ill and unconscious and where death is imminent.

The AMD can be made by any person, aged 21 years and above, and is not mentally disordered. The AMD form is a legal document which must be completed and signed in the presence of two witnesses before it is returned to the

Registrar of AMDs. The patient's doctor must be one of the two witnesses, while the other witness must be at least 21 years old. In addition, both witnesses must not have any vested interests in the patient's death.[26]

Disruptive Technologies

Technology to Improve Utilization

At the heart of many initiatives to save costs and improve efficiencies is technology.

Lois Avery writes that Khoo Teck Puat Hospital (KTPH) in Singapore has been using data analytics to identify patterns of use of subsidized beds.

> *"What we discovered was that 20 per cent of people admitted to the wards contributed to 80 per cent of repeats and only 10 per cent of the cases were actually health related – the majority were social issues," said Dr. Wong Sweet Fun, Director of the AIP Programme.*[27]

As a result, KTPH, a public hospital, selected 400 people to participate in the aging-in-place pilot in 2011 to help patients adapt to alternative methods of accessing community healthcare. It aimed to reverse the growing demand for subsidized hospital beds, targeting patients with a history of three or more admissions over a 6-month period. KTPH took these analytics and created tailored in-home healthcare plans that avoid the need for those patients to be admitted to hospital. The average admission rate fell from 3.5 times in 6 months to 1.3.[27] KTPH took data analytics further in a larger study in 2013 by mining data from the national e-Health system, which has a single record for each patient that is accessible by any medical center. Combining these data with geospatial data technologies, KTPH started to map patterns in community health, identifying problematic hot spots.

Lois Avery goes on to explain:

> *This allowed the team to implement proactive solutions such as community pop-up clinics and health and wellbeing talks in strategically positioned locations to reach those deemed at Risk.*
>
> *"The team screened 4,000 people in north Singapore, aged 40 years and above, for conditions such as high cholesterol and diabetes," said Dr. Mike Wong, who worked with KTPH's analytics team to develop a unique data dashboard designed for doctors and nurses.*[27]

These preemptive "well-care" measures reduce the likelihood of conditions developing that require "sick-care" medical interventions.

According to Lee Chew Chiat, Executive Director, Consulting and Public Sector Industry Leader, Deloitte Southeast Asia, the potential for data mining technology to benefit the healthcare industry today extends much further. In addition to predicting profiles of frail or elderly patients who are likely to be re-admitted into hospitals, data also allow medical professionals to balance drug efficacy and cost; and determine the locality of disease - dengue fever, for example - for better control.

"Having consistent basic information of a patient or a consumer is critical in healthcare. It is the foundation and since we have the foundation, Singapore can be a good test-bed," said Lee.[27]

Smart Healthcare

In a 2015 MOH budget initiative paper stating its ambitions for smart healthcare in Singapore, the MOH planned to leverage technology to enhance the delivery of healthcare services.

Apart from anticipating the needs of consumers and providers, IT also augments the healthcare workforce and enables people to better self-manage their health. This potentially improves effectiveness of our healthcare professionals and brings about greater productivity. We plan to leverage appropriate technologies to support different segments of our population, and to avail the right tools to help our people and their caregivers manage their health.

1. *For the well and at risk, we planned for Health Hub to be the one-stop platform to help Singaporeans learn more about their health and accompany them in their healthy lifestyle journey.*
2. *For those with chronic conditions, smart applications and telehealth solutions would help them better monitor their vital signs so that they can proactively manage their conditions from home.*
3. *For our seniors, we plan to deploy sensors and response system to help them age in place successfully and giving peace-of-mind to caregivers.*
4. *We are also leveraging Telehealth to bring healthcare services closer to Singaporeans of all ages so they do not need to travel and queue at the clinics. For example, tele-rehab services are currently under clinical trial to help post-stroke patients recover at the convenience of their homes.*
5. *We plan to link up providers across all sectors to achieve our vision of "One Patient, One Health Record" so that healthcare professionals can provide better shared care to patients near their home.*[28]

Technology-Enabled Homes

The Singapore-based company, Napier Health Solutions, started a pilot study in 2015 with the HDB of Singapore to bring cloud-based healthcare delivery into people's homes. Called "Napier myCare Solutions for Aging-In-Place," their solution integrates tele-monitoring of vitals, tele-alert of abnormalities, tele-consult for physician–patient video consultation, and tele-rehabilitation to track a patient's physiotherapy regime. The algorithms behind the system have been developed in collaboration with the same healthcare professionals who man the call center dashboards monitoring patients to ensure meaningful data are provided. They can do trend analysis, create automated reminders, produce care plans, and quickly triage the patient over a video phone if the panic button worn by the patient is activated. They can then send an appropriate caregiver to the home or arrange appointments or admissions to the local clinic or hospital.

The pilot covers 4000 homes and uses simple mobile phone technology that requires only the simple installation of movement sensors and a base Internet of Things (IoT), to which a simple glucose meter, blood pressure meter, weighing scales, and wearable panic button can be connected wirelessly. Most of these are now available over the counter at pharmacies. In an interview, Napier Health Systems (April 2015) said that they expected 1 health professional at the call center to be able to monitor about 500 patients on average. But the system would allow sharing between dashboards to iron out peaks and troughs in demand. There will also be facilities to give family members a role in the patient's care and provide them with peace of mind up to a point. For many families, this may enable them to return to work rather than having to provide round-the-clock care.

Some of the most significant issues for the elderly include depression, loneliness, and a feeling of isolation, which have not yet been addressed in the Napier Healthcare myCare scenario. Nevertheless, robots are moving beyond simply carrying out tasks by being taught to empathize with people, thereby making progress toward dealing with these pervasive sociopsychological issues in aging.

The Napier system is an example of how telephone companies are coming together with technology companies and venture capital to provide huge value to the consumer, disrupting the traditional healthcare market.

As we move from a patient-centered approach to a period of consumer engagement towards 2020, our healthcare system will become increasingly virtual and decentralized. Smartphone technology and applications are increasingly making available a wide range of personal monitoring capabilities and telemedicine opportunities to interact with healthcare professionals remotely. We will start to look for smart homes that integrate with this technology. Consumers will also expect to be able to compare the cost of procedures and outcomes at the touch of a button as well as access insurance that gives them an incentive to stay healthy. It's likely we will see more healthcare services conveniently located in retail settings in the same way we have seen pharmacies, as a way to create convenience while keeping costs down.

This consumer engagement will start to promote wellness as new players join the health information technology (IT) supply chain to personalize healthcare. IBM's Watson supercomputer uses algorithms to extract from the vast amounts of data that is being collected at a rate that doubles each year, to help providers/insurers such as Wellpoint in the United States to diagnose and predict on a real-time basis. These systems are proving to be more reliable than doctors alone due to their ability to compare vast amounts of data. Using this data bank and computers to aid diagnostics, the emphasis will shift toward generalists, shared learning, education, and data-led rather than opinion-led decisions and leadership.

Master Planning

The built environment has much to contribute to a population's health. The Singapore government, through its HDB, has been able to promote various initiatives. Increasingly, these initiatives are including support facilities such as elder day care, clinics, and kindergartens. They are close to transport and amenities such as cycle paths, park connectors, open spaces, and sports facilities. Additionally, streets and public transport are being made barrier free. Not only are these outdoor amenities the lungs of the city but they also promote physical activity, helping to encourage healthier lifestyles among the population.

In 2009, HDB launched SkyVille @ Dawson in Queenstown, a scheme that includes a multigenerational living scheme whereby extended families can apply jointly for a four-room or five-room loft unit paired with a studio apartment. By not physically isolating the elderly, who will make up increasing numbers of the population, the master plan can make significant contributions to combating loneliness and depression. This further encourages aging in place.[29]

Realigning Incentives to Reduce Costs and Improve Outcomes

It is not just technology that is paving the way for a paradigm shift in how healthcare is delivered. Home monitoring, tele-consultation, tele-rehabilitation, and robotics clearly have an enormous role to play, but changing incentives is equally important. Traditionally, hospitals and doctors have been paid on a fee-for-service or targets model, regardless if it is in the United States or the NHS in the United Kingdom. Too often, the number of beds in the system has been a measure of the quality and capacity of the system. These reactive and outdated metrics have only served to reward medical professionals to over-test and overprescribe, treating diseases rather than preventing them. The shift is toward rewarding medical services for managing and keeping populations healthy.

Jeremy Lim suggests that Singapore needs to incentivize family practitioners to focus more on wellness than sickness by paying them a community-based budget (calculated on the epidemiology of that community), rather than payment for services.[30] He adds:

> *A quality bonus can then be instituted to reward doctors who achieve exemplary disease control and quality of life for their patients.*[30]

Healthcare Insurance and Payment by Results

Developed countries are leading the way in reducing the average length of stay in hospital by increasing the number of procedures done on a day-case basis, reducing demand for inpatient beds. They are also enabling more treatment in a primary care setting or even at home. This reduces the overall cost of a procedure. Health insurance and government co-payment policies in Asia as a whole, with the exception of Singapore, have been slow to respond to these changes in the delivery of care that use minimally invasive techniques and anesthetics to reduce recovery time. They continue to link payment to inpatient stays for procedures, ignoring the savings they could make if they kept up with developments in medical procedures. This skews the investment in the healthcare infrastructure in many countries toward building more beds than are actually required.

From an incentive point of view, insurers and governments are also slow to reward measures taken by individuals to maintain a healthy lifestyle and do regular screening. Again, wearable technologies are increasingly able to reliably monitor and verify a person's healthy activities. For consumers, before they become patients, there is an opportunity to vote with their wallet and buy products from the more enlightened insurers who should be able to offer lower premiums to those who make an effort.

A report from Oliver Wyman explains how an enlightened healthcare provider in the United States is tackling the issue:

> *In 2008, when physicians from CareMore, an independent medical group based in Cerritos, California, heard news reports of a brutal heat wave, they began contacting their elderly emphysema patients. Physicians worried that the scorching heat would drive their at-risk Medicare Advantage patients to the emergency room. So when patients said they had no air conditioner, the physicians purchased units for them. The theory was that the roughly $500 cost paled in comparison to the cost of an emergency-department admission. As it happened, this non-medical "intervention" kept CareMore's patients out of the hospital. But if they had needed to go and lacked transportation, CareMore would have offered a free ride.*
>
> *CareMore has an expansive, counterintuitive approach to healthcare. The group fends off falls by providing patients with regular toenail clipping and by removing shag rugs—a common household risk for the elderly. Patients engage in iPhone conference calls with healthcare professionals and are remotely monitored with devices that feed data automatically to doctors; for example, patients with congestive heart failure are given a wireless scale that reports their weight on a daily basis—a key step in preventing hospitalization. They have singing pillboxes that chime when it's time to take medications.*[31]

CareMore, which comprises both a medical services group and an insurance group, has recognized that too much money is spent on the 5% polychronic ill Americans and too little on preventing them becoming sick in the first place; as illustrated in the pyramid diagrams in Figure 14.2. The trick is to invert the pyramids. In the short term, you have to center care on the top 5% polychronic patients, but over the long term you invest in wellness and prevention at the bottom of the pyramid (Figure 14.2).

Another example is the Camden Coalition of Healthcare Providers, a community coalition that targets patients in a poor Medicaid population who are at the highest risk of their already chronic condition

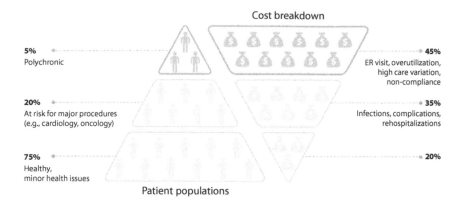

FIGURE 14.2

The upside-down pyramid (Today): Cost by clinical segment. (From Main T, Slywotzky A. The Volume-to-Value Revolution [Internet]. Oliver Wyman; 2012 [cited 2015 July 15]. The upside-down pyramid (Today): Cost by clinical segment (p. 7). Available from: http://www.oliverwyman.com/insights/publications/2012/nov/the-volume-to-value-revolution.html#.VaWZkV-qqko.)

going into an unstoppable downward spiral. A report by Oliver Wyman explains:

> *Camden Coalition identifies at-risk patients and neighbourhoods by geo-mapping hospital data and provides local community clinics with outreach nurses and social workers whose job is to build patient relationships—using home visits, counselling, and free transportation as part of their toolkit. This aggressive management approach has reduced hospital admissions by 40 percent and Medicaid spending by 56 percent.*[31]

SUMMARY

Singapore's achievements over the last 50 years have been nothing short of miraculous, not least in the sphere of healthcare. It continues to look to developed economies for their experiences and adapt to change and the challenge of providing quality healthcare in an affordable way. With an aging society, an increase in NCDs, and bed crunch, it is managing a rolling program of expansion and renewal without having to depend on private finance partnerships to help fund it. It is diversifying the way that care is delivered, investing in telemedicine and multidisciplinary team care tailored to suit the individual to prevent, diagnose, and treat diseases.

It is expanding primary care, lower-cost ambulatory care settings, ILTC beds, and home care to reduce the demand for acute hospital beds and provide the right care at the right size in the right location.

The roll out of the universal electronic patient record is nearing completion, which provides a single electronic record for each patient accessible from anywhere within the public health system. The private providers will ultimately need to be party to this for a truly integrated approach. It raises the issue of whether patient records should be owned by the patient and go with them whichever system they find themselves in.

The government is also addressing the shortage of healthcare professionals by expanding the number of places it can offer to medical students, nurses, and allied professionals. There are now three medical schools in Singapore turning out around 500 new doctors each year. We can expect to see an increase in specialist centers for emergency medicine, cardiology, and cancer, where teams are well drilled in what they do best. These will be combined with research facilities for clinical trials, training, and developing new techniques in situ.

The focus on improving and right-sizing the health system in Singapore is all coming at a cost. Finance Minister Tharman Shanmugaratnam, in his 2014 budget speech, committed to increasing government spending on healthcare from S$4billion in 2011 to S$8billion by 2016 and S$12billion by 2020. However, to stop health costs spiraling out of control, the Singapore government's strategy is to rebalance the system by incentivizing the doctors.[33]

At the same time, the government does not expect its revenue to go up as a percentage of GDP. It anticipates an overall rise in government expenditure by 3.5% of GDP by 2030, including increases in infrastructure and education as well as social and healthcare spending.[34] Given the low base of healthcare spending as a percentage of GDP, this increase will still keep it well below that of other developed countries. However, even if the government maintains a vibrant economy and a fair and equitable system of taxes and transfers that favors the middle- and low-income brackets, it will likely have to raise taxes on assets and the better off. Having said that, median Singaporean workers' tax burden in 2014 was one-third of their counterparts in the United States, leaving plenty of room to manoeuver.[35]

The Singapore health system continues to reexamine, propose, and adapt to changing circumstance. This evolution combines with learning from and adopting international experience that best applies to its situation. Its responsiveness bodes well for its future as it continues to provide its world-class health system at a relatively low cost.

During a decade of major healthcare investment in new acute hospitals and intermediate and long-term care facilities to make up for a shortfall in bed capacity, Singapore is now turning its attention more toward primary care and wellness. As with many developed countries, the future focus of healthcare is shifting away from expensive acute settings and more toward health systems and personalized health that is predictive and thus enables people to take preventive measures and ultimately manage their own health. It will be interesting to see how developing countries take advantage to fast track the development of their systems, leveraging on the exponential growth in technology related to health and its relatively low cost to make quantum leaps in their systems.

The future is less about how well we design our hospitals and more about how well we design the infrastructure that supports an integrated health system.

REFERENCES

1. The World Bank. GDP per capita (current US$) (Internet). 2015 (updated 2015 July 27; cited 2015 August 16). Available from: https://www.google.com.sg/publicdata/explore?ds=d5bncppjof8f9_&met_y=ny_gdp_pcap_cd&idim=country:GBR:USA:DEU&hl=en&dl=en#!ctype=l&strail=false&bcs=d&nselm=h&met_y=ny_gdp_pcap_cd&scale_y=lin&ind_y=false&rdim=region&idim=country:GBR:USA:DEU:SGP&ifdim=region&hl=en_US&dl=en&ind=false.
2. The World Bank. Health expenditure, total (% GDP) (Internet). 2015 (cited 2015 July 26). Available from: http://data.worldbank.org/indicator/SH.XPD.TOTL.ZS.
3. The World Bank. Life expectancy at birth, total (years) (Internet). 2015 (cited 2015 July 26). Available from: http://data.worldbank.org/indicator/SP.DYN.LE00.IN.
4. The World Bank. Mortality rate, infant (per 1,000 live births) (Internet). 2015 (cited 2015 July 26). Available from: http://data.worldbank.org/indicator/SP.DYN.IMRT.IN.
5. Beng, Y. C. Homes for a nation—public housing in Singapore. Ethos (Internet). 2007 April (updated 2013 December 10; cited 2015 July 26); 2. Available from: https://www.cscollege.gov.sg/Knowledge/ethos/Issue%202%20Apr%202007/Pages/Homes-for-a-Nation-Public-Housing-in-Singapore.aspx.
6. Lim, J. Reforming health care in Singapore (Internet). Singapore: The Straits Times; 2013 December 29 (cited 2015 July 30). Available from: http://yourhealth.asiaone.com/content/reforming-health-care-singapore/page/0/0.
7. Lim, J. *Myth or Magic: The Singapore Healthcare System.* Singapore: Select Publishing; 2013.

8. Ministry of Health, Singapore. Costs and financing (Internet). 2014 (updated 2015 January 14; cited 2015 August 16). Available from: https://www.moh.gov.sg/content/moh_web/home/costs_and_financing.html.
9. The World Bank. Health expenditure, public (% of total health expenditure) (Internet). 2015 (cited 2015 July 30). Available from: http://data.worldbank.org/indicator/SH.XPD.PUBL/countries.
10. Ministry of Manpower. Summary table: Income (Internet). 2015 June 4 (updated 2015 July 6; cited 2015 August 16). Available from: http://stats.mom.gov.sg/Pages/Income-Summary-Table.aspx.
11. Economic Intelligence Unit. Industry report: Healthcare. 2015 January.
12. Lim, J. Reforming health care in Singapore. *Straits Times.* 2013 December 27.
13. Improving Healthcare Affordability (Internet). Ministry of Health, Singapore; 2015 March (cited 2015 August 16). Available from: https://www.moh.gov.sg/content/moh_web/home/pressRoom/pressRoomItemRelease/2015/ministry-of-health-budget-initiatives-2015/_jcr_content/entryContent/download/file.res/Factsheet%20on%20Improving%20Healthcare%20Affordability%20(Mar%202015).pdf.
14. Ministry of Health, Singapore. MOH to publish data on total operation fees for common procedures to give more information to help patients and families (Internet). 2014 September 1 (cited 2015 August 16). Available from: https://www.moh.gov.sg/content/moh_web/home/pressRoom/pressRoomItemRelease/2014/moh-to-publish-data-on-total-operation-fees-for-common-procedure.html.
15. The World Bank. Fertility rate, total (births per woman) (Internet). 2015 (cited 2015 August 16). Available from: http://data.worldbank.org/indicator/SP.DYN.TFRT.IN.
16. Ministry of Social and Family Development. Chapter 1: demographic realities: opportunities and challenges (Internet). Committee on Ageing Issues; 2006 (cited 2015 August 16). Available from: http://app.msf.gov.sg/Portals/0/Summary/research/Chapter%201%20-%20Demographic%20Realities.pdf.
17. Developing a Sustainable Population: What China can Learn from Singapore, (Internet) by Patrick Thelen (2013). http://asiapacificarts.usc.edu/(X(1)A(u7GFvPkp0wEkAAAAZDI5YWQ4NTItNjg2NS00MDdmLTgyMDgtYjJlZTliZThjOWJjPI_FrjZLMG-f9xbQsNkUUfRQNQo1))/w_apa/showarticle.aspx?articleID=18867&AspxAutoDetectCookieSupport=1.
18. Alemayehu, B. and Warner, K. E. The lifetime distribution of health care costs. *Health Serv Res.* 2004 Jun; 39(3): 627–642.
19. Developing a Sustainable Population: What China can Learn from Singapore, (Internet) by Patrick Thelen (2013). http:// asiapacificarts.usc.edu/(X(1)A(u7GFvPkp0wEkAAAAZDI5YWQ4NTItNjg2NS00MDdmL TgyMDgtYjJlZTliZThjOWJjPI_FrjZLMG-f9xbQsNkUUfRQNQo1))/w_apa/showarticle.aspx?articleID=18867&AspxAutoDetectCookieSupport=1.
20. Diabetes UK. Can you reduce your risk of diabetes? (Internet). 2015 (cited 2015 August 16). Available from: https://www.diabetes.org.uk/Guide-to-diabetes/What-is-diabetes/Know-your-risk-of-Type-2-diabetes/Can-diabetes-be-prevented/.
21. The Heart Foundation. Reducing your risk (Internet). 2015 (cited 2015 August 16). Available from: http://www.theheartfoundation.org/heart-disease-facts/reducing-your-risk/.

22. Pearl, P. Hospitals may be disappearing in the era of health care reform (Internet). *Forbes Business.* 2013 November 15 (cited 2015 August 16). Available from: http://www.forbes.com/sites/robertpearl/2013/11/14/hospitals-may-be-disappearing-in-the-era-of-health-care-reform/.

23. The World Bank. Hospital beds (per 1,000 people) (Internet). 2015 (cited 2015 August 16). Available from: http://data.worldbank.org/indicator/SH.MED.BEDS.ZS.

24. Ministry of Health, Singapore; Building capacity, increasing access (Internet). 2015 March (cited 2015 August 16). Available from: https://www.moh.gov.sg/content/moh_web/home/pressRoom/pressRoomItemRelease/2015/ministry-of-health-budget-initiatives-2015/_jcr_content/entryContent/download_0/file.res/Factsheet%20on%20Building%20Capacity,%20Increasing%20Access%20(Mar%202015).pdf.

25. Seow, J. He's in better shape, thanks to home nursing. MYPAPER. 2015 June 11.

26. Ministry of Health, Singapore. Advance Medical Directive (AMD) (Internet). 2013 (updated 2013 August 16; cited 2015 August 16). Available from: https://www.moh.gov.sg/content/moh_web/home/policies-and-issues/advance_medical_directiveamd.html.

27. Avery, L., Fenton, P., and Quek, C. How big data can drive patient behaviour change (Internet). 2015 (updated 2015 February 3, cited 2015 July 15). Available from: https://www.edb.gov.sg/content/edb/en/news-and-events/news/singapore-business-news/Feature/how-big-data-can-drive-patient-behaviour-change.html.

28. Ministry of Health, Singapore; Raising quality, transforming care (Internet). 2015 March (cited 2015 August 16). Available from: https://www.moh.gov.sg/content/moh_web/home/pressRoom/pressRoomItemRelease/2015/ministry-of-health-budget-initiatives-2015/_jcr_content/entryContent/download_1/file.res/Factsheet%20on%20Raising%20Quality,%20Transforming%20Care%20(Mar%202015).pdf.

29. Singapore Government, Housing Development Board, Press Release: Rejuvenation of Dawson Estate, 27 Jun 2014, . http://www20.hdb.gov.sg/fi10/fi10296p.nsf/PressReleases/9D3A3E2768F96C9448257D04001A810B?OpenDocument.

30. Lim, J. For best outcomes, pay GPs the right way. TODAYonline. 2015 June 19.

31. Main, T., and Slywotzky, A. The Volume-to-Value Revolution (Internet). Oliver Wyman; 2012 (cited 2015 July 15). Available from: http://www.oliverwyman.com/insights/publications/2012/nov/the-volume-to-value-revolution.html#.VaWZkV-qqko.

32. Main, T., and Slywotzky, A. The Volume-to-Value Revolution (Internet). Oliver Wyman; 2012 (cited 2015 July 15). The upside-down pyramid (Today): Cost by clinical segment (p. 7). Available from: http://www.oliverwyman.com/insights/publications/2012/nov/the-volume-to-value-revolution.html#.VaWZkV-qqko.

33. Singaporehealthcarespendingtoreach$13Bin2020,ReportonSingaporeBudget2015. Healthcare Innovation: By Eden Estopace.2015-02-25. https://www.enterpriseinnovation.net/article/singapore-healthcare-spending-reach-13-b-2020-1454783661.

34. Healthcare spending may reach 3.5% of GDP in 2030. By S. Ramesh, 01 Mar 2012. http://www.channelnewsasia.com/news/singapore/healthcare-spending-may-reach-3-5-of-gdp-in-2030-8444706.

Afterword

V.K. Singh and Paul Lillrank

This book discusses the hospital, one of the most central institutions in the world. Like the factory, the bazaar, the shopping mall, and places of worship, it is a structure where demand and supply meet. The hospital is where people go to receive help for diseases and wounds.

All such institutions face the changes that come with modernization. This means, first and foremost, that more resources are available to fulfill more needs. When more can be done, more is asked for. From this, follows organization, division of labor, specialization, and standardization. Efficient high-volume production changes the relation between patient and caregiver.

Before the advent of modern medicine, the hospital was a place where people went to die. Those with decent dwellings preferred to be cared for at home. With modern medicine came specialized resources, heavy and expensive equipment that required a fixed location. All flows met at the hospital. Several authors contributing to this book have discussed how advances in information and communication technologies have the potential to reverse the logic of centralization.

Changes in the patterns of morbidity amplify this trend. An increasing share of the demand is for cases that reflect the ups and downs of chronic conditions. While the emergency department is still the nexus of the general hospital, not everything can be managed by the logic of urgency and severity. With an increase in low-intensity care episodes, patient flow requires more attention. In manufacturing, focus has shifted from the factory to the supply chain. Likewise, in healthcare the focus is moving toward the full cycle of care. Just adding floor space is not the solution.

In the practice of management there are two problems. The first is "just do it"; the second, "Do I know what to do?" In other words, there are the "known knowns" that require implementation, and the "known unknowns" that require innovation.

Management is not an exact science. Managers operate in the real world, which is marred by variability and decay. Variability finds its way even into the most controlled environments, such as the clean rooms of semiconductor manufacturing and the operating rooms of hospitals. All structures, be they mechanical or behavioral, tend to fall apart. In preventing variability and decay from getting the upper hand, there is sufficient knowledge of what to do; or what should definitely be avoided. Some of the issues discussed in this book, safety and environmental efficiency, have a sound theoretical and practical basis. Accidents happen and to err is human, but there is a thin yet still visible line between predictable and unpredictable events. If hand hygiene is lax, infections will occur; if hazardous waste is not disposed of promptly and properly, problems will follow. There are best practices backed up by solid evidence. In such areas, the primary task of management is to "just do it"; show leadership, inspire people to do their best, and stay firm on central principles. To the extent that a hospital is a production unit it follows the factory logic.

As has been pointed out by many authors of this book, a hospital is more than a site that produces clinical interventions. It is a healing environment that generates experiences of being cared for. In issues of human behavior and emotions, the scientific foundation is fuzzy. A perfect procedure can leave an unsatisfied patient, if bedside manners are rude. A medical outcome below expectations can leave a positive experience, if it is perceived that everything possible was promptly and respectfully done. However, some experiences, good and bad, can be predicted from evidence. These are waiting time and integration. A smooth, even flow will, other things being equal, leave a better impression than an unpredictable sequence of stop-and-go. If it seems that nobody is in charge of the whole patient case, experiences will be negative.

This is the area where hospital design and patient process management intersect. A hospital is engaged in mass production founded on the division of labor, specialization, and standardization. Demand, however, can't be standardized; a hospital has to deal with a variety of issues. The core questions therefore are, how to design a facility and a process management system that can accomplish a reliable, high-quality, safe, and swift patient flow under the constraints of variable demand and specialized assets. This book has sought to contribute to the development of more and better theories and evidence-based methods for this purpose.

Index